THE PRACTICE OF LOVE

THE PRACTICE OF LOVE

Break Old Patterns, Rebuild Trust, and Create a Connection That Lasts

LAIR TORRENT

ROWMAN & LITTLEFIELD
Lanham • Boulder • New York • London

Published by Rowman & Littlefield
An imprint of The Rowman & Littlefield Publishing Group, Inc.
4501 Forbes Boulevard, Suite 200, Lanham, Maryland 20706
www.rowman.com

86-90 Paul Street, London EC2A 4NE, United Kingdom

British Library Cataloguing in Publication Information Available

Library of Congress Cataloging-in-Publication Data

Names: Torrent, Lair, 1970– author.
Title: The practice of love : break old patterns, rebuild trust, and create
  a connection that lasts / Lair Torrent.
Description: Lanham : Rowman & Littlefield, 2022. | Includes
  bibliographical references and index.
Identifiers: LCCN 2021042822 (print) | LCCN 2021042823 (ebook) | ISBN
  9781538139356 (cloth) | ISBN 9781538139363 (epub)
Subjects: LCSH: Love. | Married people. | Interpersonal
  relations—Psychological aspects.
Classification: LCC BF575.L8 T67 2022 (print) | LCC BF575.L8 (ebook) |
  DDC 152.4/1—dc23
LC record available at https://lccn.loc.gov/2021042822
LC ebook record available at https://lccn.loc.gov/2021042823

For Jake and Jasper
because of
Ashley

CONTENTS

LIST OF FIGURES

ACKNOWLEDGMENTS

To my amazing and beautiful wife, Ashley, who poured over every word, paragraph, and page of this book from start to finish. If not for your love and support and your extraordinary editorial eye, this book would not have happened. Thank you for helping me make a dream come true. Your turn.

Thank you to Hugo Lilienfeld for being there for Ash and me all of these years. You were one of the first to help me believe that this book had possibility. Thanks for your belief.

Suzan Lemak—thank you for your kindness, your generosity, your Toughlove, your wisdom, your raised eyebrow, and your laugh. Wherever you are, you are always with us and around us. Thanks for reminding me that I'm good.

Julie Winter and Jon Child, thanks for helping to mold me into the clinician I am today. Without you, and Helix, none of this would've been possible.

To Ellen Gregory, Elena Hull, and Christina Curtis, thanks for taking a chance on me and making me a part of the Midtown family.

Brian Malloy, you literally put a roof over my head and food and wine in my belly. Without the support of you and Jess, this practice and this book might not have been possible. And thanks for listening to me drone on endlessly about "my book," "my book," "my book" like it was the Fields Medal. Only a best friend makes sacrifices like that.

Thanks to everyone at the Nordlyset Literary Agency: Nathan Vogt, Isabelle Bleeker, and especially Jennifer Thompson, who found me in the forgotten and discarded bin. You believed in me and this book when few others did. Thank you for your endless support and tireless efforts.

And finally, thanks to all of you who made life difficult for me from time to time. Intentional or not, you gave me the resiliency and fortitude to push past what I believed was possible and create a life worth living. In your way you've had a hand in this, so thanks for being shitty—you know who you are.

PREFACE

I do not offer this work from the faulty precipice of the grandiose healer or the artifice of the fully analyzed therapist. Instead I offer it as a fellow traveler, working and practicing, trying to do it a little better tomorrow than I did it today.

* * *

"So, how did the week go?" I braced myself for the answer. I could tell by the looks on their faces and the energy between them it hadn't gone well.

"We've certainly had better," Molly said quietly.

Bill nodded in agreement.

"Really?" I said. "I'm surprised. You seemed so connected last week. I felt confident we were headed in the right direction since you both have been doing so well with the communication techniques. Tell me what happened."

And they did: Bill had been traveling for work again, and upon his return, Molly had a lot to say. In their kitchen, the room tacitly agreed upon to host such discussions since it was farthest from the kids' rooms, Molly began. "Once again, I didn't hear from you all week. Did you ever think to check in? If not with me, at least with your children?"

Bill replied, "How many times do I have to say it? Between meetings, flights, and the time difference, I just didn't have time. I don't know why this has to be a referendum on how I feel about you or the kids."

Molly tried to remain in control. "Hold on. Before this gets out of hand, can we at least try what we learned in therapy?"

Steeling himself, Bill tried to use the tools he learned in session. "Okay, what I *think* I heard you say is that when I'm away for work, you don't hear from me enough. What I *think* I'm getting from you is that you don't feel I understand you at all. Is that correct? That no matter how hard I try, I never really get it right? Molly, it hurts my feelings when I don't feel appreciated. I bust my ass all week, and then I come home to this, not to mention I don't think you've touched me in a month."

Molly took a breath to ground herself. "It must be hard to feel so unappreciated by me. And you're right. I don't feel heard or understood because no matter what I say, it feels like I'm a terrible wife who never wants to have sex. Am I hearing you right? Well, Bill, it's hard to feel like having sex when I'm never a priority. Did you ever consider that? So, I'm sorry if I'm not the dutiful wife waiting here for you in a night-gown made of fucking Saran Wrap!"

Bill pounded his fist on the kitchen table. "So, as usual, this is my fault. None of this is your responsibility? I work hard to support this family, to build this business I thought *we* wanted, to make the kind of money we want to make. Do you think I like being away all the time? I thought this was what we talked about—I thought this is what we agreed on."

In my office, they finished the story and sat in stone silence. The air was thick with disappointment and trepidation. Molly looked at me with tears in her eyes. "You're right," she said. "We left here last week feeling awesome, but it seems like when we are on our own, all of our work goes out the window. We always end up in the same place, circling each other and getting nowhere."

It was hard to see them struggle after feeling so hopeful. I was frustrated and disappointed, and, despite their best efforts and mine, I was failing them. My heart sank as I thought about the other couples in my practice who also do well in the office but fail to thrive on their own. With all their efforts and good intentions, why wasn't it enough? I considered myself a highly trained and skilled couple's therapist. What was missing from my work? Why couldn't I help them?

This led me to consider questions outside of my practice. With all of the therapies, couple's workshops, and self-help books available, why aren't couples reporting a dramatic increase in overall satisfaction, and why is the divorce rate holding steady at 50 percent? I needed to know what was missing.

For far too long, we have assumed that we should innately understand how to love each other. Relationships have fallen into the basket of things that we should just know how to do. But we are not born knowing how to make a relationship work any more than we are born knowing how to file taxes or buy insurance, and there are no classes in high school or college that teach us how to do this.

And so I began to dig. After an exhaustive exploration of both clinical and popular methods, I came to realize that many of these modes were good but based on statistics and in my experience not quite good enough. The clinical models, such as psychoanalysis/psychodynamic therapies, cognitive-behavioral therapies, Gestalt, and humanistic therapies, were initially developed for individuals then retrofitted to meet the needs of couples and families. On the other hand, the popular psychology approaches proved to be either too simple or too complex to apply in real-life situations. And so, with a combination of apprehension and disbelief, I wondered, had I discovered a blind spot in my field?

I sought the counsel of colleagues, supervisors, and mentors, all of whom, when pressed, would admit to similar results. One elder and very well-known therapist and writer in the field said flatly, "Welcome to the world of couple's work." There seemed to be an implicit understanding in my profession that this is how couple's therapy can and probably will go. Sure, there will be a few success stories, but most couples will follow the statistics, meaning just shy of half of all marriages will end in divorce or separation. There is a popular belief that divorce rates are falling, but this isn't actually true. Fewer people are getting married today, so the raw number of divorces is falling, but the percentage of marriages that fail remains steady. When I came to fully understand the startling deficiencies of couple's therapy both in practice and self-help literature, I came to one inconvenient and incontrovertible truth: This was never going to be good enough for me or for the couples I was trying to help. I recalled the words of Harvard Medical School's Elvin Semrad, a forefather of modern therapy, who once said, "Let your patients be your textbooks," and so that's what I did. I let my clients teach me what was needed. I went back to the proverbial drawing board, and here's what I discovered.

There is a glaring blind spot in the world of couple's therapy. To date, we have not provided a method for working with couples that is simple enough to be used outside the therapy office, yet sophisticated enough to help repair the complicated issues couples face. We have been too focused on the symptoms. Poor communication, cyclical arguments, lackluster sex lives, and an inability to build or rebuild trust are indicative of a much deeper problem. We simply cannot learn to communicate more effectively, feel connected in the bedroom, stop fighting to win, or feel safe enough to be truly vulnerable to each other until we address what has been missing in all of this: how to "show up."

I poured over my research and my training spanning everything from the clinical to the mystical. What I found most effective for the couples I work with, and in my own marriage, for that matter, was a combination of the knowledge I culled from my training in Western psychology and the profound inner work made possible by the practices of mindfulness and Buddhist psychology. I recognized that through mindfulness, partners could become more self-aware and better able to bear witness to their thoughts and feelings, getting them out of their knee-jerk responses to each other. When mindful, we can skillfully choose our responses and have access to our most connective and most compassionate parts of self. From here, we can re-author a more loving narrative about our partners while learning to understand their unique wants and needs in a relationship.

Through trial and error, I distilled this work down to five key components or Five Practices that, if implemented correctly, gives couples the tools necessary to make their relationships work. The Five Practices consist of:

Mindfulness: Which brings partners into the present moment and out of their knee-jerk reactions to each other;

Parts of Self: To help partners find the part of self that is open to connection, empathy, and understanding;

The Narrative: A means of interrupting the negative stories we tell about our partners, which can become concretized beliefs;

Choosing: A conscious practice of choosing one's partner, which develops trust and intimacy; and

Personal Responsibility: This is designed to eradicate the behavioral contracts that keep couples locked in turmoil and resentment, and it is the foundation for all the other practices.

On the path of life together, couples often lose their true north. They lose connection. Our relationships have to be a daily practice if we want them to thrive. We have to treat them like we treat anything that we want to succeed at by giving them time and attention. Couples who come to me will often ask, "It shouldn't be this hard, should it?" My answer is always the same "Yes, yes it should, but not for the reasons you think."

This book brings together concepts and tools to help couples heal for the long haul. It offers strategies that are simple enough to be used when emotions run high but also sophisticated enough to treat the complex problems couples face. This book will take you and your partner on a step-by-step journey to healing, and you will come away with a deeper understanding of yourself, your mate, and your relationship. The techniques that make up the Five Practices are brought home to you through relatable anecdotes from real couples as well as concise explanations of the concepts. Each practice is followed by exercises geared toward both the individual and the couple. The practical sections ask each partner to truly take responsibility for their part in the work and how they show up in the relationship. This is also a crossover book for therapists, offering clinicians a new and innovative way to meet their clients' needs.

WHO IS THIS PROCESS FOR, AND WHO IS IT NOT FOR?

Before we begin, I want to be clear that this book and the process are contraindicated if there is abuse in your relationship. If you are experiencing mental, emotional, physical, or spiritual abuse, the Five Practices will not fix the problems you are facing and would be inappropriate to apply. To do so would only serve to validate an abusive relationship.

Healthy relationships are difficult because they ask us to take responsibility for ourselves. They ask us to be compassionate when we want to point the finger, to be brave enough to listen when we want to yell, and to be vulnerable when we want to shut down. What is more, we have to be willing to do all of this when we don't want to. Our push-button society has created a need for a quick fix. If a couple can't find one, they wonder if something is wrong with them. Difficulties in your relationship are not necessarily an indicator of how "meant to be" your union is. Life cycle events, such as getting married or having children, are supposed to be joyous, yet they offer a host of stressors that can weaken even the strongest bonds. A better gauge of your "meant to be–ness" is your willingness to work on the problems that arise. I will tell you the same thing I tell the couples that come to my office: "I do not sell the fifty minutes a week we spend together. I sell a practiced relationship." In like kind, I am not selling you this book. I am selling you a practiced relationship. As long as a client's work exists only inside the walls of my office, or, in the case of the reader, between the pages of this book, it will all be a big waste of time, energy, and money. The work we do in our relationships cannot be a one-off scenario; it has to become a priority that we consciously work at and give attention to.

You have to practice these every day, you have to practice them all the time, and you have to practice them when everything inside is telling you not to. This is where my clients find the most difficulty. I liken it to driving when a car's power steering has given out; it feels like a monumental task to change direction. Here, we are building new habits and getting out of old patterns. The good news? The good news is that studies show that in just six to eight short weeks of repetition, we begin to take advantage of the plasticity of the brain. This means, when we consistently practice something new, we begin to form new neural pathways, effectively changing our brains. So yes, you can teach an old dog new tricks.

ABOUT THIS PROCESS

This book is sectioned into five basic parts that make up the Five Practices. Each practice is a lesson providing the reader with all of the knowledge and understanding necessary to use these strategies in real time, when it counts and when it's hard. Each practice is sectioned into four chapters that are labeled The What, The Why, The How, and Exercises. The What chapters give you a solid definition and working knowledge of each practice. The Why chapters give you an in-depth reason each practice is so important to the health of your relationship. The How chapters offer you a firm understanding of how to integrate each practice into your life. Finally, the practical section outlines specific exercises that you can implement in your life to make a deeper and more heart-centered connection with your partner.

As best as you can, stay flexible and be realistic. Tailor your practice to fit your life with the understanding that the only way to get this process wrong is to not do the work. With this in mind, I say practice well, practice badly, but practice.

Part 1

PRACTICE 1: MINDFULNESS

> Between stimulus and response there is a space. In that
> space is our power to choose our response. In our response
> lies our growth and our freedom.
>
> —Viktor Frankl

"I think you can do this shit at home on your couch for free" were my exact words. Dispensing with the psychobabble, I took my therapeutic kid gloves off and told my clients the truth.

It was my third session with Tom and Nick. I'd spent the first few sessions as I usually do, getting to know the couple, providing some psycho-education around the upcoming work, and watching what probably unfolds at home happen in front of me.

Couple's therapy can feel a lot like playing *Star Trek* chess. If you are unfamiliar with the reference, and I'll bet many are, *Star Trek* chess does not happen on a flat, one-dimensional board; instead, the game happens on multiple levels. When I first started working with couples, it was hard to keep everything straight. As the therapist, I must consider how the multilayered dynamic is unfolding in front of me. There is the problem that brought the couple in the door, which is usually a symptom or symptoms of something bigger. Then I must consider each individual's life story, wounding, and any therapeutic interventions as well as any projections that might arise both in me and in the clients.

I like working with couples for many reasons, not the least of which is you can be far more directive as a couple's therapist than you can with individuals. In individual therapy, there is a lot of guiding—an often slow unfolding of insights that hopefully lead to revelatory moments. With couples, I have to be willing to take risks earlier on in the process. I have to come out from behind the clinical curtain from time to time and give them my honest opinion, especially if they are locked in conflict and hurting each other. This morning I watched Nick and Tom and knew the bloodletting needed to stop.

Nick was angry. "Come on, Tom, how hard is it to pack a fucking bag?" He turns to me. "How hard is it? The poor kid is out on a field trip and she has almost nothing she needs. I asked him to do one thing—one thing!"

Tom shook his head. "*I Thought I Packed It All*. I made a mistake. I guess you've never screwed up?" He looks at me. "This one never makes a mistake. Mr. Perfect here. Have you met my husband? He's type A." He looks back at Nick. "So, I guess I'm now responsible for *your* job too?"

Nick's head turns like it's on a swivel. "My job? My *job*!? Last time I checked she was your kid too."

"No, don't worry, Nick, I got it. I'll go to work for eight hours a day and then come home to this! You're acting stupid."

Nick tries to contain his obvious rage. "Now I'm stupid? *You* are calling *me* stupid?"

"No, I didn't call you stupid. I said you were *acting* stupid."

"Well, you're acting like an idiot."

It was unclear whether they had petered themselves out or become aware of my obvious silence. I looked at them both, raising my eyebrows as if to say, "Are y'all done?"

Nick broke the silence. "Well? Aren't you going to say something?"

Tom seconded his thought. "Yeah, aren't you supposed to tell us what you think? We want to know what you think."

And that's when I said it. "I think you guys can do this shit at home on your couch for free. Frankly, I think you're both better than this. Tell me, how is this going—treating each other this way?"

They asked an honest question, so I gave them an honest answer.

I pause to let my comments sink in. "How do the kids feel when you fight like this?"

They look at each other knowingly.

"Do you think we might try doing something different? Because from where I'm sitting this doesn't look like it's going well." I reposition myself in my chair and lean forward. "Here's the thing, fellas, if you don't do something different, it's only going to get worse. I mean, you might not get divorced but that's probably not great news, because living together this way isn't going to be any fun, for anyone."

Both their mouths were agape at my honesty. Then the corners of Nick's began to curl into a slight smile. He looked at Tom. "Wow! Toni never said anything like that in therapy."

"Maybe she should have," I replied.

Toni was their former therapist. They both liked her and felt she'd done them a lot of good. I agreed, initially Toni was exactly what these guys needed. She was warm, kind, and mothering. But now Tom and Nick no longer needed the motherly presence of Toni, they needed someone to keep them in line and help them establish healthy boundaries of what was acceptable and unacceptable behavior. Tom and Nick needed me to help them reconfigure the culture of their relationship.

For my taste, the word "culture" is thrown around too often. Every company, organization, and team talks about their culture. As much as I don't love the term, it is an apt description of where I like to put my focus as a couple's therapist. Culture is our agreed-upon behaviors, beliefs, and values. It is the generally accepted way of being and living that is endorsed often without thought. And here we have the key phrase, "without thought." Although Tom and Nick loved each other and were committed to their marriage and family, the culture between them was a mindless one. From what I witnessed, they weren't kind to each other. Their comments were sharp, their retorts pointed. When they spoke about the more serious issues like sex, the kids, or money, their words were draped in sarcasm disguised as "just a little humor." However, when tensions ran high, the gloves came off and the mudslinging began. Today in my office was a perfect example.

The problem was Nick and Tom each operate on autopilot in their relationship. Caught up in life, short on time, energy, and sometimes money, they interact mindlessly. Speaking in sharp tongues became the accepted shorthand in their relational culture—their tacitly agreed-upon way of interacting.

Another client in a similar relationship as Nick and Tom once asked me, "Isn't this just how it is for couples after a certain number of years? I mean, isn't this how couples end up for the most part?" I have to admit, in my experience her assessment was pretty accurate. Couples on autopilot, left to their own devices end up doing what I call "practicing badly." It might start out as bickering, or snide jabs that turn into toxic arguments, a lackluster sex life, or any other form of maltreatment. Whatever the modus operandi, these behaviors do not lead to reverence and compassion, two pieces crucial to a heart-centered connection.

If we want to do anything well, we work at it—we practice the fundamentals to do that thing better. Our relationships should be no different. The first step to better relational practices, healing, and reconnection for couples isn't a date night, learning to communicate better, or even sitting in a therapy office for hours and hours hashing out who did or said what to whom. There is little traction to be gained in any of that. The first step for all couples who want to practice well, who want to make a heart-centered connection, has to be mindfulness.

1

WHAT IS MINDFULNESS?

Mindfulness gives you time. Time gives you choices.
Choices, skillfully made, lead to freedom.

—Bhante Henepola Gunaratan

I know I'm not anyone's first choice. People talk to parents, siblings, friends, clergy, or even their boss before they dial my number. An antiquated stigma shadows couple's therapy. Many of us feel shame admitting we need support; others never want to be one of "those" couples that need help to make it. The truth is, being in a relationship is challenging to everyone at times, even for me, and I'm a therapist who is married to a therapist. When a couple is ready and makes the difficult decision to go to therapy and consciously work on their relationship, they are anxious to roll up their collective sleeves and jump right into skill building. Their vision of the process is usually out of a movie. They imagine themselves tête-à-tête with their partners squaring off with the therapist acting as referee while they dig directly into their issues and each other. When I introduce mindfulness as the first fundamental skill to healing, some clients become frustrated and perplexed. They wonder how a practice so insular and focused on the self can be important to couple's work. Most hope therapy will be a place they can safely point out everything their other half is doing wrong. Secretly hoping to be deemed the good one, they find shining a light on their partner's foibles comes easy. When I turn the tables on this vision and start by asking each individual what they are thinking, feeling, and experiencing, let the puzzled looks and head-scratching begin.

Mindfulness is the skeleton key, the universal remote, an all-access pass to making a heart-centered connection. Without it, we are lost. It is the backbone of my work with couples and is an ever-present concept throughout this book. Mindfulness is integral to the execution of the core skills we will explore, and it is conceptualized in the Five Practices. The Practices are strategies uniquely designed to help couples reconnect.

In both my personal and professional opinion, mindfulness has the potential to change everything. When we are mindful, we change the focus from our partner's behavior, to our own. When we push our internal pause button, we harness the power to alter our habits and become aware of what we are thinking and feeling. If we are going to make changes to our behaviors that last, we must first develop the ability to see our lives and our relationships from the "witness position."

One client came in complaining about mindfulness. "I just don't understand what you mean. The concept is too out there for me. The *witness*? I feel what I feel, I think what I think."

"Yes," I replied. "But who is the one inside you that is watching. What part of you sees all that you feel and experience?"

The witness position is the essence of mindfulness. It is a frame of mind that affords us space between our emotions and our reactions, a place where we can observe our experiences without judgment. Since the concept of mindfulness is easily misunderstood and often hard to pin down, I find it helpful to first talk about what it is not, before explaining more in depth what it is.

WHAT MINDFULNESS IS NOT

During one onboarding conversation with a new client, I asked, "Do you have a mindfulness-based practice of any kind?" This prospective client replied that he did. In fact, he had a robust mindfulness practice. His meditation cushion was located in his bedroom and he used it twice a day, almost without fail, meditating for twenty minutes in the morning and at night before bed. He said he was drawn to my work as a therapist because of the mindfulness component.

"That's great," I said. "Sounds like my practice might be a good fit for you. Now, tell me again why you're calling?"

Without missing a beat, he replied, "My lawyer told me I needed to complete eight sessions of anger management due to a road rage incident I was involved in a few weeks ago."

This is not mindfulness.

At first glance, this philosophy from a foreign land can feel strange and mercurial to our Western minds. There has been a lot of confusion and misunderstanding with respect to the practice. For instance, it's a common misconception that mindfulness is meditation and that meditation is mindfulness. The terms have been used interchangeably for some time. However, these concepts are by no means synonymous. Mindfulness is the intended byproduct of a meditation practice. The idea being, the more we meditate, the more mindful we become. Evidenced by the example above, this is not always the case. For those who have tried meditation and found it wasn't a fit, have no fear, sitting cross-legged on a cushion and listening to your breath for what seems like an inordinate amount of time is not a prerequisite to leading a more mindful life or for using the Five Practices in your relationship.

Written off by the psychological community throughout the seventies, eighties, and nineties, mindfulness was relegated to the fringe of society and thrown into the New Age bin even though it's not a New Age concept. In fact, mindfulness has been around for about 2,500 years, but because of its lack of quantitative research, it was discredited in psychological circles. However, in the last decade mindfulness has enjoyed a host of solid trials bringing it to the forefront of self-help and therapeutic circles. It's made the cover of *Time* magazine twice and is supported by heavyweights in the field such as Oprah, Deepak Chopra, Dan Millman, Eckhart Tolle, and Tara Brach, to name a few.

THE MIND IS NOT MINDFUL

Our brains do not live in a mindful state. In fact, the brain defaults to a mindless mode called automatic pilot where it tends to wander. As an example, if you've ever had the experience of reading a book only to get to the end of a page, paragraph, or chapter and remember almost nothing you just read—this is automatic pilot. If you've ever had the experience of driving to work and, though you arrive there safely, you remember little if any of the trip, this too is automatic pilot, and is the antithesis of mindfulness. Harvard psychologist Ellen Langer has been at the forefront of mindfulness studies since the early seventies. According to Dr. Langer, "Most of us are not even there enough to know we aren't there."[1] Our brains are wired to wander and unless we have something particularly interesting or evocative to focus on, we default to a mindless state, especially when the people and situations in our lives are no longer novel.

Some years ago the Dalai Lama, the de facto spokesperson for mindfulness, was on one of his first tours of the United States. A reporter asked his holiness what he thought of our Western culture. In his typically compassionate way, the Dalai Lama stated simply, "You are all so distracted." Now more than ever, our phone-crazed, likes-driven, social media–aholic culture is not helping the matter.

At this point, you might be thinking, okay, but what's wrong with a little mind wandering? After all, everyone needs to check out from time to time to get a little brain break. Truth be told there is a good bit wrong with allowing our brains to go on automatic pilot, especially for couples. And while new studies continue to challenge the notion that a wandering mind leads to low mood or depression,[2] what we know for certain is that while on autopilot we are subject to our own knee-jerk reactions. In this state, we fall prey to our habituations and old patterns of thinking and acting. A mindless couple—a couple comprised of two individuals chronically on automatic pilot—is a couple in trouble. If this is you, you might not divorce, however, you will probably languish in an unfulfilling relationship or spend the next few decades driving each other crazy.

WHAT MINDFULNESS IS

Picture for a moment a person standing on a bridge looking over a river. They are simply standing on the bridge, perhaps leaning on the railing, regarding the water. They see the ripples, maybe some rocks or fish within. They feel and smell the moisture in the air and hear the water as it passes beneath. In this image the water is not actually water, it's representative of this person's thoughts and feelings. The bridge is mindfulness. In this example, the person is simply witnessing their thoughts and feelings from a distance, from the bridge. An example of what mindfulness would not be is if this person fell or jumped into the water/feelings.

If they did jump in, they would immediately be caught in the current of their emotions—they would be awash in their thoughts, possibly drowning in the river of their own experience.

Take a moment to experience mindfulness.

Read through this exercise two or three times before trying it.

> Take a deep breath in through your nose and into your belly, letting your abdomen expand.
>
> Now release the breath, letting it flow out through your mouth.
>
> Repeat this in-and-out breath two more times.
>
> Now allow yourself to breathe easily and freely.
>
> Bring your awareness to your thoughts. Just notice them.
>
> Notice what thoughts come up.
>
> It might be some event in the past or in the future.
>
> Whatever your thoughts are, just make note of them.
>
> Then bring your attention back to your in-and-out breath and back to the moment.
>
> The moment, the now is found in the breath, not in the thought.
>
> Your goal here is not to change anything but to bear witness—to observe your thoughts.
>
> Now take in another breath and focus your attention on the sensation of the in-breath as it goes deeper into your belly.
>
> Notice what you are feeling emotionally as well as in your body.
>
> What feelings and sensations are you aware of?
>
> Again, as with your thoughts, we only want to notice what you are feeling.
>
> You might notice that you are hungry or tired or even resistant to this exercise. You may notice that you are sad, angry, or happy for some reason.
>
> Whatever the case, notice your thoughts and feelings. Allow them to come and go like passing clouds.
>
> This is the present moment. This is mindfulness.

I give this guided meditation to my clients because mindfulness is a concept that is best felt rather than explained. Mindfulness is a pause in the mind's natural process of recognizing thoughts and feelings, judging them as good or bad, reacting to them, and then sorting them for storage in our memory banks. Mindfulness allows us to step back and observe this process—to be aware of what is happening for us mentally, emotionally, and physically without reacting. Later you will see the benefits of this practice when used in the difficult moments we encounter with our partners.

In my former life, I was an actor. Obviously not a particularly good one, or I wouldn't be writing a book on couple's therapy. One of the first lessons they teach you as an actor is to never act with kids or dogs. Why? Because a child and a dog are never trying to be present, they just are. In their natural state they are in the moment, in the now. If you are standing on stage with either one, *trying* to be in the moment, it's going to look effortful and you are going to be a bad actor.

Mindfulness is a practice that helps us to be in the present. It's a gentle way of focusing the mind that allows us to get in touch with the now. It's been called a "magic pill." I'd like to tell you that it's magic, that in one application mindfulness will cure all that ails you and your relationship, but it won't. Having said that, the benefits of a mindful practice can feel magical when couples begin to use it, but the key word I keep using, and the word I will continue to use throughout this book, is *practice*. Mindfulness is and has to be a practice if we are to gain all of its benefits. Because of the brain's default mode and because our minds are wired to wander, we have to practice to stay focused and in the moment. Mindfulness is a simple skill made difficult in large part because it's so hard to remember to do it.

We begin the practice of mindfulness by paying attention to our thoughts, feelings, and bodily sensations on purpose. We do this by bringing our gaze inward as you did in the exercise above. As best we can, we do this without judgment and without allowing our minds to move to thoughts of the past or the future. Put simply, mindfulness is looking with curiosity at our inner experience. It may feel a little weird at first because we are socialized to look externally for confirmation and validation of our experiences. Mindfulness flips the script on this and brings that outer gaze inward. This practice provides a natural pause as we stop and bear witness to what is happening for us. In my time as a therapist and corporate consultant, I have come to one irrefutable truth: If you want to excel at anything, whether it's business, sports, art, music, or your relationship, you must first learn to be a witness to your own inner experience.

The benefits of mindfulness are many, and the practice has been adopted by CEOs of Fortune 500 companies, professional and Olympic athletes, and the US Marines, as well as actors and performers from the stage and screen. All of whom are trying to achieve excellence in their respective fields. They are using this tool to take their careers and lives to the next level. It's hard to believe that the simple act of noticing our thoughts and feelings, rather than reacting to them, can be so beneficial but it can. In trials around the country and around the world, mindfulness has proven to reduce emotional exhaustion, psychological distress, depression and anxiety, occupational stress and overall stress, as well as physical pain. It also significantly improves emotional intelligence, relaxation, sleep, compassion for self and others, creativity, and overall health. While all these sound great and are certainly interesting benefits for the individual, why is mindfulness so important for couples?

2

WHY IS MINDFULNESS SO IMPORTANT FOR COUPLES?

Kindness can manifest as compassion, as generosity, as paying attention.

—Sharon Salzberg

WE ARE ALL CLAY BUDDHAS

A number of years ago in Thailand, a group of monks were moving a rather large, ancient, clay Buddha. In the move, the statue dropped and some of the clay began to break away. The monks were of course alarmed that they were damaging this ancient artifact. As they examined the place where the clay had broken away, they noticed something surprising. The Buddha wasn't made of clay at all; in fact, it was actually made entirely of gold. They came to understand that many centuries ago during a time of war, the monks in the area were afraid that the invading armies would steal their golden statues. In an effort to hide their treasure, they covered it in clay. Over the years the inner gold was forgotten and what was inside was lost.[1] The analogy here is fairly obvious. During times of turmoil and difficulty, as the world and the people in it begin to feel more and more dangerous, we put on an outer layer of protection. In doing so, we forget our inner gold. The practice of mindfulness reminds us of our true nature.

At our essence, we are beings capable of tremendous kindness, compassion, empathy, and understanding. These are qualities that are essential for couples who want to make a heart-centered connection. These are also qualities that can feel inaccessible when we are trying to protect ourselves from the vulnerability of love. I tell my clients, the people we love the most in the world can feel the most dangerous because they are uniquely designed to break our hearts and somewhere inside, we know it. As we sense this inherent danger, we begin to consciously and unconsciously take countermeasures and heap on protective layers of clay, so to speak. The practice of mindfulness gives us the ability to shut down our automatic response to wall off and protect. It gives us access to our inner gold—our inner nature of kindness and compassion. As a clinician, I see mindfulness as a missing link in couple's therapy and a reason couples have experienced such poor results.

FROM KNEE-JERK RESPONSE
TO COMPASSIONATE CHOICE

Mindfulness is fundamentally linked to compassion. When someone is compassionate, they tend to act with benevolence and are willing to help others in an effort to end their suffering. Researchers have said that mindfulness practitioners tend to be more compassionate. For many years the actual link between mindfulness and compassion remained somewhat of a mystery. I and others in the field of Eastern thought surmised that mindfulness leads to compassion because it puts us in a position of choice. Let me be clear on this point: We don't get to choose our thoughts and feelings, they come up as they do, and it's how we deal with them that matters. The brain is a structure so complex that 95 percent of its operations happen at the subconscious level. It has developed over the centuries to filter and sort literally billions of bits of information in seconds. Mindfulness allows us the ability to hack this complex system. When mindful, we can choose the way we react to our thoughts and feelings, affording us some authority over how we communicate, the words we use, and the tone we employ. Now the latest research is backing up these assertions with respect to mindfulness and compassion. MRI scans show that after just eight short weeks of mindfulness practice, the amygdala, a region of the brain associated with stress, fear, and emotion, actually shrinks, while the prefrontal cortex, an area of the brain associated with higher-order functions such as awareness, concentration, and decision making, thickens. Adrienne Taren, MD/PhD, cognitive neuroscientist and researcher, says that "mindfulness practice increases one's ability to recruit higher order, prefrontal cortex regions in order to down-regulate lower-order brain activity."[2] What this means in layman's terms is our knee-jerk, emotional responses can be negated through mindful practice and replaced with more compassionate reactions.

This is a particularly powerful tool with respect to relationships. When practicing mindfulness, we can respond from our most emotionally intelligent and healthy sides of self.

When the words hurt, when our partners bump into our wounds, it's normal to become defensive. Whether our protective measures are to fire back in anger or to ice the other out, you can bet these off-the-cuff, very primal responses are decidedly lacking in compassion. If this becomes a habit in a relationship and a primary mode of dealing with difficult issues, scar tissue will form. Your lover, who formerly hung the stars and the moon, will soon become someone to fear, dislike, or even hate. Watching couples in this dynamic brings to mind the Edgar Allan Poe quote "That years of love have been forgot in the fever of a minute."[3]

Mindfulness can help to stop all of this. As we push pause on our reactions, we are able to assess our options for a retort, as if they were unfolding in front of us like a color palette going from our least compassionate knee-jerk reaction to our most compassionate loving responses. Barring any sociopathic tendencies, if given the choice, the human condition can lead us towards compassion. Mindfulness practice clears the path to this innate capacity. If there is one element that a truly loving and connected relationship needs, it's compassion. Ironically, when couples begin to struggle and begin to react from their wounds, it is usually one of the first things to go. When compassion leaves a relationship, as it had in Nick and Tom's case in chapter 1, the gloves come off and formerly loving partners are now open to an array of unhealthy habits and behaviors that erode connection.

Nick and Tom

"You mentioned that we should 'try something different.' What would that entail?" Nick asked with a hint of resignation in his voice.

Fresh off their recent volley of pointed jabs about field trips and whose job is whose, Nick and Tom had for the moment stopped bickering, but the energy between them was still tense.

"It would entail slowing down. Stop the finger-pointing. Take the focus off your partner and bring it back to yourself."

"How do we do that when we are obviously driving each other crazy?" Tom asked.

"Let's start with what you notice. I asked a minute ago how this was going. It wasn't a rhetorical question. Ask yourselves, 'How is this going?'"

Tom said, "Not good."

"Really bad," Nick replied.

"Right! That's really important information that you are not paying enough attention to. When what you're doing isn't working, when it's not going well, it's the first sign that it's time to try something new. But you two are on autopilot doing the same thing over and over expecting that, somehow, something different is going to happen. Now, let's bring some awareness to how you're feeling."

Mirroring their last responses, Tom said, "Not good."

"Really bad," Nick replied. "I'm angry, really angry."

Tom continued. "Me too."

"Okay, so you're angry. I think that's pretty evident. I'm wondering what else you are aware of? What else is in there besides anger?"

"I feel really misunderstood," Nick offered.

Tom looked at him. "I don't think you like me anymore."

"I'd like each of you to take a deep breath and notice where in your body you feel what you are feeling."

Following my direction, both men took in a deep belly breath. Immediately, Nick's eyes filled with tears as he put his hand on his heart.

"I feel it here. I feel it right here. It's like my heart is breaking."

Tom put his hand on Nick's back to comfort him as he held his own emotions in check. Conserving words, Tom spoke in a clipped fashion so as not to break. "Yup, me too, chest, heart."

Nick said, "I'm sad. I'm sad we've treated each other this way. I feel like we're losing *us*."

Tom replied, "I know I haven't been the best version of myself in a long time."

"I want you to keep your awareness on your bodies. Notice what's there. Notice how the energy between you has shifted."

Tom reached over and held Nick's hand. "I'm sorry. Truly."

Nick, smiling through his tears, replied, "I know. I'm sorry too." With a wry grin on his face, he said to Tom, "And I do like you. I just like you better when you're like this."

DE-ESCALATING THE COUPLE CYCLE

If you were to thumb through the big book of couple's therapy models, like the one I had to study in graduate school, you would notice that de-escalation is the first step in almost every form of therapy. The question for the therapist is, how do you get couples to de-escalate, especially if they are triggered or have developed the habit of living in reaction to each other?

When our buttons are pushed, we experience a stress response. Our heart begins to race, our breathing becomes shallow, blood stops flowing to the extremities, and stress hormones are produced. We go into survival mode—into a part of ourselves that knows only how to defend against a predator. It is a survival mechanism that dates back to our early ancestors, who frequently had to run from bigger, stronger, faster, and scarier animals. And while we are no longer in the food chain, we can say with some assuredness that when in survival mode our options for responding to our partners are reduced to something like fight, flight, freeze, and appease.

As we saw with Tom and Nick, in order to interrupt this process, we must insert a mindful pause. In the pause we take a breath, then evaluate or name what we are thinking and feeling. This simple process lets the air out of the balloon, so to speak, and calms a triggered nervous system. From a physiological perspective, a pause and a few deep breaths activate the parasympathetic nervous system. It tells the brain that the threat is over. Our breath becomes deeper and slower, our blood pressure lowers, and our body begins to calm.

When I began teaching couples how to use mindfulness, I noticed that de-escalation was no longer a necessary first step in the work of reconnection. Through mindfulness practice, each partner showed up already de-escalated, nervous systems less triggered, and emotions in check. If at any point in the work emotions ran hot, we had a common practice and language that would lead to a cooldown.

As an example, let's say your partner does or says something that hurts you. Most of us have a knee-jerk response to defend ourselves, especially when it's our romantic partner who hurts us. However, our knee-jerk response is often our least compassionate response. When we employ mindfulness, we pause and notice our inner experience. When we do this, we become aware of what we are thinking and feeling and our desire to retaliate. We can then explore possible responses and the ramifications of each. Mindfulness helps us engage one of the most important tools for couples, emotional intelligence, the capacity to be aware of, control, and express our emotions in a thoughtful manner as well as navigate our relationship fairly and empathetically.

WHAT ABOUT RESENTMENT AND ANGER?

It is far easier to be mindful of our thoughts and feelings as well as our reactions when we are in relationships that are not hampered by years of poor practice and ill-treatment. It's another thing altogether to be the calm center of the universe when we are carrying years of pain and wounding.

Mindfulness is not an exercise in emotional bypass. Paying attention to your thoughts and feelings in an effort to de-escalate the tensions in your relationship does not mean you suddenly stop being hurt. In fact, mindfulness gives us an opportunity to truly understand, not only why we are angry, but the pain that lives underneath the anger.

In my work with anger management, I have come to see anger as a secondary response to a primary emotion, usually fear, shame, or sadness. For the most part, our anger is the body's way of saying "No, this is not okay." It is a protective measure against further hurt. As a clinical intern, I was the only man and the most likely candidate to head up the Men's Anger Management Department in an otherwise female practice. Thrown to the wolves, my anger management groups rarely centered on managing anger, but, instead, focused on the injuries and vulnerabilities that lived beneath the fury. To get these highly enraged and sometimes violent men to gain control of and understand their emotions, I asked them to stop focusing on their anger and instead pay attention to the thoughts and feelings that lived below the rage. With mindfulness, I witnessed these men learn to regulate their outbursts and began to heal the wounds that fueled their paroxysms.

In relationships that are both full of scar tissue and mindlessness, our options for communicating about our pain are severely limited. Conversations can and often do become volatile, brimming with the ire that lives under our protective measures. These discussions are typically one-note and leave little room for couples to move forward. In my experience, this is when communication devolves down to something akin to "Well, what about you?" with a partner responding, "No, what about *you?*" Sometimes to show my couples just how far down the communication maturity scale they have fallen, I will stop the "What about you"s and say, "Have you tried, 'maybe you are, but what am I?'"

We have to learn to talk about our anger rather than through it. When we speak through anger, we attempt to protect ourselves by wounding others. We resort to hurling expletives and name-calling, or withdraw and shut down altogether. Our conversations feel a lot like the conversation I witnessed between Nick and Tom, one where there is little space for insight or thoughtful consideration of their partner's position. In situations like this, I ask couples to take a breath, to feel their feet on the floor, or to notice the chair underneath them. This pause in the action has a grounding effect that titrates the nervous system. It clicks off the fight, flight response. Once settled, I ask couples to mindfully speak about how they feel—to talk about their feelings as if they are describing something that is sitting in the chair next to them. When we speak about our anger and hurt rather than through it, our discourse is less blaming. Conversations become less incendiary because the description of our pain and resentment seems more personal to our own experience and less critical of our partner's. In stark contrast to the conversation with Nick and Tom, when we talk about our anger and hurt rather than through it, we speak from an emotionally intelligent side of self. From this mindful place, our words are not chosen to inflict pain but to help our partners understand how we have been injured. There is an inherent vulnerability in this way of communicating. It says, in essence, I want to do something different, I want to change the game and chart a new path.

There is a popular notion that no one can make you feel anything, that you and you alone are responsible for your emotions. For me, this line of thinking is convenient and amounts to New Age fascism. People can absolutely hurt our feelings. This is especially true when that person is someone who is supposed to love us. We are not responsible for the way people treat us or how it makes us feel. We are, however, responsible for how we react to that hurt.

REWRITING THE BRAIN'S OLD PROGRAMMING AND THE ALL-ACCESS PASS

We've established that mindfulness can help couples get out of their knee-jerk reactions and help to de-escalate arguments, but how do we change our habits with each other?

We are creatures of habit, that's not news. Humans create habits both good and bad all of the time; in fact, our brains are geared toward automation. The human brain is a powerful machine that is always processing information. In order to sort all of the data coming in, the basal ganglia, a part of the brain associated with learning and both habit and emotional formation, and the prefrontal cortex, a brain region implicated in decision making, work in concert to turn repeated behaviors into automatic responses. Once a behavior has turned into an automatic response, the brain can rest, at least on that issue. The pull to automate is a boon as habit formation allows the brain to move on to new business. As an example, consider parents in the morning as they prepare themselves and their children for the day. As the sun rises on our house, my wife resembles a comic book superhero. She is simultaneously preparing herself for her day and her clients, probably fielding texts and phone calls, dressing children, breaking up fights, soothing feelings, some of them her own, directing childcare, and monitoring screen time, while preparing several sumptuous yet nutritious meals in an effort to give me time to write this book. She does most of this without having to consciously think about any of it. She, as with so many busy parents, is able to do this Cirque du Soleil–like performance because of the brain's ability to turn a behavior into an automated routine. While this sounds like a superhuman skill, as I alluded to in the "What Mindfulness Is

Not" section in chapter 1, automatic pilot is actually more of a bane than a boon for couples.

For the brain, budding love is like a shiny toy just out of the box, fresh and new. The brain has yet to go on autopilot as we endeavor to court and win our potential partner's heart. After the dopamine blast of the new relationship wears off and the stressors and responsibilities of life kick in, our partner begins to take a backseat, as other more urgent matters steal our attention. Like so many things in our lives, our thoughts, feelings, and considerations of our relationships can fall victim to our brain's natural tendency to automate. Couples that come to offices like mine are usually suffering from the side effects of autopilot. At best, these mindless relationships leave partners feeling complacent, bored, not considered, or taken for granted. At worst, autopilot causes toxicity, resentment, and ill-treatment that can border on mental, emotional, or verbal abuse.

Mindless couples are couples in trouble. Caught in negative-feedback loops, they are destined to strengthen these patterns through neural conditioning, or Hebb's Law. Hebb's Law, or the Hebbian Postulate, is a theory in neuroscience that stipulates that neurons that fire together wire together. Hebb's Law proposes that when we think the same thoughts and have the same experiences time and again, the neurons that consistently fire off in unison get used to working or "firing" together.[4] Based on this principle, couples who don't interrupt their negative patterns are unconsciously creating neural pathways in their brains that support negative thoughts and behaviors toward their partners. If left unchecked, we resent our partner as if they were our enemy. On autopilot, we create a narrative about our relationship that lacks kindness, consideration, or empathy. Mild annoyances in the beginning slowly turn to disdain. When our partner tries to connect with us, we see them through the lens of apathy and contempt. Unable or unwilling to change, our patterns eventually create neural pathways in our brains that move in the direction of hating the person we once swore we loved.

A CULTURE OF REVERENCE

Almost twenty years ago, my wife, then-girlfriend, and I were bartenders in New York City during our late twenties and early thirties. Needless to say, we had more than our share of fun and tequila-filled nights. Truth be told, some of those nights were not all that much fun. They ended in arguments fueled by too much booze, immaturity, and a lack of reverence for each other. We both did and said things we would prefer not to remember. One morning after a particularly rough verbal go at each other, we woke up hungover, tired, and ashamed at how we'd behaved. As we tended to, we spent the morning talking about and processing the events of the night before. We both felt terrible, and on that particular morning, lying on my futon, we made what seemed to be a small promise in my crummy apartment on 61st Street and 1st Avenue. We promised to never call each other a name again. The name-calling was infrequent but for my taste and hers, it was happening too often. It was bad practice and a bad habit easily assumed. Something inside of me knew it was the precursor to the type of relationship I didn't want, a relationship where the rules of engagement were subject to how angry you got. If we weren't careful, this would become the type of relationship where in the heat of battle, love and reverence for each other would be tossed aside.

And so the promise was made, no name-calling, ever. I have to admit I wondered, could I do it? Could I promise to always treat her preciously no matter how angry or hurt I became? Being mindful of the way we spoke to each other became a part of our practice as a couple. It's not that things were suddenly perfect because they weren't. We struggled as most new couples do trying to find our way together. We were tempted to break our promise when emotions ran high but we held fast to our oath. What we had unwittingly created in our relationship that seemingly insignificant morning was reverence. Reverence is a feeling of deep respect tinged with awe and veneration. It rarely makes the list of top ten things people need or want in their relationships, but it is foundational to love that stands the test of time. We all have people in our lives that we are careful with, people we treat mindfully. It might be a parent or grandparent, a young child, or a trusted best friend. We might even save this type of treatment for a boss, a colleague, or a client. Unfortunately, in my experience, our romantic partners are often low on the list of people who receive our reverence.

Years ago, I sat in session with a woman who spoke terribly about her husband, who sat inches from her. She talked about how lazy he was, his intellect or lack thereof, as well as the awful way he'd parented his children from a former marriage. His demeanor and the way he let her run roughshod over him through the session said he was a man who had stopped arguing long ago. He had given up fighting his case and had let go of any attempts at changing her mind about him.

I let the conversation go on for a short time to get a sense of what must happen in their home. At a certain point, I stopped her and asked, "What is it you do for a living again?"

"Physical therapist. Why?"

"I wonder, would you ever speak to any of your patients the way I just heard you speak to your husband?"

The look on her face became one of annoyance as the conversation shifted to her. "No, never," she replied in a way that suggested my question was ridiculous.

"Why?" I asked.

"Because I have a license I need to be concerned about."

"So you're telling me that your P. T. license is more important to you than your marriage license?" For the first time in the session, a smile began to crawl across her husband's face.

To varying degrees most couples struggle with a lack of reverence, but why? If we have a choice, and I would argue most of us do, why would we choose to live in a relationship that lacks this key ingredient to happiness and connection? And if we can do it for some people in our lives, why wouldn't we do it with the person we sleep next to, made a life with, and maybe even created other people with? The answer, as sad as it might sound, is because we don't have to. You see, we know our partners are invested. Through time, kids, familial connections, monetary ties, mortgages, marriage certificates, and all of the other trappings of a relationship, we are pretty sure they aren't going anywhere anytime soon and it makes us lazy. We figure "They'll be fine, I'll make it up to them," or worse, "They'll get over it." Because our partners are heavily leveraged in us, we figure we have a lot of chances, plenty of shots, and enough at-bats to get it right. Here's the truth: We don't actually have that many chances to get it right. Lack of reverence leaves marks that look like scars. You might be saying to yourself, "Yeah but we aren't like that couple. We don't talk to each other like that." Okay, but do you treat your partner with the same kindness and consideration with which you treat your best friend, colleague, or client? Do you treat each other preciously and with reverence? If you don't, I have more news: It makes your relationship average, boring, and nothing special.

Something happens in a relationship when we lay down the cudgels and put our partner's heart in the china cabinet. When we decide that the usual ways of defense are no longer welcome or appropriate, hearts begin to open because it's suddenly safe for them to be open. Ashley and I had no idea that our promise to each other would forever alter the culture of our relationship and foster a space where love might have the chance to take root. If not for the practice of mindfulness, our story would have gone in a different direction. Without mindfulness, this story would be a forgotten instance from a time where the romanticism and naivete of young love let us dare to consider the impossible. This might sound overstated but it's true; mindful practice in your relationship has the potential to make what might seem impossible very, very possible.

ATTUNEMENT

It's wonderful to be loved, but it's profound to be understood.

—Ellen DeGeneres

It was the end of Ashley's and my second year at the Helix Training Program in New York City. Helix was a four-year training in psychospiritual counseling. Its eclectic approach to therapy made it feel more like we were attending the Hogwarts School of Witchcraft and Wizardry than some stuffy clinical program. Helix satisfied our insatiable need to know about the mind, body, and spirit, and the interplay of these fundamental pieces. It gave our need to understand those pieces guidance and direction, and, by the end of the second year, we both showed signs that we were geared for and gifted in this line of work.

I rose one morning to find Ashley, as I often did in those days, dark and despondent. I used to say the Helix Training motto should have been *"If you can't work your own shit, how can you help anyone else work theirs?"* because Helix asked us to gut ourselves and walk the same path to healing we were going to ask our clients to walk. It sounds great in theory until you get on the path, and that's where I found Ashley that morning, on her beautiful and terrible path toward healing. She sat in our living room curled up in the overstuffed chair with one of my old T-shirts stretched down over her knees. Tears streamed down her face. I sat down on the couch across from her. "Are you okay? What's wrong?" I asked. The subject of our conversation escapes me now, maybe because I wasn't really listening—maybe because I just didn't want her to hurt anymore. Whatever the case, when she was through sharing her deep and excruciating pain, a pain she could barely share with herself let alone another person, my response was, "Why don't you try using your tools?" referring of course to the multitude of tools and skills we had been trained to use at school. I mean, it made sense, right? I figured we had all of this knowledge—she should just use it on herself. Problem solved.

I may not remember why she was crying that morning but I will never forget the look on her face, which was a mix of disbelief, anger, fear, and abandonment. I wish I could say I regretted the words once they'd left my mouth. I wish I could say it was a momentary lapse in judgment and that I regained my composure and self-corrected immediately, but I didn't. I wanted to fix her. I didn't want to be present for her process and I didn't want to take the time to understand her pain. I wanted the person I loved more than anything not to hurt anymore, and, as admirable as that is, it was not at all what she needed. Glennon Doyle in her book *Love Warrior* says, "You have to be known to be loved."[5] In that moment, Ashley desperately needed to be known by me. She needed someone to tell her, "I see you. I hear how hard all of this is. I love and understand you." Unfortunately for her, for me, and for us, I missed this chance because I was caught up in the need to have the answer to her pain. I missed this chance, not because I didn't care but because I was not paying attention to her with purpose. I was not attuned to her.

Attunement is mindfulness's little-known cousin. While mindfulness is the act of turning our gaze inward, attuning is turning that gaze outward, in an attempt to become mindful of others. When we attune to others we can understand their inner world, we focus our attention not only on their words but also on patterns in their energy. "The subjective side of attunement is the authentic sense of connection, of seeing someone deeply, of taking in the essence of the other person in the moment. When others sense our attunement with them, they experience 'feeling felt' by us."[6]

In romantic relationships, attunement is our capacity to perceive, understand, and be present for our partner's emotions. It is the state of being where we put aside our own agendas in an attempt to truly grasp and fathom the depth of another's experience. As evidenced by the quotes referenced in this section, when we attune to our partners, it makes them feel loved because they feel known and understood. But here's the rub: Feelings tend to make most of us uncomfortable. Because of this discomfort, we tend to pathologize feelings in our culture. If we aren't feeling good, we believe something must be wrong and we should take measures to stop those feelings immediately. Pop-psychology tells us not to feel what we are feeling. The ever-popular Law of Attraction tells us that we can't feel bad. If we feel bad, then we are not vibrating at the level of the thing we want to attract, and in this, we risk not manifesting *that* thing into existence. Okay, but what do I do with my gut-wrenching fear, grief, and shame?

Years ago, I asked, no, I begged my therapist to give me a prescription for anxiety medication to help me get rid of some difficult feelings. I was about to ask my first wife for a divorce. My life was a mess and I was about to hurt a good person. My shrink responded by saying, "Your heart is broken. Sad and despondent are really appropriate emotions for this situation. You should feel this." As much as I hated it, I knew she was right, and I did not take medication to bury the feelings.

In Buddhism, the image of the lotus flower is used to symbolize the human condition. To fully understand this image, we must remember that it includes the flower and the mud it grew from. It includes not just the light but the dark of life as well. However, in the West we tend to focus on the pretty flower, forgetting that if not for the dirt, mud, and darkness, there would be no bloom. Life provides suffering, and we need to feel sad, angry, or despondent from time to time. When someone we love is struggling, it may seem antithetical to tune in and be present, especially when we are sure to feel de-skilled and ineffectual in the process. Very often this type of experience can create feelings of avoidance, frustration, or, in my case, a strong need to fix or save.

Sitting across from Ashley that morning, it was news to me that I was not being asked to do anything with her emotions. The practice of attunement can feel like a cruel prank; I mean surely we are required to do more than just sit on our hands and "be present"? But that is exactly what I did. I attuned to her and learned to do less, listen more, and allow my innate compassion and empathy for her to flow. Her feelings were no longer inconvenient or annoying, they were simply her feelings. They came and went like passing rain. It is my job to be with Ashley through the storms, to be present and curious about her suffering. As her partner, it is my job to be a witness to her life. She is not a project for me to fix. As a matter of fact, when I took my tool belt off, I learned Ashley is capable of using her tools when she needs to and she will use them when she is good and ready.

This brings me to another important and elemental point in this concept of attunement: listening. We established earlier that in order to be loved we must first be known. I'll follow that with, if we are to be known we must first be heard. I don't believe it's too far a stretch to say that most people aren't good listeners. We have a natural tendency to want to speak and be heard first. In conversation, most people are thinking about what they are going to say next even as their partner is speaking. As I stated before, the human brain is geared for automation and sorting information. It is not, however, geared toward listening. This is why it can feel strange and wonderful when someone, anyone, listens and asks clarifying questions in an attempt to comprehend our experience. This type of attuned listening is in part what makes therapy so appealing. To truly stop, to push pause on everything else, and be present for another's experience is a cognitive, behavioral effort; in other words, it is a mindful effort.

In my practice, teaching couples to be mindful is job one, helping them to attune to each other is a close second. In relationships where mindfulness and attunement are at a deficit, there is a compromised ability to go to any real depth. Romantic partners are left feeling alone, angry, abandoned, and resentful as if they are speaking their life's experiences into an abyss where no one cares and no one is listening. As you will find out later in Practice 3, the Narrative, a lack of attunement, and its accompanying behaviors, corrode our interpersonal connections.

When we don't feel seen or heard by our loved ones, we begin to create negative and toxic narratives about our partners that dramatically impact our beliefs about who they are and who they are not. However, when we attune, we say, in effect, I am here for you—I care and will bear witness to you and to your life. Not only do you matter but you can count on me. This type of effort in the direction of the ones we love strengthens the bonds between us and develops deep and long-lasting trust.

We *are* beings capable of tremendous amounts of kindness, compassion, empathy, and understanding. This is the treasure we have to offer to the ones we love. However, like those clay Buddhas, we hide and protect our treasure, especially when we feel vulnerable. When we are mindful of our partners, we move past our natural pull towards shutting down or walling off. There is a duality in our experience of romantic love; while we desperately want to connect at the heart, opening our hearts can feel excruciatingly exposing. Mindfulness helps us hold space for this dichotomy.

In this chapter, I have outlined the benefits of this discipline. Now it's time to practice. In the upcoming chapter, I will outline in detail how to use mindfulness in your life and in your relationship. For now, begin to consider your thoughts and feelings. Notice your inner world from a new and different lens—the lens of the witness. Take a breath, push pause on your reactions, and just notice. And oh yeah, breathe.

3

HOW TO PRACTICE MINDFULNESS
IN YOUR RELATIONSHIP

Just watch this moment, without trying to change it at all.
What is happening? What do you feel? What do you see?
What do you hear?

—Jon Kabat-Zinn

MR. MIYAGI'S DOJO

A few weeks had passed since I had seen Tom and Nick. Today they
sat on my couch closer together, the energy between them very
different from our previous session.

Nick laughed. "You Miyagi'd us."

It was obvious they shared a joke I wasn't in on. I didn't mind but
I was curious. "I don't understand."

Tom, trying to clear up my confusion, said, "You know Pat
Morita, *The Karate Kid*. Wax on, Wax off."

"I know the movie, sure, but how did I 'Miyagi you'?"

Tom explained further. "You know, all the mindfulness stuff. Having us do the mini-meditations, the mindful walks, mindful eating. I
never realized how quickly I wolf down my food."

Nick laughed again and swatted at Tom playfully. "You're just
realizing that, *really*?" He turned to me. "I try not to get my hands too
close when he's eating for fear of losing a finger." Rather than be offended, Tom nodded his head knowingly.

I was amazed. The shared kindness and lightheartedness between
them was either new or had resurfaced from the beginning of their
relationship. Gone were the pointed verbal jabs and eye rolls. They were

playing off each other like a comedy team. I could see for the first time the attraction that initially drew these two men together.

Nick and Tom's reference was, of course, to the 1980s movie *The Karate Kid*, where Mr. Miyagi, played by Pat Morita, teaches a teenage boy, Daniel, played by Ralph Macchio, the art of karate. However, as everyone who has seen the movie knows, Mr. Miyagi takes a rather unorthodox and circuitous approach to his teaching. Rather than punches and kicks, Daniel is tasked with a series of seemingly meaningless and mundane chores. He paints fences, waxes cars, and sands floors, all of which he believes are unrelated to his expressed desire to learn karate. As the plot of the movie moves forward, Daniel is surprised that his chores were actually the building blocks of his skill set as a karate champion.

Nick and Tom's allusion to Mr. Miyagi was fitting. Couples in my practice can feel a little like Daniel when I ask them to engage in practices that feel irrelevant to their expressed desire to connect with each other. In this latest session, Nick and Tom were feeling the effects of mindfulness practice in their relationship. They were learning to de-escalate tense conversations by pausing and choosing their reactions to each other. The space between them was kinder, compassionate, and full of reverence.

As I stated in the beginning of chapter 2, there is an expectation of what couple's therapy looks like. Rather than prescribe cliché couple's exercises, I offer breathing spaces, routine tasks done with consideration, meals eaten in contemplation, and attention paid not to the partner but to the self. In short, I offer mindfulness practice first, often, and throughout my work with couples from beginning to end, and the results are often astounding.

Mindfulness applied to couple's work offers a new experience and a redefinition of therapy. But it begs that the bulk of the effort happens outside of the therapy office. I like to tell my clients that while your experience in session will of course be mind-blowing and wonderful beyond your wildest expectations, if the majority of your labor exists within the confines of your appointment, you can be sure your relationship will not get a whole lot better.

To this end, you must endeavor to put mindfulness on your proverbial table every day, all the time. It's easy to go on autopilot and forget to be aware, that's what the brain is wired to do. When you make mindfulness a part of your daily routine, you begin to see the benefits rather quickly. Studies show it takes as little as six to eight weeks to see the rewards of mindfulness, but many of my clients report seeing the needle move in the right direction even sooner.[1]

The following are a few examples of mindfulness-based exercises and how they can be used in your life and in your relationship.

TIME

To become more mindful in your relationship is to be mindful in your daily life. This means taking a little time every day to set an intention. For our purposes, your intention is to be more mindful and aware of your thoughts and feelings and to be more present for your partner. Oprah Winfrey opens her podcasts with the statement "One of the most valuable gifts you can give yourself is time. Taking time to be more fully present." My interpretation of that is time *to* ourselves and time *for* ourselves. This is time to contemplate, time to journal, and time to read inspiring material. My suggestion to jump-start your mindfulness practice is to set aside a little time every day just for you. It can be as little as ten or fifteen minutes up to and beyond an hour. Dr. Joe Dispenza, author of *Breaking the Habit of Being Yourself* and *Becoming Supernatural*, gives himself upwards of two and a half hours every morning of personal time to prepare himself for his day. Obviously, most of us are not this time affluent, but whatever time you can afford, take it, make room for it, and then guard it. This might mean that you have to get up a little earlier or go to bed a little later, but the end result is worth it.

Taking time to contemplate life, your day, and, yes, your relationships sets the stage, as it were. We can plan and mentally prepare for whatever work or the tasks of our day as well as ask, "How do I want to interact with my partner?" "How are we doing?" "Do I/we need to do something different?" I encourage all of my clients to adopt the practice of taking mindful and intentional time every day. I ask them to journal about their thoughts and feelings so as to be more aware of them. I urge them to read books or articles on self-help, healing, relationships, or any topic they find inspirational, informative, or educational.

When we start or end our day in this fashion, we tend to be better prepared for whatever life throws at us. We are more self-aware and able to act with emotional intelligence when situations become triggering. Many of my clients report that when they begin their mornings by reading, journaling, or just thinking about their day, they are less reactive and more mindful and aware of themselves and of their partners. Personally, I like to give myself an extra thirty minutes to an hour of this reflective time. I typically start with a breathing space, where I can get a sense of what I am thinking and feeling. I will read excerpts from my favorite books and consider taking one of the concepts I read out into my life for practice. Towards the end of my time, I will set an intention for close relationships in my life. I ask myself, "How do I want to show up for my wife, for my kids, and for my clients?" Most of us simply arrive in our lives and to our relationships in whatever state, mood, or mindset we happen to be in. Without intention and time to set that intention, our relationships are subject to the vagaries and stressors of life.

THE THREE-TO-FIVE-MINUTE
MINDFUL PAUSE, NAMING, AND NOTING

The pause can be taken anywhere. It can happen at your desk, on a crowded bus or train, or standing in line at the bank. Some clients report they don't even have *that* kind of time to devote to the practice, especially not three times a day. To that, I will say, "Really? When was the last time you looked at or posted to social media?" If you have time for social media or to surf the internet, you have time to take a few mindful pauses. For people who say they can't find the time or they can't seem to remember to do it, my response is that there is a good chance you don't want to. I know that might sound harsh, but I believe we do what we want to do and we don't do what we don't want to do. Put simply, it's a choice to prioritize other things over this practice and your relationship. If this is true, you might consider skipping to the section of this book titled "What If They Refuse to Own It?" in chapter 19.

In the beginning, I ask clients to set alarms on their phones that go off in the morning, at noon, and then once more in the evening. This is a routine I still use when I feel my mindfulness practice has gone off track. Mindfulness is a practice that can best be described as simple but not always easy. The pauses last anywhere from three to five minutes in length. The only other requirement is to name or note whatever feeling is present or arises. For example, if anger arises, I coach my clients to say softly to themselves, "This is anger, this is my anger, I am angry." If sadness is the prevailing feeling, I have them repeat to themselves, "This is sadness, I am so sad." I have them do this until their nervous systems begin to settle. Naming is a traditional mindfulness-based technique that helps us become less reactive or hijacked by our emotions. "A shift in our experience takes place when we find the right word to describe it. When we are called by our correct name or our experience is correctly named, we relax and breathe easier from being understood."[2]

Naming brings our attention inward and directs it to the only thing we have control over: ourselves. As we take our power back through naming or noting, we feel less compelled to place blame or to fire back. All of this can lead to a pronounced de-escalation of our triggered nervous systems. Naming might not rid us of problematic or uncomfortable emotions in total, that's not what it's meant to do. When we name or note a feeling, we are simply stating this is what is true for me right now. In our culture, we spend an inordinate amount of time trying not to feel how we feel. In this way, naming can seem antithetical to our usual way of processing emotion.

"A successful relationship depends upon us recognizing our own painful feelings and emotions inside—not fighting them, but accepting, embracing, and transforming them."[3]

Pushing pause on our knee-jerk reactions should be a fundamental tool for any couple. These types of mindfulness exercises not focusing directly on the couple have a way of softening the space between partners.

After the three of us shared a laugh about Nick's Miyagi joke, he said, "Mindfulness practice might not solve all of our problems, but it certainly gives us a new way of dealing with them. I would pause, and then just notice how I was reacting to the things he (Tom) would do or say. Then I'd take a breath and think, 'How do I want to talk to him? How do I want this to go?'"

In support, Tom said, "Before I knew it, it was like the old days again. I would see Nick not reacting—he stopped being snippy, the way he used to be. I could see him trying to do something different and it made me want to try harder too. I practiced the mini-meditations religiously throughout my day and I swear it makes a difference."

For Nick and Tom, mindfulness worked as a salve to the tensions between them. It paved the way for new and different discussions about old topics that at one point were deemed too sensitive and off-limits.

MINDFULNESS OF EVERYDAY TASKS

In many mindfulness-based courses, everyday tasks are done with awareness to help make the formal practice of mindfulness more understandable and user-friendly. For many, mindfulness can be confusing, leaving us to wonder "Am I doing this right?" Learning to perform the mundane chores of life from a more present place not only makes mindfulness accessible, it also allows for innumerable opportunities to practice throughout our day. I ask individuals to choose a few routines that are often performed on autopilot and without much consideration or thought. Examples of these routines are showering, taking out the trash, going for a walk, or eating a meal. The instructions are simple. Choose a task and slow it down, perform it mindfully. This means, as best you can, keep your focus on the task at hand. As your mind begins to drift, and it will, gently bring your attention back to whatever you are doing in the moment. If you are washing dishes, notice how the water feels. Bring your attention to your hand as it moves over the dish. Feel the sponge in one hand and the dish gripped in the other. If you are taking a walk, notice how it feels to move your body in this way. Notice your environment, what do you see that you might have missed before? A good rule is to try to note five new things in the experience that you were once only vaguely aware of. With mindfulness, repetition is our friend. When on autopilot it is easy to forget to be aware. The goal is to strengthen your mindful muscle and to make you aware of when you go on autopilot. With our mindful muscles strengthened, we are less likely to have a knee-jerk reaction.

WHAT WOULD LOVE DO?

When Nick and Tom's interactions became overly emotional and teetered on reverting to toxicity, I gave them a technique I call "What

Would Love Do?" "What Would Love Do?" is a practice I ask couples to employ when things are bad and getting worse. It is a simple, fail-safe technique that if used properly will save both partners from creating further chaos or injury.

In this approach, the first person to become aware that things are going to a bad place is the anchor. I ask the anchor to take a deep breath and ask the question, "What would love do now?" and do that thing. It might mean they reach out physically to hug or hold a hand, take responsibility for what they've done or said, or validate their partner's feelings rather than continue to argue the point. Whatever the case, "What Would Love Do?" is an interruption and a reminder that our goal is to make a heart-centered connection, not to destroy each other. I want to point out that this technique can be difficult at first because it can feel like we are giving up in the middle of the fight. It can feel like we are abandoning our argument and to some degree giving in. Rest assured, "What Would Love Do?" is not giving in. This technique is merely a recognition that we are heading in a bad direction, maybe a direction we have gone before. "What Would Love Do?" is an understanding that we need to reset and begin from a place of kindness and compassion.

For some, this technique might feel like a Band-Aid; however, I see it as a course correction. What love would actually do moves us in an entirely different direction from where we are headed. The biggest advantage to this approach is that it affords us an opportunity to stop hurting each other and to ask how much further down the road of pain we want to go.

I can report both for my clients and for myself this question can feel like a bucket of much-needed cold water in the face. It wakes us up to the chaos we are willfully creating, but it's not always easy to implement. Thankfully, the question itself puts us in a mindful place and highlights the underlying link between mindfulness and compassion. It is my belief and experience, with few exceptions, that when we are faced with inflicting more pain or acting through our innate kindness, the human condition will lead us inexorably toward our compassion. The practice of "What Would Love Do?" puts this choice in the forefront of our minds in the moments we need our benevolence most.

THE MINDFUL BREAK

All couples experience conflict. From time to time, conversations become intense enough that one or both partners need a break from the action. These situations necessitate a strategy—one that allows for a pause in the conversation while acknowledging the abandonment that can be felt if a partner leaves the exchange abruptly.

Like so many couples, Nick and Tom had bad practices in their relationship when things got heated. One tactic Nick used was the "violent leave." The violent leave happens when someone storms out of an argument or difficult discussion. This type of leave usually begins with some kind of grand proclamation such as "I don't know if I can do this anymore!" or "Maybe we should just rethink our entire relationship!" It is then punctuated with an exit and a slammed door. I refer to this leave as violent because there is an underlying violent component to it. When we take it apart, we see that there is a statement made that brings into question if the relationship can or will continue. This statement is a tactic used to inflict fear to gain the upper hand and is in essence a form of violence.

Whether the door used is an exit to the outside or to another room is inconsequential. The leave to another room is only marginally better because regardless of the exit, an abandonment without warning is, by its very nature, again, violent. While this might sound like an overstatement, the message is, "I'm capable of discarding you, vacating the premises and this relationship." The partner that leaves is giving the other a taste of what being left would feel like.

This type of leave can be particularly difficult for people who have abandonment histories. For those who have been wounded by abandonment, the feelings the violent leave can engender are regressive and can bring the pain of their childhoods rushing back. Childhood is a time when we are powerless and at our most vulnerable. People with an abandonment history can have reactions to the violent leave that seem out of scope with the current moment. For relationships where one or both partners have an abandonment history, learning to use the Mindful Break is extremely important.

When I couched the violent leave as a tactic that is unfair, out of bounds, and violent in its way, the pushback I received, and the argument Tom countered with, was "What am I supposed to do, just sit there and endure bad treatment?" The answer is, of course, no. No one should be forced to sit in proximity to anyone whose behavior you cannot abide. However, making a grand statement that calls into question the validity of the relationship and then abandoning your partner cannot be the answer either. This is especially true if the goal is to make the relationship better. When clients need a break from the conflict and time to gather their thoughts, I offer the "Mindful Break." The Mindful Break allows for time away but dispenses with the grand proclamations and the abandonment of the "violent leave."

STEPS TO THE MINDFUL BREAK

Step 1: Take a few breaths and bring your attention and focus inward for a moment. This is a moment to stop engaging in the conflict and use your breath to bring your triggered nervous system back to center.

Step 2: Name what you are feeling. Remember when you do this, you give yourself space from your feelings. You might say to yourself, for example, "I'm angry," "I'm hurt," or "I need to leave the room."

Step 3: Tell your partner as compassionately as you can what you need and what you are going to do next. "I could use a break from this conversation" or "This back-and-forth doesn't seem to be going anywhere constructive. Is there any way we can take a break from it?"

Step 4: Tell your partner that you are going to take a break. Then promise to return in an agreed-upon amount of time. For example, "I'm going to take my break but I will be back in _____ minutes/hours or in the morning and we can talk more then." Establishing the agreements and language used around the Mindful Break outside of conflict is a useful strategy. Here you can negotiate agreeable time frames for breaks that work for both partners and the words used in asking for the time away. Taking proactive measures eradicates the element of surprise.

It is the ambiguity of the violent leave that can feel cruel and heartless. In contrast, it is the specificity of the Mindful Break that can feel quite kind and loving. Taking the time to be specific about a needed break from the conflict and then to name when you plan to return denotes care and compassion. This will feel like a tidal shift from the current conflict and can serve to reset the conversational table going forward. For Nick, Tom's willingness to use the Mindful Break let the younger parts of him know that he was not being left forever. It acted as a clear and healthy boundary for any disagreements going forward.

For Nick and Tom, the work was by no means over. They were enjoying the afterglow and de-escalating effects mindful practice can bring to a relationship. By taking the time to practice these simple but powerful tools, they acquired the knowledge necessary to radically redefine their connection. With a foundation of mindfulness, they opened the door to the other four practices and with them a whole new world of possibilities.

As you dive into this material, you may experience some resistance. Please understand resistance to the new and different is normal. If and when it comes, simply name it and notice it. Be present with your resistance and watch if it fades or asserts itself in each new practice. Now, I invite you to practice mindfulness in your life and in your relationship.

4

MINDFULNESS EXERCISES

Thích Nhất Hạnh said, "If you love someone, the greatest gift you can give them is your presence. How can you love, if you are not even there?"[1] Mindfulness is the practice of paying attention on purpose to what's going on inside of us mentally, emotionally, and physically from moment to moment. When we practice mindfully, we are better able to regulate our emotions, effectively stopping our knee-jerk response to each other. Practice 1 teaches us how to be more present in our relationships. When we are present, we can be more aware of our own behaviors as well as better attuned to our partner's needs.

In this chapter, I offer a number of exercises that will not only bolster your understanding of mindfulness but will help you use it in real time. These techniques are designed to give you a working knowledge of this concept. Take time to get to know and understand mindfulness practice and all of the benefits it can afford you.

THE PRACTICE

1. Time
2. Three-to-Five-Minute Breathing Space
3. Attunement: Notice Five New Things
4. Awareness of an Unpleasant Experience
5. Mindfulness of an Everyday Task
6. What Would Love Do?
7. Stealing Time

EXPLANATION

1. Time

     Make a commitment of time to yourself and to your mind-fulness practice. Take time every day to pay attention to your thoughts and feelings. Meditate on them or journal about them. This is an opportunity to learn to listen and pay attention. Remember, this is not a chance to fix or judge yourself; it is time for understanding. As you gift yourself this time, notice how it is affecting you and the people around you. Are you more engaged and present? Are you more aware of your thoughts and feelings? Are your reactions different? Has anyone noticed a change in you?

2. Three-to-Five-Minute Breathing Space

     This exercise asks you to pause three times a day, every day this week, and notice your thoughts, feelings, and bodily sensations. It can be helpful to set an alarm or download a mindfulness app with a reminder that goes off mid-morning, midday, and again in the evening.

     Sit for three minutes in a comfortable position and bring your focus to your breath. Pay attention to your inhale and your exhale. Notice if your mind wants to drift off or jump around. When and if you get distracted, bring your awareness back to your breath. You might find it difficult in the beginning to quiet your mind or focus. This is normal. If you become frustrated, try not to judge yourself. Instead, note the frustration and then go back to your breath.

     After three minutes, take a moment to contemplate your experience. Did your mind slow down or speed up? Do you feel more relaxed or more agitated? What did you become aware of? There are no wrong answers. You can record your thoughts and feelings in a journal. Remember, the hardest part of mindfulness is remembering to do it. This exercise is designed to help you keep mindfulness in mind.

3. Attunement: Notice Five New Things

     Dr. Ellen Langer says if you want to become more mindful in your relationship, simply notice five new things about your partner. These can be five things that are not necessarily "new" but are aspects of them you paid little attention to before. When we attune to our partners, as outlined in chapter 2, we begin to notice things about them. For example, you may notice a new hairstyle or article of clothing, a note of sadness in their voice, or a shift in their energy. You may also notice something they've done that seems routine but has never garnered a "thank you." Attuning to your partner tends to make them feel seen and understood.

Set an intention to attune and notice things you have not seen before. Kindly and compassionately communicate what you see. It takes almost no effort to be considerate in this way; again, the hardest part of this exercise is remembering to do it.

4. Awareness of an Unpleasant Experience

When unpleasant people or events come into our lives, we tend to stew on them. Typically we go on autopilot, thinking about what happened. We imagine and have fantasies about what we should have done or should have said.

Unpleasant events have a way of pushing our buttons. As a practice try to recall something or someone that was notably unpleasant. Notice how it makes you feel to recall the experience. What does this event make you think? What does it make you want to do or say? What do you feel in your body? What fantasies does it conjure up?

Now use Naming and Noting as outlined in chapter 3. Just simply name what the feeling is. "I'm angry, I'm so angry," "I'm so hurt," or "I feel so guilty. This is guilt." As best as you can, don't let the dialogue go further than what you are feeling. Notice what happens in your body when you focus your attention not on the person or situation, but on the raw feelings.

5. Mindfulness of an Everyday Task

Everything we do can be made into a mindfulness exercise. Pick one task each day this week to perform mindfully. Tasks could include eating a meal, taking a shower, driving to work, brushing your teeth, cleaning the house, and the like. As best you can, bring moment-to-moment awareness to the task at hand. Focus your mind on each movement or aspect of the task.

Notice if and when your mind begins thinking about something else and simply bring it back to your task. Notice how it feels to be totally present and in the moment. Notice how it feels to drift off. This practice is like doing a mindful push-up. Every time you drift off, it is like the release to the floor, whenever you bring your mind back to the task at hand, it's akin to pushing your body back to plank position. Every time you drift and come back you are strengthening your mindful practice.

6. What Would Love Do?

What Would Love Do? is a method I use to de-escalate difficult situations. However, its practice can be useful during calm moments as well. When you are with your partner, ask yourself "What would love do right now, in this situation?" Love might reach out and hug your partner or hold their hand. Love might offer help or consultation. It might ask you to listen deeply, to not fix but to attune to your partner and be present.

Notice how this practice makes you feel. Is there any resistance to the action love would ask of you? If so, why? Whatever love would ask of you, remember to do it mindfully and with reverence.

7. Stealing Time

I try to put mindfulness on my calendar every day. If I don't have time to meditate, I'll use the time when I am commuting, waiting on line, or in a doctor's office, or while I'm on hold to practice. These formerly wasted moments of life can be golden opportunities to become more acquainted with mindfulness. The more we practice mindfulness, the more we get in the habit of switching off autopilot—coming into presence both for ourselves and our partners. There will always be excuses not to practice. These exercises are designed to make it easy but you have to choose it. In short, you gotta wanna.

Part 2

PRACTICE 2: THE PARTS OF US

> Remember, you are the child kicking and screaming and
> the one that holds that child with compassion. You are the
> one who judges and attacks and the one who forgives and
> atones for the attack.
>
> —Paul Ferrini

Liz's cheeks flush and her back straightens. My question about their homework doesn't embarrass her; she's angry. "Well, I *noticed* I was horny and wanted to have sex with my partner, that's not news. I also *noticed* that John didn't do any of the homework."

"That's not true, Liz. I did my homework, I noticed my thoughts and feelings."

"Really?" Liz shoots back. "Because I *noticed* you didn't reach for me at all this week, not once."

John replies, his tone calm, "You didn't reach for me either, sweetie."

"I don't want to be the one constantly reaching, John. I want you to reach for me, for a change. I want to be kissed, and not like my brother would kiss me, not a peck on the cheek. I want to be kissed passionately. I've all but given up on the idea of *actual* sex."

Liz and John are smart, kind, generous people with interesting careers and robust social lives. More importantly, they are genuinely interested in working on themselves and their relationship. In our first session, Liz described John as "an amazing man in a sea of not great guys." She felt lucky to have found her "diamond in the rough." For John's part, he appears to not only love Liz but also has a deep and abiding respect for her. After four years together, the banter between them was still connective and playful. However, when the subject of sex came up, the issue they came to work on, the warm feelings between these two loving partners began to cool. Their sex life had been on a steady decline for two years. Sex was now relegated to vacations or when they'd had too much to drink.

The week before, I'd given them homework. I asked them to use the mindfulness-based exercise in Practice 1, to notice and become aware of any sexual thoughts or feelings they experienced toward each other. The understanding was that they didn't have to act on their feelings unless they wanted to. The second part of their assignment was to notice moments when they could be more physically connected. This could include hand-holding or cuddling on the couch or in bed. I wanted Liz and John to become aware of the feelings that came up around touch. Were there any barriers or a need to pull away? If it felt safe enough, could they ford the physical gap and reconnect through these small moments? More than anything, I wondered how they would react to the homework. Would they actually do it?

Liz turns to John. "I wonder if you're even attracted to me anymore. If that's it, tell me." Her voice grows louder. "Just fucking say it! If you don't want to be with me anymore or sex is just done for you, you need to tell me. I need to know what I'm dealing with! Are you gay?"

John's face glazes over. When he speaks, it's not to me or Liz but to his hands folded in his lap. His voice in stark contrast to hers is quiet. I watch as he chooses his words carefully. "That's not it. I'm not gay and of course I'm attracted to you. I want this part of our relationship back as much as you do."

Liz glares at John's bent head. "If that's true, what are you going to do about it? I want to know what your plan is because I'm sick and tired of being the only one who seems remotely alarmed by the fact that we are not intimate anymore—that this part of our relationship is dead! And by the way, can you fucking look at me?"

John doesn't answer but instead seeks refuge in his chair.

It's not only about what a client is saying or not saying in the room. I was trained to use my empathic nature to read a client's energy. On the surface, John looks like an adult man. In his professional life, he's a doctor and a leader who makes life-and-death decisions almost daily. But now, John is a little boy waiting for a parent to ground him.

"John, how do you feel when Liz speaks to you like that?" I ask.

Without looking up from his hands, he replies, "I feel bad. I'm sad she feels this way. I want to fix it and make it better for her—for us." He peers up from under his eyebrows in Liz's direction, checking for her approval.

Liz sighs. "I don't want to do this to him."

"Do what to him?" I ask.

"Do this; I mean look at him." She gestures toward John. "He looks like a child who's been scolded."

"Maybe he is."

While a client or couple's self-diagnosis is compelling and important for timelines and context, often the presenting problem that brought them in isn't the problem at all. The real issue—the problem that lies beneath the surface and the thing few therapists are talking about—is, how we "show up." By "show up," I mean, what side of our personality comes out when things get tough.

We are not the single organisms we see staring back at us in the mirror. In fact, we are made up of subpersonalities or parts of self that have their own beliefs, experiences, motivations, desires, and agendas. Left to their own devices, these parts will speak, act, and make decisions of their own volition. In order for us to get to the root of dysfunction in a relationship, we must start with an understanding of the parts of us that show up to our partners, especially when we feel our most vulnerable.

5

WHAT ARE OUR PARTS?

I'm still learning to love the parts of myself no one claps for.

—Rudy Francisco

The Russian Matryoshka Doll, or nesting doll as it is informally known, is an apt representation of our parts of self. At first glance, the nesting doll seems to be a single wooden statue, however, when we look inside, we see there are many wooden figures hidden within, descending in size. The Matryoshka Doll is said to represent Mother Russia and the significance of the matriarch in the family. The doll is also believed to be symbolic of life because it shows us the many faces, experiences, beliefs, and selves that are held within a single person. Like this popular Russian souvenir, we have many parts hidden within what appears to be a singular being.

When I first explain parts work to clients, they're frequently puzzled. The initial and recurrent response is, "But I'm just me." To that, I will offer, "Yes, you are you, but there are different versions of you in there. It's my job to help you get to know as many of them as you can."

When our parts shift, one part takes the seat of consciousness over another, changing our perspective and mindset. This shift happens naturally depending on the people, places, or situations we encounter, but because we live a large majority of our lives on autopilot, it generally goes unnoticed.

To give you a clear sense of your parts, consider for a moment the part of you that goes to work. There is a specific part of your personality that comes out when you perform the tasks related to your job. If you think about it, your work self probably has a distinctive feel, maybe even a specific way of thinking. If you are particularly good at your job, and the people at work praise and reward your efforts, this side of you is probably quite confident and self-assured. It could be said perhaps, that this part of you moves in the world in a particular way, a way that might feel different from other sides of you that show up in your personal life, for example. Now juxtapose your work self with the side of you that shows up with your family. You might notice a surprising contrast between these versions of you.

When I brought the incongruity of his parts to my client Mark's attention, he said, "Wow, you're right. The part of me that shows up with my family would never survive at my job, and my family would never tolerate who I become at work." Mark worked in finance on Wall Street, a notoriously cut-throat environment. To survive at his job, Mark had to find a part of himself that could survive in that world. He described his work self as "a part of me that takes no prisoners. There is very little room for mistakes or vulnerability at my office." Aware for the first time of the difference in his parts, Mark laughed and said, "I never thought about it before but I *am* two totally different people. The guys at work would never believe what a softy I am at home with my wife and kids."

For some, parts of self can feel overwhelming or induce fear. Some clients wonder if I'm suggesting they have DID, or Dissociative Identity Disorder, formerly known as Multiple Personality Disorder. It should be noted there are important differences between DID and our parts of self. DID is a mental illness that stems from major childhood trauma involving physical, emotional, or sexual abuse. While those with DID experience the presence of different personality selves, their severe dissociation creates a disruption in their perception as well as a breakdown of memory or what's known as dissociative amnesia. These are gaps where the sufferer loses time and the memory loss is beyond what would be considered normal forgetfulness.

It has been argued that our parts of self are not really parts at all but merely evidence of our ever-changing moods. However, throughout the vast history of psychology, theorists in the field have found the idea of subpersonalities to be a useful way to understand the psyche. Going back as far as Freud's id, ego, and superego and Jung's complexes, we find the concept of subpersonalities employed to illustrate how the mind processes our experiences. Throughout Jung's writings, he described the mind not as a singular object but as an organism made up of subpersonalities that act independently of one another. Therapy models such as Gestalt therapy, Transactional Analysis, and Cognitive-Behavioral therapy also use a similar schema to describe our internal process. Noted therapist Virginia Satir liked to say we have an internal "parts party" happening inside all of us. The latest brand of parts-related therapy is Richard Schwartz's IFS, or Internal Family Systems. In Schwartz's model, our parts are examined through a systemic lens and are seen as an internal family of interrelated parts of self. Suffice it to say, no matter how they dice it up, experts both old and new agree we all have parts of self. My goal is not to give you a graduate degree in psychology but to afford you a working understanding of some of your parts and how they affect your ability to connect with your partner.

For a moment, consider the different sides of you. Notice not only the work and family version of you but also the side of you that shows up to social occasions. Does your inner extrovert come out at happy hour or is it your introvert? What side of you shows up to controversy? Do you want to wall off and run or do you dig in for the fight? What side of you comes out most often in your relationship? Are you open, loving, and compassionate, or does the exposure of love cause you to show up in a shut-down and defended side of self?

Pop culture would have us believe love is made up of rainbows and unicorns, but anyone who has felt its sting knows the truth. The exposing nature of love is something we all understand. Love can gut us and leave us feeling broken and bleeding on the floor, causing more than one of our inner parts to become activated. In her book *Daring Greatly*, Brené Brown captured how fragile we can feel in the face of opening our hearts.

> I define vulnerability as uncertainty, risk, and emotional exposure. With that definition in mind, let's think about love. Waking up every day and loving someone who may or may not love us back, whose safety we can't ensure, who may stay in our lives or may leave without a moment's notice, who may be loyal to the day we die or betray us tomorrow, that's vulnerability. Love is uncertain. It's incredibly risky. And loving someone leaves us emotionally exposed. Yes, it's scary and yes, we are open to being hurt but can you imagine your life without loving or being loved?[1]

Well, when you put it like that, Brené, yes, yes I can imagine it. It seems the universe has a cruel and unusual sense of humor. You see, love doesn't only expose the compensated adult parts of us to vulnerability, love lays us bare to our oldest and deepest wounds. I can think of few things that expose our core wounding as much as our romantic relationships. What is more, we actually go looking for it. We have an innate and compelling need to heal the wounds of our childhood.[2] We look for and are drawn to the love we've known, usually the kind of love we have received from our parents. Good or bad, connective or rejecting, tender or toxic, we seek what feels familiar, and this unconscious desire to heal ourselves brings forth the wounded parts in all of us and puts those parts front and center in our romantic relationships.

In response to this exposure, the protector parts of us will rise up in defense of the wounded self. This is the dynamic that lies beneath the surface of all the issues couples face. Each partner's wounded child seeks healing, while simultaneously, their defended parts battle for their safety. With all of this in mind, let's take a look at each of our cardinal parts; the wounded child, the defender, and the inner critic, what motivates them, and the jobs they perform.

THE WOUNDED CHILD

When we're born, we're not only naked and vulnerable, we come into this world asking questions—such as: Am I safe? Am I loved? Do I matter? Am I enough? As infants, we ask these questions nonverbally and energetically. As we grow and mature, we continue to unconsciously ask these questions of our parents, family, extended family, and then our community while moving through the formative years of our lives. These questions give us a sense of our world and our place in it. When one of them is not answered in the affirmative, when experience says in effect that you're not safe, you're not loved, you're not enough, or you don't matter, you suffer a core wound. If this experience happens consistently and/or traumatically, the psyche splits and forms a different aspect of our personality known as the inner child or wounded child part of self.

The wounded child is a single part or group of parts that are both young and in pain. Forged in the fires of the traumas of our youth, they are caught in a time warp and frozen at the moment of injury. When the wounded child takes over the seat of consciousness, we feel powerless, childlike, and overwhelmed.

Before I had any formal training as a therapist, I came into contact with my wounded child one morning as I crested the hazy space between deep sleep and consciousness. A memory of when I was seven years old came rushing back. In the memory, I sat on the school bus in the front seat just to the right of the driver and my mother was on the steps of the bus. I could only see the top of her head but her voice was clear. The other kids were silent and listened. It was rare for a parent to breach this space, and it was even rarer for anyone to give Mrs. Johnson, the driver, a good sound talking-to, but that's just what Mom was doing. I heard her say, "He sits in the front with the rest of the kids his age, not in the back with those animals. They beat on him and I won't have it! If you have a problem with him, you come to me, and trust me, I'll handle it, but he's not to be put back there again. They are twice his age and they have no business handling him that way—he's a little boy."

The doors shut, Mom was gone, and the bus was silent. Mrs. Johnson peered down at me and said, "Get in the back." The bus erupted in cheers and laughter. I refused her command and almost on cue one of her henchmen grabbed me by the collar and dragged me to the floor of the bus. He then picked me up and slammed me into an empty seat.

"Fucking weak," I whispered as I lay there twenty-plus years later in my half-dream state. I'd had this memory many times over the years and always came to the same conclusion. The thought, "How could I have been so pathetic?" was followed by feelings of shame.

The wounded child holds our inner secrets, which are often laden in shame. Whether we label the traumas of the past as either big "T" or little "t" makes no difference. If we get the message we are not loved, we are not safe, we do not matter, or we aren't enough, we don't blame our parents. Instead, that blame rebounds onto us and solidifies our inner belief that we are broken. We experience our brokenness as shame. In his book *Healing the Shame That Binds You*, John Bradshaw perfectly explains the experience of our shame-based wounded child parts: "Shame masks our deepest secrets about ourselves; it embodies our belief that we are essentially defective. We feel so awful we dare not look at it or ourselves, much less tell anyone."[3]

We typically do not walk through our adult lives thinking of ourselves as children; we don't want to feel weak, helpless, or exposed. However, the wounded child is like an old injury that acts up from time to time when the weather is bad. To a degree, we've become accustomed to the discomfort. The pain lives close but under the surface until someone bumps into it. Let's say, for example, you had a parent abandon you emotionally or physically when you were six years old. By this theory, there is a wounded six-year-old part of you who is trapped in that abandonment experience. This part will become triggered at the mere thought of a partner leaving you or betraying you in some way. When this wounded part takes over, you may feel defenseless and vulnerable. Your attachment to your partner may feel tenuous and unsafe. You might feel jealous or worry your partner is not as invested in the relationship as you are—that you love them more than they love you. Whatever the catalyst, the wounded child steps up to warn of potential dangers, signaling that defensive measures need to be employed. Typically, we take refuge from the feelings associated with the wounded child and enlist our inner defender or our inner critic parts of self. Unfortunately, these defensive measures rarely leave us with open hearts, minds, or ears. When our countermeasures are deployed, our inner child is shoved aside, banished, and suffering in the shadows of our subconscious minds. The wounding of our childhood is recapitulated and the experience is, once again, left unprocessed and unhealed.

When we consider Liz and John's sexual dysfunction, we see a prime example of how the wounded child can present itself. In our session, John, a grown man, is reduced to a little boy waiting for a parent to ground him. In fact, Liz said as much at the time. I would argue that in that moment, and in others like it, John becomes compartmentalized in a younger, wounded version of himself.

John's mother was verbally and sometimes physically abusive. She raged at her children daily; that, for me as a clinician, smacked of Borderline Personality Disorder.[4] He said it was not *if* you triggered her anger, it was *when*. As a result, John walked on eggshells and tried to appease his abuser. When that didn't work, he would freeze and make himself small until the storm was over. He became fearful of confrontation, especially with the women in his life, and tried to avoid it at all costs. Now, John's wounding had found its way into his marriage. His historical fear of never getting it right with his mother, of always disappointing women, was now playing out in the bedroom with Liz. When Liz became frustrated or angry with his disinterest in sex, John would revert to his old strategies of shrinking, freezing up, and pacification. Liz's anger triggered John's abused inner child as well as the appeasing parts of him responsible for protecting him from more pain. Unfortunately, none of those aspects of John were capable of meeting his wife's needs for physical intimacy.

For John, the question "Am I safe?" was never answered in the affirmative. As a result, John and Liz's dynamic left them fighting for their relational lives, caught in an unconscious dance involving their wounded and defensive parts.

THE DEFENDER

While the wounded child is forged in the traumas of our youth, our defender parts spring forth from a need to protect us from further pain. During the maturation process from child to adult, we find some agency and our ability to protect ourselves. We do this through the formation of defender parts of self.

Our defenders heed the warnings of the wounded child. They recognize that some of our most fundamental needs were never met and their job—their sole purpose for existing—is to protect our hurt, inner children. These parts act like a protective older sibling we might never have had. When the world and the people around us prove to be unsafe, they step in and say in effect "That's it! This kid has had enough and we aren't going to take it anymore!" The defender is able to draw boundaries. They can say "no" or leave an uncomfortable or even dangerous situation. Whatever the threat, like a faithful bodyguard, the defender will jump in front of our wounded children to save the day. While our defender parts perform an important role in our lives, left ungoverned, their efforts to guard our hearts can impede our ability to connect.

In the case of Liz and John, we see both of their defenders coming to the rescue of their wounded children, effectively stifling their communication and making the resolution of their sexual dysfunction near impossible. In their session, John's defender tried in vain to pacify and not provoke Liz. The more he tried to defend through appeasement, the more incensed Liz became. John was inadvertently sending Liz the message that her feelings didn't matter—a message that hearkened back to her childhood wounding.

As a young girl, Liz's parents subjugated her feelings. Whenever she expressed an opinion that went outside the familial norms, her feelings were summarily dismissed. Rather than being curious about their daughter's obvious intelligence and willingness to question the status quo, Liz's parents ignored her, shut her down, punished her, or shut her out. Because of this treatment, Liz received the message that she and her feelings did not matter. In response to this consistent and traumatic treatment, two things happened. First, a part of Liz's personality split off and became a wounded child part. Second, as Liz got older and began to individuate, a side of self that could protect the wounded child came forth. The defender in Liz could fight for her, and that is exactly what this part of her was doing in her relationship with John. Liz would yell, scream, and demand. She did everything short of shaking John to get him to show her that she mattered. Unfortunately, her anger was an echo of John's abusive mother and did not pave the road to the emotional and physical connection she longed for with her husband.

Types of Defenders

Your defender parts will employ a multitude of tactics in their attempt to keep you safe. Some defenders will use control to micromanage your life or the people in it. This type of defender seeks refuge from vulnerability in perfection. We see this in those we think of as "Type A," people who try to create the perfect home or the perfect relationship or try to be the perfect partner. This is a tireless and never-ending pursuit of safety through perfection that is unattainable. This type of defender may also try to manage their partner's feelings while neglecting their own. This strategy says, I'll be okay as long as everyone else is okay.

Some defenders will protect us through consumption. This protective part shows itself in all forms of addiction. Whether through alcohol, marijuana, drugs, food, money, shopping, gaming, or sex, this part wants to anesthetize the pain of the wounded child. Its intention is to save our fragile hearts by making us numb.

Devin had a devoted partner who loved him dearly; however, he couldn't refuse sexual liaisons with other women. Rather than relegating himself to the moniker of yet another bad guy who cheats, Devin came to see me. As it turned out, Devin had been hurt deeply by a father who made him feel as if he was never good enough and by an ex-wife who left him for another woman. Devin's inner child believed love and connection were a dangerous endeavor. To guard the little boy inside, Devin's defender used sexual consumption to keep his relationship in the shallows.

One of the more popular strategies of our defenders is emotional bypass. Emotional bypass is a diversion or a way to sidestep unresolved emotional issues that we've deemed too difficult or too intense to confront. Bypass can take on many faces: the emotionless intellectual, the jester, the passive aggressor, and the angry fighter, to name just a few.

A former client named Sam used her intellect and her interest in psychology as a means to bypass the tremendous sadness and grief of her inner child. Calling her defended part "The Professor," she intellectualized her feelings about her parents and her upbringing. Both her mother and father suffered from depression and were unable to show her the kind of love and attention she naturally longed for as a child. Sam studied psychology in an effort to understand not only her parents' experience but her own, and this became the predominant way she dealt with difficult emotions. The Professor allowed Sam to bypass her feelings through clinical reasoning that ultimately made it difficult for her to connect deeply to herself or to her wife.

Another client admitted when things get tense, he bypasses his feelings with humor. Referring to his wife, he said, "I clown around with her to avoid how I feel and to avoid fights. I don't want to make our home anything like mine was growing up." His wife, on the other hand, complained that nothing was ever taken seriously, not even sex. "I can walk into our bedroom in lace underwear, begging for sex, and he will squeeze my boobs and make honking noises."

I have a defender part my wife likes to call "Mitch" who uses anger to bypass my inner wounding. Born to a fifteen-year-old mother, in abject poverty, the world and the people in it were often cold and scary. Bullied by adults, coaches, teachers, and other children, rather than collapse I found a big burly bodyguard inside of me that is really good at only one thing: defending me and those I love. The angry defender is a common strategy, especially for men in our society. For many of us, there is a deep and enduring fear that if we show our vulnerability, we cease to be masculine. Underneath our anger is a vast well of pain that takes the face of a wounded child who longs to know that they are safe and loved.

The defender I refer to as the "trophy hunter" lives in the pursuit of the shiny and new. Addicted to the dopamine haze of new experiences, this defender will put achievements and people alike on their proverbial mantel, never willing to dive the depths of intimacy and vulnerability. A client, Kyle, had suddenly and abruptly stopped catering to the physical and emotional needs of his partner once she said "I love you" and committed to him. Though he professed to love her deeply and even married her, once she was committed the luster of her was gone. She had become another trophy won, and he stopped nurturing her and the relationship. Different from Devin's defender, Kyle wasn't pursuing other women, he was pursuing other hobbies and projects at work, which became more important than cultivating his connection to his wife.

Another defender is what one of my clients called his "Eeyore" part of self. This client experienced tragic loss in his childhood as well as in his adult life. Rather than being hot and explosive like "Mitch," Eeyore's defense was to become sullen and remote—to collapse under the weight of possible vulnerability. This side of self pervaded my client's relationship and acted as a wet blanket, as it were, to all entreaties by his wife for fun, closeness, and intimacy. The prevailing narrative of this defender is "Why bother?" or "What's the point?" This part is closely related to what is known in psychological terms as a Masochistic core conflict or an Endurer character style. This is a defender that "wins" by saying "no" even to situations and experiences that might arguably be good for them. Beyond tragedies, this defender also finds its origins in an overbearing parent or parents. These are people whose will and choice were routinely taken from them and who now find strength in saying "no." This defensive tactic is, in effect, an attempt to say "fuck you" to the world, but it ends up playing out as a fuck you to themselves. Clients who discover that their partner's defender behaves in this manner report never being able to bring new things up directly. Instead, they must convince their mate that "it" was their idea. At its core, this part believes that hope is dangerous and does what it can to guard the wounded child within from further disappointment.

THE INNER CRITIC

Our defender parts try to keep us in an emotional Shangri-la, a place where shame, fear, and sadness don't exist. Here the wounded child is sufficiently sequestered in the shadows, safe to some degree from harm. As you can see, defenders show up in many different ways, however, there is one whose strategy is so divergent from the others that it warrants its own category. Meet the inner critic, the only defender that actually turns on the self.

Everyone hates their inner critic. To a person, when I mention the critic, they say some version of "I hate that part of myself" or "I wish I could just get rid of that side of me altogether." The critic's goal is to keep us safe, but it meets this objective through a toxic narrative that usually involves self-hate, shaming, belittling, guilt, or mental or emotional self-flagellation. This part essentially says, "Stay inside, lock the windows and doors and keep your head down. It's a dangerous world out there and you're not fit for it. Don't go on that date, don't expect your needs to be met, and don't even think about asking for deep love and connection."

Although it can seem counterintuitive, I want my clients to listen to their inner critic and become familiar with their critic's tactics. I ask them, "Who does your inner critic's voice sound most like?" Often the critic's voice is that of the parent or person who made them feel unloved, unsafe, not enough, or as though they didn't matter. In psychological terms, this is also known as an introject. The introject is an aspect of the abusive or neglectful parent that has been unconsciously absorbed into the self. The introject/inner critic holds the view and opinions of the not-good-enough parent and carries the abuses from our past into our present.

Dan's chief complaint was that his girlfriend, Jessi, was too negative. "She's always down on herself, especially about her body. I love the way she looks, but she picks herself apart, then she picks at me, and then the relationship. This happens all the time and usually in that order." Dan went further to say he had a hard time loving Jessi because she rarely let his love in. When I asked Jessi the foundational questions, she stopped on "Am I loved?" Her eyes filled with tears as she pondered my inquiry. People cry in my office for many reasons, and one of the biggest reasons is the truth. When we land in our truth, our nervous system reacts and our body releases the pent-up energy of our bottled-up feelings. Jessi believed she was unlovable. Nothing was ever good enough for her cold and perfectionistic mother. Jessi's intrinsic goodness as the beautiful child she was, was never part of the equation. Love in her home was conditional. In order to keep up with her mother's demands around her grades, her body, and how well she performed in sports, Jessi developed an inner voice that sounded much like her mother's, an introject that became her inner critic. This part prevailed in her relationship with Dan. She was never good enough, not good enough for Dan, and not good enough for love.

The inner critic does not reserve its toxic narrative for us alone. This faultfinder will see flaws in almost everyone and everything we come in contact with and ensures our safety by keeping love and our would-be lovers at a safe distance. Jessi's inner critic saw Dan as unworthy. If he wanted Jessi, flawed and unlovable as she was, he must of course be terribly flawed as well. The inner critic's philosophy about potential partners is "I would not want to be a member of any group that would have *me* as a member." For Jessi and people like her, the critic sets off a never-ending cycle of self-sabotage, where compassion for self and the love of a partner is rejected. The critic then points to their low self-esteem and the inability to let love in as more evidence of their brokenness.

We are a complex array of intertwining parts of self, each with their own beliefs, narratives, experiences, motivations, and desires. As I said earlier, I will focus largely on the wounded child, the defenders, and the inner critic, but throughout this work, you may become aware of other parts of you. There is a part of you that shows up in all the different aspects of your life. Using Practice 1, Mindfulness, you can push pause on your brain's natural tendency to go on autopilot. From this more mindful and aware place, you can begin to get to know your parts of self and the profound effect they have not only in your relationship but also in your life.

6

WHY ARE OUR PARTS
SO IMPORTANT?

Your task is not to seek for love but merely to seek and
find all of the barriers within yourself that you have built
against it.

—Rumi

At the beginning of our next session, John asked, "Do you have any
recommendations for a good sex therapist in town?"

"I'm happy to give you some names, but I have a few thoughts on
the subject if you're open to hearing them."

There was a reluctance in their mutual nod of agreement as if
they'd made a tough decision they didn't want to go back on. Liz and
John had decided that their work with me had been helpful but that
another, more drastic step needed to be taken. As therapists, we never
want to take a client's autonomy. It is often useful in my profession to
employ the wisdom of the Tao-te ching. Authors Greg Johanson and
Ron Kurtz explain in their book, *Grace Unfolding: Psychotherapy in the
Spirit of the Tao-te ching*, that if there is simply a disagreement between
what the client wants and what the therapist offers, the therapist must
set the client free to seek what they want elsewhere: with no blame, no
guilt, no subtle message that they need to stay to take care of our need
to be good therapists.[1] Clients have to be agents in their own healing. I
want the people in my practice to understand that they can come and go
as *they* need to—that they decide. However, there is a delicate balance
between supporting their autonomy and asking them to explore and to
dig deeper when the work of therapy gets hard. Sometimes you need to
fight for the client, especially if there is work to be done that you can
see but they cannot.

Responding to their inquiry about a sex therapist, I said, "If I'm honest, I don't know how much a sex therapist is going to help you. I think something else is playing out here. It's my thought that your inability to connect in the bedroom is symptomatic of another problem. This issue is also to blame for why you're having such a difficult time communicating." Their collective body language told me they were waiting for the big reveal. "The real issue is how each of you is showing up."

A "PART" OF THE PROBLEM FOR COUPLES

Many writers and researchers believe that relationships unfold in stages. They use this evolutionary process to explain the friction and discord many couples face. There is a honeymoon stage when your brain is flowing with dopamine and you believe your sweetheart has hung the moon and the stars. Then, depending on the list you're reading, there are a few middle stages, with ominous names like "The Reality Stage," "The Crisis Stage," "The Work Stage," or, my favorite, "The Disappointment Stage." With few exceptions, these phases of relationships are said to involve frustration, instability, and fear. If you manage to navigate the turbulent waters of the middle stages, you might get to "The Commitment Stage," when you apparently, with some reservation, accept your partner and your relationship as both flawed and sometimes awful. Wow, where do I get in line for that experience?

There is a certain resignation inherent in our levels of relational development. The researchers attempt to normalize the turbulence and suffering by saying, in essence, that this is just how relationships go for us humans. What the authors of these stages and so many articles and books on relationships have yet to realize is the role our parts of self play in the difficulties we encounter in our romantic connections. In my opinion, no matter the stage, when relationships go bad, our parts of self are at the root of the issue.

The dopamine blast of new love is not sustainable in the brain, that's true. Eventually, the rose-colored glasses come off and we "step in it" with each other, we make mistakes, and feelings get hurt. A better way to explain the middle stages of a relationship, when things go off the rails, is to say that our inner wounded children get triggered, the pain of the past bubbles up, and our defender parts swoop in and take over. Walled off and compartmentalized, we are in a desperate fight to keep our hearts safe. This process happens under the surface and is mostly unconscious. It's guised in the typical issues couples face that, left unchecked, become malignant. Sooner than later, we are habituated to this way of interacting with each other. Some are not sure what the first issue was; some can't forget. As a clinician working with couples, I believe the focus should be on the parts of us that show up when things get difficult.

The parts of us that typically show up to the difficult times are the protective and wounded sides of self. Unfortunately, these parts of us don't have access to compassion, empathy, or understanding. When we are in the wounded or protective parts of self, this is who we believe ourselves to be. We are locked in that compartment and see the world through that lens, a lens that is colored by fear and contraction. We have little or no experience of our other sides of self and have only the skills and abilities of our fear-based parts at our disposal. This has significant implications with respect to our ability to make a heart-centered connection.

Connecting is simply not a skill these parts possess—it's not something they are geared to do. As a matter of fact, in an effort to keep us safe, they are designed to do the exact opposite. If you try to connect or have a collaborative conversation from the wounded child or defender, it is akin to trying to send an email from your Instagram account. In fact, evolutionary psychologist Robert Kurzban said the brain developed as a compartmentalized, modular, problem-solving organism analogous to a smartphone or to a Swiss Army knife. Using Kurzban's examples, if we want to create a loving relationship, we have to make sure we are in the app/part of self that has that ability. Using the Swiss Army knife analogy, we can't expect to be able to cut a rope with a corkscrew, as it were. Unfortunately, that is exactly what couples do when they try to connect from their wounded or defended parts of self.

The importance of our parts and the roles they play in our lives didn't land on me in any of my romantic relationships. This understanding found me via a more circuitous route, through my licensing exam. The Marriage and Family Therapy National Exam is a notoriously difficult two hundred–question standardized test. While studying for the exam, I'd failed an alarming number of practice tests, and, despite three years of graduate school, almost two thousand face-to-face client hours, as well as untold numbers of group and individual supervision sessions, if the practice tests were any indicator, I was going to fail to be licensed.

I pictured the creators of the exam as a group of shadowy, mustache-twisting figures with diabolical grins or as cold, emotionless clinicians in white lab coats. Whatever the image, my narrative about their intentions was less than positive.

Though not an example from a romantic relationship, the exam gave me firsthand experience of just how compartmentalized we can become when triggered. It is a prime example of how being in the wrong part of self can leave us de-skilled and unable to access the capabilities we need in the various moments of life.

Historically, I was a terrible test taker, let alone the standardized version. My belief about standardized tests: They are composed of totally unfair questions and a bunch of ridiculous answers, whose chief design is to trick you into failure. As the exam drew near, I became despondent as my professional and financial future hung in the balance. I could not understand how I was performing so badly. I'd been at the top of my class, carried a 3.98 GPA all through grad school, read the books, attended the lectures, and wrote the papers. I knew my stuff, but where was the information I'd learned? It was in my brain, I was sure, but where?

One afternoon, I sat angry and scared, practically slumped over my desk, when I began to think about mindfulness, the parts of self, and the work I'd been doing with my clients during my clinical internship. After all, I had been asking them to use mindfulness to become aware of their parts in the difficult times in their relationships and in their lives. Could this stuff work for me? At that moment I stopped and took a breath. I used what would later become Practice 1 of this book, Mindfulness. I began to pay attention to how I was feeling and what I was thinking, and I realized how scared and powerless the test made me feel. I was angry at the evil and dastardly test makers. From the witness position, I began to understand that the fear I was feeling was old and that of the wounded child within me. As a kid, I was not a strong student. For me, doing well in scholastics was an entirely adult experience and was therefore compartmentalized in my adult parts. Through this mindful lens, it was also clear that my anger was an expression of my inner defender, who, right on cue, had shown up to protect the scared, wounded kid in me from the vulnerability of failing. The idea occurred to me that neither my scared kid nor my defender had ever spent a single minute in grad school or sat with a client. Like Kurzban's smartphone example, I was compartmentalized, the information I now needed was in another part of my brain in a different app. If I could find the part of me that had done the studying, gone to class, and sat with clients, I would find the side of self who knew the answers.

I jumped up, took a breath, and went to my closet. I put on the same clothes I would normally wear to see clients and took a seat in a chair in my living room. I pretended to have a conversation with a client. I imagined how it felt to sit across from someone in process. I asked and answered questions out loud to my imaginary client. As I did this something inside of me began to shift. Suddenly I was not angry and scared. I felt confident, the way I did while sitting with clients. When I was sure something inside of me had changed, I got up and walked from the chair to my desk. I walked slowly and carefully so as not to disrupt whatever I had managed to shift in my brain. As I reread the questions from the exams I failed, something miraculous happened. Where before I saw nothing but tricks designed to lead me astray, I now saw questions that acted like bread crumbs guiding me to the answers. I felt like Will in *Good Will Hunting*, an unlikely genius able to solve the unsolvable equations. I was now in the right "app" of my brain. I'd shifted into the part of me, the compartment of my mind, that held information and experiences I needed to meet the demand. The implications of this practice with clients landed on me even then. I knew this experience would become the backbone of the work I now do helping couples create lasting, healthy, and happy partnerships.

Just as the test sparked parts of me that could not access what I learned in school, romantic partners are triggered into parts of self that have little or no access to love, compassion, empathy, and understanding. Once the slide into a wounded or defender part happens, they are locked in a compartment of their minds—sealed off from the sides of themselves that house their ability to connect. This shift in parts dramatically affects all aspects of relationships, including one of the most important, our ability to communicate.

COMMUNICATION

Trying to remain calm, Debbie asks her husband, "Why are you giving Larry money?"

"What?" Pete replies.

"I know everything. I talked to the accountant."

"Alright, ya know what?" Pete answers. "I don't want to get into some nasty fight, so can we talk to each other the way the therapist told us to talk to each other?"

"Fine, fine." Debbie breathes, centering herself as she tries to find the language they have learned in therapy. "It makes me feel sad when you are dishonest."

Pete matches her effort and says robotically, "I understand it makes you feel bad when I am dishonest with you. It hurts my *feelings* when you treat me with *contempt* and corner me and try to trick me into lying."

Debbie, nodding her head in what looks like agreement, responds with "Okay. It makes me sad when it's so easy to trick you into lying because you're such a lying shit-bag."

Pete stammers, "That's not . . . You can't do that. The therapist said you are not allowed to judge me."

"That's not a judgment, that's just a fact."

Regaining his composer, Pete says, "Fair enough, sometimes I withhold truth, that is true. But it's only because I am scared to death of your crazy-assed, illogical overreactions."

Debbie counters, "Well, it hurts me inside and triggers me, when you're such a dishonest shit, that you are lending your father money without telling me, while your record company is going bankrupt and we're on the verge of losing our fucking house!"

Pete and Debbie are not my clients, but there was a time in my career where they could have been. This is a scene from the movie *This Is 40*, starring Leslie Mann and Paul Rudd. When I first saw this part of the film I was stunned. The accuracy of the writing and the depiction of a couple struggling with a communication strategy made me think the movie's writer, Judd Apatow, must have learned this type of clunky communication device in a therapist's office only to have it fall apart when trying to use it in real life.

Couples tell me all the time they have communication problems. My pat response is, "I don't think that's true, in fact, you communicated that you have communication problems just fine." What these couples have is a part-of-self problem. Our parts of self dramatically affect our ability to communicate, especially about emotionally charged topics. Problematic communication is a leading reason partners report feeling unhappy or unfulfilled.

With communication playing such an integral role for couples, one would think there would be a therapeutic technique designed to meet this need. However, there has yet to be a method effective enough to take communication off the lists of why relationships fail.

Non-Violent Communication, Active Listening, and other communication devices like these have been developed to give struggling couples a method of communicating when emotions run high. Each of these techniques requires partners to listen first, to use "I" statements, or to talk about what they heard in a non-judgmental way. All of these techniques can prove quite effective. I should know, I have used most of them with my clients and in my own life. Here's the thing, these techniques only work if everyone is on their best behavior and playing by the rules. But what happens when one or both partners cannot or will not play by the rules?

Couples have a funny way of not playing by the rules when emotions run high. Therapists can apply these conversational techniques with success while in the confines of the session, however, what this amounts to is false hope. Clients leave their sessions sure they have acquired skills in discourse that will serve them when the subject matter gets tough. The scene from *This Is 40* falls into the category of funny because it's true. Once outside the security of the therapist's office, there is no one to referee—no one to give direction. More often than not, couples become de-skilled in the face of their overwhelming emotions. As their protector parts take over, the communication device goes out the window or, as we saw with Pete and Debbie, they weaponize the technique itself.

In the psychological community, we have put the cart before the horse with respect to couple's communication. For years therapists have created and implemented scores of techniques and practices designed to bring couples together. As well-intended as these therapists may be, they have failed to consider the importance of who shows up to the conversation. Knowing what part is here has to be of paramount consideration.

You cannot ask a client to use "I" statements, to listen compassionately, or to be non-judgmental if they are entering the conversation in a wounded, critical, or defended part of themselves. When one of these sides takes over our consciousness, we see everyone and everything from a guarded perspective. Through this lens, the world and the people in it can be seen only as dangerous. Our emotional toolbox shrinks, limiting us to the skills available in that compartment of our brain. This brings to mind the smartphone reference I made earlier. Trying to connect and allow our partners to feel heard and understood from our hurt and guarded places *is* analogous to trying to send an email from our Instagram account, we simply do not have that capability in that part of self.

To illustrate this idea, I use a Venn diagram. Each circle represents one partner, with the middle or almond-shaped area indicating any conversation or interaction. Imagine, all your parts of self are sitting in one circle; your work self, family self, and social self as well as your defender, critic, and wounded child. Your partner's parts occupy the opposing circle. As an interaction begins, your and your spouse's parts become activated. As the wounded child feels hurt or sees the possibility of further wounding, the inner critic or the defender enters the shared area in an attempt to save the wounded child. At this point, the brain has compartmentalized. The parts present in the conversation are either skilled protectors or wounded

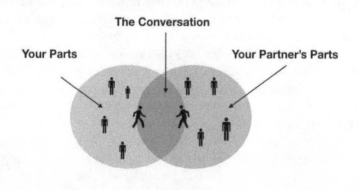

Figure 6.1.   Venn Diagram.
Courtesy of the author

children who don't know how to connect. They lack the ability to listen, to show compassion, or to empathize. For these sides of us, vulnerability is a weakness. As long as these parts are present during the interaction, communicating or reaching your partner is almost impossible.

This example shows why the current communication devices are inadequate and are not meeting the needs of modern couples. Good communication can happen only when our wounded and defended parts have stepped aside, allowing our more compensated parts, or "the healthy self," to take over.

The healthy self, or the wise self, is the part of us that sees through the lens of loving—kindness, benevolence, and generous assumption. When we show up in the healthy self, we can listen with a mind that is open to being changed and we are able to take responsibility for what we have done and said. This part is self-regulated, self-aware, positively motivated, and emotionally intelligent. As such, this side of self is the right "app," so to speak, for connective communication. Making sure we are speaking from this part becomes the first and most important step in a couple's communication. We will cover how to find the healthy self later in chapter 7, "How Our Parts Work." For now, it is enough to understand how essential our parts are to healthy discourse and to making a heart-centered connection.

BIGGEST MISTAKE MOST COUPLES MAKE

It is no secret that communication between partners can devolve rather quickly. I see it all the time. Something is done or something is said and suddenly two people, seemingly in love and emotionally intelligent, are regressed into their wounding and defenses. Beyond being unaware of parts and how they show up, the biggest mistake most couples make is their inability to validate what they don't agree with.

Validating a thought or feeling you agree with is easy; the hard part comes when your partner expresses a thought or feeling that you take issue with. Carl Rogers was one of the most influential psychologists in American history and the founder of the Humanistic Psychology movement. Rogers revolutionized the profession with his concept of client-centered therapy. In his view, we rarely permit ourselves to truly

understand people because understanding is an inherently risky under-
taking. Rogers said, "If I let myself really understand another person, I
might be changed by that understanding. And we all fear change. So as I
say, it is not an easy thing to permit oneself to understand an individual,
to enter thoroughly and completely and empathetically into his frame of
reference. It is also a rare thing."[2]

Sara and Matt entered therapy over what seemed like an ordinary
couple event. Matt took a work call on their big night out, leaving Sara
waiting for him alone at the table in the middle of a romantic restaurant.
This experience was just one of many that made Sara feel passed over for
work and ultimately unimportant. In their session, Matt and Sara unpacked
compelling stories full of reasons why the other was in the wrong. From
my seat, I could see both sides: after all the call had to be taken and she did
feel abandoned—*again*. Nevertheless, what these two were arguing over
was actually irrelevant, though convincing either of them at the moment
proved difficult. What was of grave importance was how each person felt.
It is not the therapist's job to choose winners or losers—to make one partner right and the other wrong. If there is a victor there must also be the
vanquished. This is a losing scenario for everyone involved, including the
therapist. It is the job of every therapist to help couples find their way to
understanding each other—to empathize and to be compassionate to each
other's experience. This is where Matt and Sara were making the biggest
mistake most couples make. They could not—would not—validate the
other person's feelings. To do so would be too risky.

At this point, I think I know what you are thinking, and yes, there
are situations where one partner is wrong and the other is clearly in
the right; a clean house is simply better than a dirty one, drinking and
driving is obviously not okay, and there is no question that screaming
and calling names or lying is out of bounds. I'm not saying that every
situation fits neatly on the dividing line of amicability. Having said
that, even the most obviously lopsided scenarios can be leveled when
we stop fighting to be right and put our partner's feelings first. Deep
down, we want our partner to argue for us and not the topic at hand.
We want to know that our feelings and experience are more important
than winning. Until we feel understood, it is near impossible to enter
wholeheartedly into vulnerability.

For most couples, we can actually substitute one problematic issue for another, and the conversation will end up down that same road. It's like a jagged little pill but it's true, by and large, that the facts are immaterial; what is very material, however, is how our partners feel. Speaking only to the facts says, in essence, here are some really good reasons why you shouldn't feel the way you feel, and here's why what you're saying doesn't matter. When we lean into the facts and not how our loved ones feel, we send the message that we care more about being right than we do about their hearts. This has the added effect of leaving them feeling misunderstood and ultimately unloved.

When we are locked in our fear-based parts, we will not risk our hearts long enough to consider another's position—it's far too dangerous. Our defender or critical parts know if we entertain another's position, if we consider for a moment that they might have a point, we risk change, and as Rogers noted, we fear change and because of this fear we will not "enter thoroughly and completely and empathetically into [their] frame of reference."[3]

The only way to avoid making the biggest mistake most couples make, the only way we can learn to validate a thought or a feeling we do not agree with, is by mindfully showing up in the part of self that has this capability. In our healthier, wiser sides, we can hear things we don't like, we can listen to opinions we don't agree with, and we can validate, at the very least, that our loved one is having the feeling they say they are having. From this place, we can acknowledge that they are hurt and that we hurt them even though we did not mean to.

This brings up our intentions. Validation proves even more difficult when the feelings our words or actions create are in direct opposition to our intentions. Unless a couple has fallen deeply into resentment and discord, our intentions are rarely to inflict harm. Our partners will report feeling hurt by us, but because hurting them was the furthest thing from our minds, we will argue vehemently for why their pain is illegitimate. It seems inconceivable that anyone could feel wounded by our words or deeds when our intentions were the exact opposite.

Matt and Sara didn't need to assess who was right or wrong, they needed help creating a space where both of their experiences could be true. This was a place where Sara could see that her husband had no

"right" choice that evening and Matt could understand that, despite his good intentions, his wife did, in fact, feel abandoned.

As I coached Matt on how to bring his open and loving side to the table, he said, "From this part of me I can see her point. I totally get it now. No one likes being left like that and I do it to her all of the time for work. My boundaries are not good with my job and she deserved better than that." Matt went further. "I noticed something else when I got out of my fighter self: like you said, empathy doesn't actually require agreement. When she's hurt, whatever our differences may be, I need to let her know I care that she's hurt, not try to prove her wrong."

Most of the time, when one person makes the shift to a more open and loving side of self, the space between partners begins to soften. As Sara saw Matt shift, she began to soften as well. "I do feel passed over for work a lot. But, or *and*, I should say, I know he's in a difficult position with his business, and that was especially true that night. I could have tried harder to see that."

When we are able to push pause and get out of the noise, we can mindfully pull back into our wiser parts. From this vantage point, we have a clearer view of ourselves and the dynamic in our relationship. Rather than caught up in the judgment of the inner critic, the tactics of the defender, or the pain of the wounded child, we see, maybe for the first time, through the lens of our healthy, adult self. It is clear who in us is hurt and what needs our attention. The question that most people have at this point and the question I am sure you have is, how? After we become aware of our parts of self and the way we are showing up in our relationships, how do we make the shift from one part to another?

7

HOW OUR PARTS WORK

No problem can be solved from the same level of consciousness that created it.

—Einstein

LIZ AND JOHN

The night prior to our session, Liz approached John for sex. They went on a date and had a great time together. The wine flowed, and the conversation was connective. When they got home, Liz wanted to cap off the evening by making love with her husband. John sensed her expectation and moved toward her sheepishly. Liz became frustrated and angry. Rather than lash out, as usual, she simply stopped, turned her back to John, and went to sleep.

Liz and John passed their general physicals, which ruled out the usual physiological suspects. Neither fit any of the categories of sexual dysfunction of arousal, desire, pain, or orgasm disorders. What John and Liz had was a parts-of-self problem. Both were pinging off of each other, going from their wounded child parts to their protector parts and back again. When Liz wanted sex, John became triggered into his wounded child as he sensed her powerful and adult needs. Fearing he might "get it wrong," John became submissive. His passive, childlike approach made Liz feel abandoned and like she didn't matter enough for him to try harder and "to be more of a man," as she put it.

Similar to my experience with the licensing exam, both John and Liz were in the wrong app. They were compartmentalized and unable to access the knowledge, experiences, and abilities necessary to make a sexual connection. The adult, healthy parts, the parts of them that could be open to physical connectivity and vulnerability, were sidelined. What made matters worse, both Liz and John were making this way of interacting habitual. By reacting to each other in the same way over and over, they were reinforcing a cycle of disconnection, poor communication, and resentment. As I explained in chapter 2, Hebb's Law: Neurons that wire together fire together. Like many couples, Liz and John were reinforcing brain patterns that kept them on a relational merry-go-round.

"Liz, can you tell me what part or parts of you are here right now?"

"Well, I'm going to take a wild guess and say it's my angry defender part, right? I'm angry and hurt, and I feel like I don't matter. But none of this is news."

"These are the parts that show up in the bedroom with John. I want you to close your eyes and take a breath." Liz complied. "What are you thinking and feeling?"

"I'm thinking we're never going to make this work, and I'm pissed he's not trying harder. If he loved me more, he'd be able to do it."

"What do you feel in your body?" I ask.

When you ask people what they feel, they usually tell you what they think. But emotions live in the body and not the mind. The cliché therapist question, "How does that make you feel?" is not enough to get people into and to process their emotions. I use the chakra system as a guide to help clients map their feelings in their somatic systems. Where an emotion sits in the body tells me a lot about the experience the client is having and further serves to validate their inner experience. Anodea Judith is a leading authority on the integration of chakras and therapeutic issues. In her book *Eastern Body, Western Mind*, she offers that when emotions we perceive as negative go unacknowledged, they keep us from moving forward. If we acknowledge these "negative" emotions and explore their reason for being there, we gain a deeper understanding of ourselves.[1] If, for example, someone says they feel energy or tightness in their throat, or "throat chakra," this indicates there is something that needs to be said or communicated. If there is energy or pressure in their heart center, it is often an indicator of heartache or sadness left unprocessed. If they feel it in the belly or the "power center," it is often evidence of guilt, shame, or powerlessness to change something.

Liz continued, "I feel tension."

"Where?"

"In my belly and in my heart."

As Liz made contact with the feelings in her body, she immediately began to cry. She had touched into sadness, not just the sadness she felt at the state of her relationship with John, but the deep sadness of her rejected inner child. From this perspective, the energy in Liz's chest was the heartbreak she felt at the lack of love she received from her mother. In like kind, the emotion trapped in her stomach was the powerlessness she felt to change it. These emotional experiences mirrored the ones she was now having in her present-day relationship with John.

"Liz, if it's available to you, I want you to imagine your angry defender. Can you tell me about her?"

"This seems weird. I don't know if I like this."

I reply, "I get it. This can feel like some weird shit at first, but if you can hang in there with me, I think it will feel better soon."

"She's standing tall and defiant. Her hair is crazy, and her clothes are ripped. She doesn't give a fuck!"

"It sounds like she's really been through it," I offer.

Liz's face softens. "She has. She's been so strong for so long now."

Tears begin to slip through Liz's closed eyes, and John reaches over to put tissues in her open hand.

I guide Liz further. "Liz, can you tell her how strong she's been and thank her for the amazing job she's done?"

There is a long pause as Liz silently thanks her inner warrior self. Her nod tells me the task is complete.

"Good. Now can you ask her to step aside and let you run things? Tell her that this isn't working—not for you and not for the little girl inside. Let her know that she's always welcome and that she always has a job and a place in your life. If you need protection, you will call on her, but she can't make decisions in your relationship anymore."

There was another pause as she took my direction, and then Liz broke the silence. "I see her. That little girl you keep talking about, she's here."

"How old is she?" I ask.

Now smiling through her tears, Liz replies, "Eight, maybe nine. She's wearing that purple jacket I loved so much. I remember it because I wanted to sleep in it, but my mom said I'd get too hot."

"How do you feel about the little girl?"

"I feel so bad for her. She has so many years ahead of her where no one cared what she thought or felt. I'm getting angry again."

"Your defender has returned. Can you ask her to give us a little space? Tell her we got it." Liz nods. "So the little girl. What's she up to?"

"She's looking at me. She's glad I'm here, but she's wondering when I'm going to leave again—when I'm going to abandon her."

Liz's chest begins to heave as she breaks down into sobs. John rubs her back. His touch is loving and tender but deliberate and assured.

"Liz, can you tell her you are never going to leave her again? Can you let her know that you know how hard it's been? That you love her and that she matters to you?"

Hands clasped over her heart, Liz's shoulders began swaying back and forth. "Liz, I'm noticing your body moving. What's happening?"

"I'm rocking her."

When Liz opened her eyes and came back to the room, John was no longer hiding in the couch or protected by his appeaser part. Liz was met by her adult, present-day, husband. The energy between them had shifted dramatically.

I pointed out that John was able to occupy his adult self when he knew Liz was actively dealing with her angry defended side. Her emotions would not trigger his wounding if she was mindfully watching how she was showing up. This did not mean Liz could never get angry with John. What this practice offered was a new way for Liz to express what she was feeling. Using Practice 1, Liz began talking about her feelings rather than through them. She checked in with the part of her that was speaking especially when she was hurt or upset. This would be a touchstone experience for this couple.

In the following sessions, I repeated this process with John. Mindfully, John was able to name his defender part. He thanked this part of himself and let him know that the little boy inside was no longer in any danger. He told his defender that the storm was over and Liz was not his mother. He asked his defender to step aside and let the adult in John run the show, as it were. When John's inner protector bowed out, John was able to make contact with his wounded little boy. When I asked John what his child part was feeling, he said, "She's coming. He knows she's coming. He's scared." John drew his knees into his chest and began to wrap his arms around them. I sensed he was moving into the wounded child and asked him to stand firm in his adult self. As he did, he shifted his body back to a regular seated position.

"John, I'd like you to make contact with the little boy in you."

John described his wounded child as a small boy of about eight, feeble, skinny, and unkempt. I encouraged John to speak to his child part from the loving adult man that he is.

John said, "I know how scared you are. I know how bad it was for you, but that's all over now. I'm here, and I'm going to do my best to never let anything happen to you again. I'm so proud of you. You are so strong, and you were strong for all of your siblings. You tried so hard."

John told me later that prior to this, he secretly hated the child part of himself. He felt embarrassed and ashamed of that scared boy. Now he could feel only love and admiration for him and what he had survived.

THE PRACTICE OF WORKING WITH PARTS

What John and Liz learned in session became the practice they took into their life together. These are the same skills I teach every couple and individual I work with. To take a mindful pause, to name what parts are showing up, to find the healthy self, to negotiate with the defender and/ or the inner critic, and then to reparent the wounded child. At first, this can seem overwhelming, but what has proven true for both myself and my clients alike is that this process can happen in the time that it takes to breathe in a few calming breaths. What is more, in couples where both partners have agreed to work in this fashion, this practice becomes the cornerstone of the way they speak and interact with each other. When couples make the time and effort to choose how they show up, they create a fertile breeding ground for compassion, empathy, reverence, and benevolent expectation.

The following is a step-by-step process you can use to ensure you are showing up to your relationship in your most connective parts. As best as you can, get a working understanding of these steps as they will be important in chapter 8, "Parts Exercises."

STEP 1: MINDFULNESS

We went over this step in Practice 1. However, mindfulness is a subject that bears repeating. The directive in this step is to stop and take a mindful pause before any evocative conversation, sexual encounter, date night, or any situation with your partner that you want to go well. When we use Practice 1, Mindfulness, to pay attention on purpose to our thoughts and feelings, we get to know our inner landscape. This requires a level of patience and a willingness to slow down, especially when emotions run high. Mindful awareness not only titrates the nervous system and shuts down our knee-jerk responses, it also clues us in to what parts of us are present. All of our thoughts and feelings are important indicators of the parts of us that have come out to play in any situation, so mindfulness is the first step in changing our relationship.

STEP 2: NAMING

Naming, as discussed in chapter 3, encourages us to state or name our truth. If you are angry and spoiling for a fight, searching the room for the closest possible exit, or desperately wanting to run and hide, you are most likely in a defended side of self. If you find yourself nitpicking or thinking derogatory thoughts about yourself or others, there is a good chance you are in your inner critic. Likewise, if you are scared, feeling collapsed or vulnerable, you are probably residing in your wounded child. While none of these parts of self feel particularly good, they do offer us the chance to "name" the part of us that is present. When we name the part, we cease to be that part. Naming or noting in this way unlocks the compartments of our minds, allows us to uncouple from our wounded or defensive sides, and frees us to preside in the healthy self. When we take an inner inventory, the mere act of naming begins the process of separation from our parts and has the added effect of inviting the healthy self, the wise self, or inner witness to come forward. In

Richard Schwartz's version of parts work, Internal Family Systems, or IFS, he asserts that there is a self that lives beneath our wounding and defensive measures. It is a part of us that, once our defenders and wounding have been named, will automatically come forward. As I said earlier, the healthy self is the side of us that sees through the lens of loving—kindness, compassion, and benevolent expectation—and is the natural-born leader of our parts.

I encouraged both John and Liz to find their healthy selves before every attempt at physical intimacy. By mindfully pausing and naming their parts, John and Liz learned to separate from their wounded and defended sides of self. With this practice, they changed their sexual dynamic by entering the experience of sex from an entirely different mindset. With Liz's defended, angry part aside, John was no longer triggered into his wounded little boy. This was a part of him that was scared, insecure, and had no sexual libido. With their adult selves present, sex for this couple transformed into a loving and connective experience, but only through some negotiation.

STEP 3: NEGOTIATING AND REPARENTING

Negotiating and reparenting the defended and wounded sides of us is an important next step in changing how we show up in our relationships. Whether it's sex, communication, or our normal, everyday interactions with our partners, negotiating with these sides of us is vital, but it is a step that is often skipped. When we have properly named and uncoupled from our parts and are inhabiting the healthy self, we tend to feel markedly better. From this part of us, we see our relationship from a new and more emotionally intelligent perspective. Feeling the wind in our sails, we are compelled to move forward in our relational dynamics too quickly, only to be upended by the tactics of the defended or wounded parts of us. A central theme in IFS work is that you must negotiate with these aspects of self. If this step is missed, you will be besieged upon by your inner parts, sabotaging any progress you might have made.[2]

From the wise self, we can negotiate with the defended parts of us that are attempting to keep our wounds and hearts safe from the vulnerability of love. As shown in the session with John and Liz, you must turn to your defenders and say, for example, "I see you and how hard you have worked to keep me safe. You have been an incredible protector and friend, but I need you to step aside. I need to speak with the wounded child you are protecting. I need to be able to open my heart to love and being loved. You will always have a job here, and I will call upon you if I need you, but you can't do the talking anymore."

If my words do not fit or do not feel organic to you, you may of course make this dialogue your own. The important aspects of the negotiation are to validate the job the defender was attempting, to ask them to step back, and to gain access to the wounded child. I will give more details to the negotiation process in the practice section located in chapter 8. For now, it is important to have a basic understanding of the conversation and your intention.

When discussing the process of "reparenting" our wounded child parts, I'm reminded of the teachings of Thích Nhất Hạnh, who said, "To take care of ourselves we must go back and take care of the wounded child inside of us. You have to practice going back to your wounded child every day. You have to embrace him or her tenderly, like a big brother or a sister. You have to talk to him, talk to her . . . to say you recognize his or her presence and you will do everything you can to heal his or her wounds."[3]

For whatever reason, on that morning twenty years ago, as I lay thinking about the bus incident, my words didn't sit right with me. Normally I would shake the memory off and move on to something else, effectively leaving my wounded child locked in the purgatory of that moment. Now, I saw the seven-year-old version of myself as something other than weak and pathetic. To call him "fucking weak" seemed shocking and inconceivable. Why would anyone treat a child this way?

I forced myself to stay with the image of that shameful kid. In the dreamlike state, I saw him from what I would now call the wise self or the healthy self. I imagined this adult version of me holding him and loving him. I said to my child self, "Hey, it's all going to be okay. All that's over now, and I promise I will do my best to never let that happen again. I'm so sorry I said you were weak. You've been so strong all these years and I love you so much."

In his book, Bradshaw goes further on the subject of the shamed inner child, offering that when we out our shame-based parts, we open ourselves to love and acceptance, we learn that we are not all bad, and our shame dissipates as we "risk exposing ourselves to someone else's scrutiny."[4] That morning the "someone else," the person who I exposed my shame to, was my wise self.

Acknowledging my inner child shifted something in me energetically. I had been bullying and shaming that kid in me by calling him weak for decades at that point. I was twenty-nine then and still several years away from knowing anything about parts work. All these years later I can report that the memory never resurfaces. I now understand what I did back then was a version of the work I do with clients. I had unknowingly reparented the wounded kid in me and brought the split-off part back into the fold, so to speak.

Our intention in reparenting is to give our wounded child the thing they did not get—what Carl Rogers called "unconditional positive regard." Rogers offered that we are all looking for unconditional positive regard, a sense that we are loved and accepted without judgment. From our kinder, wiser selves we can tell our wounded child that they are loved, that they are safe, and that they matter. We can also tell them that they have no responsibility in this adult love relationship and that they can go and play elsewhere. The goal is to get our parts, both defenders and wounded children, to step aside, but to do it in a loving and careful way.

Successfully negotiating and reparenting means we are free to relate to our partner from the wise self. This work strengthens this part of self, affording a visceral sense of what it is like to reside in this place of authority and self-assuredness. Once in the wise self, we are less likely to be taken over by the powerful and compelling needs of our inner parts. We are no longer reacting out of our wounding but making choices from a conscious, integrated place inside of us.

Having said all of this, it doesn't mean our wounded child, defender, or inner critic are gone for good. It just means we have rebalanced the power in favor of the wise self. Clients are sometimes frustrated that after all of this work and inner understanding these sides of self can still rise up and take over the seat of consciousness. To that I say, we are still humans. We will become triggered, we will get hurt, and our parts will try to do what they are designed to do. Though we are now more adept at dealing with our problematic parts, from time to time a side of self that is not our most emotionally mature or connective side will take over our consciousness and despite our best efforts will not relinquish control. This is what I call a mutiny.

THE MUTINY

A mutiny happens whenever a part refuses to step aside and let the healthy self take over. You will recognize a mutiny when, to the best of your negotiating abilities, a defender or wounded part won't budge. Though your intent is to be loving, kind, and understanding, you are anything but that. You might feel short-tempered or vacant, critical or judgmental, afraid or collapsed—all are earmarks of parts that won't shift. In this hostile takeover of our consciousness, these parts of us seem bound and determined to have their experience. We can quickly feel disheartened and think the practice doesn't work or at least isn't a fit. Typically, the mutiny happens because one of our parts doesn't trust that things are safe enough to relinquish the seat of consciousness. Have no fear; a mutiny is not evidence that this process doesn't work or that you are somehow uniquely flawed. We all experience a good mutiny from time to time, but when it happens, we do have recourse.

The first step in thwarting an all-out takeover is to lean into mindfulness. Once aware of a revolt, we must then push pause on any interactions with our partners. Gently and compassionately pushing pause in these situations stops the bleeding, so to speak. It keeps us from heading down those well-worn paths of frustration, resentment, and heartache. We can, for example, decide not to have that important conversation right now or we can choose not to be physically intimate. In short, we can elect to reconvene any interaction for a time after our rebellious parts have stepped aside and the wiser self has come forward. A pause in the action allows us to chart a new path and to form new habits that feel healthy and connective.

This, of course, might require some negotiating with our partners. We might say, "There is a part of me present right now that won't step aside. I don't want to do this with you through this part of me. Can we try again at another time?" Awareness on this level sends the message that we are present and willing to take responsibility for how we show up and that we are trying to make the space between us a safe one.

However, if the opportunity to postpone is not an option, mindfulness again wins the day. If the interaction between you and your partner must move forward, if the tough conversation cannot be delayed, you must do it in full awareness of the defended or wounded part of you that is present. Knowledge like this allows us to monitor our responses. It says, in essence, I know what part of me is up and I am aware that I'm filtering everything I see and hear through this part of me. As best I can, I'm not going to react from this place, and I will not believe anything this part tells me to be true. Mindful practice like this keeps us from inflicting unnecessary damage on our relationship when our parts have mutinied and we are stuck in a defended or wounded side of self.

JASON SEAVER

This brings me back to our couple, John and Liz. Although they were able to begin connecting through their adult selves, they struggled with their fair share of mutinous parts, especially Liz. Negotiating with her defender and reparenting her wounded child was only one aspect of the battle. In the end, Liz wanted to be open and vulnerable to John. She wanted to love him freely and courageously, but she was buckled by the fear that this part of her did not exist. She worried that the years of poor treatment from her family had killed her ability to love wholeheartedly.

Liz said, "Lair, what do I do if this part of me doesn't exist?"

I responded, "Let me tell you about Jason Seaver."

Jason Seaver is the name my client Tim gave to his "Wise Parent Self," the part of him who stayed calm and didn't give in to the anger or frustration of the defender when dealing with his kids. Tim came into my practice by what we call "spousal mandate." The impetus for most who seek therapy comes from an understanding that something inside needs to be healed and that something may require the support or insight of a professional. There are those, however, who require outside intervention and are mandated to attend therapy. The decree can come in the form of a court mandate, always fun, the employer mandate, or a spousal mandate. With few exceptions, the spousal mandate is a directive that says in effect, "Get your ass into therapy, fix your shit, or we're done." In Tim's case, it was his wife who made the initial call. A mandated client is often a reluctant client, and I stopped doing dog-and-pony-show therapy for reluctant clients years ago. Because a "partner call" tells me that perhaps the person they are calling for is not yet ready for the work, I handle all "partner calls" in much the same way, saying, "Tell your spouse/partner to call me when they get serious about therapy." However, in this case, Tim's call came quickly on the heels of his wife's, so I knew he was motivated to change.

Tim struggled in his relationship with his oppositional defiant daughter.[5] Mirroring Liz's comment, Tim said, "I don't think that part of me exists. The part of me that can parent this kid just isn't in there. I've looked. I don't think I actually have this side of self."

As therapists, we often meet this kind of opposition. It is an "all is lost" kind of response. In the client's mind, there is no help, no resource, and no reprieve. In cases like these, it's up to us, the therapists, to disrupt this concretized way of thinking. As an example, clients will say, "I couldn't *ever* tell anyone *ever* about this problem," to which we will say, "Yes, I understand, but if you were to tell someone, anyone— I mean if you *had* to, who would you tell?" The answers come rushing forward and the client, for the first time, feels they have the possibility of resource and support.

When I pressed Tim to name someone, anyone, who could parent his daughter calmly and compassionately, he surprised me when he said, "Jason Seaver." I was looking for someone in his life that he'd had some actual experience with, a role model he could find in a family member, coach, or teacher. Someone who we might use as an example of good-enough parenting or of wise, calm emotional resilience in the face of a storm. Tim, however, was referring to the character of Dr. Jason Seaver, played by Alan Thicke, from the 1980s television show *Growing Pains*. Tim said that "Jason always had the right answer, always knew what to say, and he always knew what to do with his kids no matter what the issue." When I asked Tim to name someone, I was grasping at straws, if I'm honest. If help was going to come in the form of a 1980s sitcom character, I would at least consider it. Tim began to refer to his inner Jason Seaver often. At first, I was concerned that all of this was really just a big exercise in "acting as if," admittedly not the most-sound psychological advice. As I gave Tim room to explore how Dr. Seaver would handle his anger and frustration, Tim's reactions to his daughter slowly began to change. With this glimmer of hope, Tim and I formed a plan, and he presented it to his wife. At the outset of one of his daughter's outbursts and at the first sign of his anger, Tim would "tag his wife in" and go into their bedroom for five minutes. In those five minutes, Tim would name the parts rushing to the seat of consciousness, quickly negotiate and reparent his parts, and ask that the wise Dr. Jason Seaver take over. Once the good doctor was present, he would relieve his wife. Tim reported that his wife was a bit skeptical of our use of a 1980s sitcom character for therapy but was heartened to see Tim finally feeling hopeful about their situation.

Tim began to use our plan, and as his angry outbursts lessened, his relationship with his wife and his daughter began to improve. Tim and his wife were now a united front in the face of what is a very difficult struggle. Couples who have an oppositional defiant child can find themselves turning on each other. Keeping couples unified in the face of life's adversities can prove difficult, but it is a first-line intervention no matter what gets thrown at them.

Although I initially had doubts that our experiment would work, as Tim began to use it successfully, I understood that this was not an "act as if" exercise. The years of turmoil and struggle had shrouded Tim's compassion for his child. He would say, "I know I love her, but I'm not sure how much I like her." The character of Jason Seaver gave Tim a model to work from and an external reference point for his own empathy and compassion, which were hidden but still alive in him.

As with Tim, I had a hunch that Liz had the ability to love John openly and courageously, but she would need to learn how to love herself first. Perhaps she needed her own Jason Seaver, an external reference point to model how to love both herself and her husband. In the weeks that followed, Liz and I worked to find her external reference point. In the end, she created a patchwork quilt of strong women that represented wholehearted love to her. These women included her favorite authors Maya Angelou, Glennon Doyle, Cheryl Strayed, and Brené Brown. Women who had not only struggled but who found the ability to love both themselves and the people in their lives. Reading their stories, Liz found permission to love the little girl inside of her.

I hate books that give the reader neat and tidy anecdotes about something as complicated as the human psyche, so if I'm giving the impression that Liz's transformation was an overnight success, it was not. Liz consistently showed up for her partner, herself, and her wounded parts. Through this work, she was able to give herself the unconditional positive regard her parents could not. Although this was a painstaking process, she began to feel a sense of wholeness and that she finally mattered.

So, "Who shows up?" should be the first question we ask. I know it's a bold statement, but in my experience, it's true. The part of you that comes to play predetermines everything in your life and in your relationship. When you struggle with your partner, you are often struggling with the need to heal yourself. Your partner and the vulnerability of love shine a light on aspects of you that are begging for attention. It's easier, to a degree, to point the finger and blame our partners or the relationship itself. It's an exercise in mental, emotional responsibility and maturity to point the finger back at yourself and ask, "What could I do better?" and "How can I show up differently?" If we do this work, we can see the things that push our buttons as invaluable clues to what needs to be healed. When in our protective or wounded selves, we can get caught up in "the noise," the "What about you?"'s or the plausible deniabilities. We have no control over anyone other than ourselves. The wise, healthy self knows this, and from this place, we can focus on our parts rather than on our partners. Now, I offer you an opportunity to practice, to look at your life and your relationship through the lens of your parts of self.

Taking these three steps of mindfulness, naming, and negotiating/reparenting ensures you will know who shows up in your relationship. But this work isn't always easy. As I have said, I hate those self-help or psychology books that wrap this often messy and painful human experience up into a nice, neat package. Yes, mindfully naming, negotiating, and reparenting your parts actually works. It can absolutely clear a path to making a heart-centered connection, but this work must be seen as a practice. It needs to be done again and again to regroove your brain's neural pathways in order to create new habits. If you do not practice, the brain's default autopilot will kick on, and you will go back to your old ways of showing up.

8

PARTS EXERCISES

> Be gentle, you are meeting parts of yourself you've been
> at war with for years.
>
> —Unknown

NAMING YOUR PARTS

As we begin the process of naming your parts of self, I want to make it clear that this is a roll call of sorts. We don't want to become fully engaged with any single part as that would take us off of the task of discovering all of whom is in there. You can think of your naming process as a board or team meeting or as a family gathering. Whatever the image in your mind, take time to notice each of your parts as you invite them to the table. It might be helpful to envision each aspect of self as it takes its seat. Notice how each part behaves.

NAMING YOUR DEFENDER

This exercise is designed to help you get to know your inner defender. This is the part of you that comes into your relationship when you feel wounded, hurt, vulnerable, or unsafe. Typically, these parts show up as a fight, flight, or freeze/appease response. You may already be well aware of how your defender shows up and the tactics they use; however, participating in this exercise will help you understand the nuances of your defender.

Steps

Take a few moments to reflect on how you have historically defended yourself with your partner or partners. What happens when you get hurt or angry? What are the stories or narratives playing in your mind? What does this kind of pain make you want to do? What emotions are coming up for you as you do this?

In a journal, write down your answers as if you were describing someone you were observing. For example, "She gets furious, and she wants to hurt back" or "I notice he always wants to run from the room—he just wants out of there. He needs to get away from the danger." Using this third-person technique will give you space from your part and your experience. As best we can, we want to cultivate this observational vantage point of your parts of self.

Now read over "The Fighter," "The Flight Risk," "The Freezer," "The Appeaser," and "The Inner Critic" sections below and notice if any one of these defensive styles is a match for you.

Note: Some people get confused if they have a "blended" fight style. A blended fight style happens when you flee until you ultimately turn and fight, as an example. The defensive tactic you eventually land on is usually your preferred defensive strategy. Everything you do before is merely you trying to do something, anything, other than using the old and tired strategies that did not work in the past.

The Fighter

- Are they quick to anger?
- Do they defend by arguing the loudest?
- Do they corner their partner verbally?
- Do they try to make their partner's feelings seem irrelevant?
- Are they quick to use the "nuclear option" ("We should just get a divorce/break up!")?
- Do they mock, call names, or act from contempt?
- Does their body become tense and rigid?
- Is there an increase in their heart rate with a rising feeling of anger or rage?
- Do they have revenge fantasies?
- What is this part's job?

If you use any of these strategies, your defender part is probably a fighter. The fighter is "weapons hot" and focuses on strategies of attack, and it sees anyone in its path as a probable enemy. This part is closed off to vulnerability at all levels and keeps you from risking your heart.

The Flight Risk

- Are they quick to use the violent leave? (as explained in chapter 3)
- Do they shut down emotionally?
- Do they go somewhere else in their mind and wait until the discussion/argument is over?
- Do they find it difficult to remember what their partner has said?
- Are they inclined to avoid uncomfortable or challenging topics and conversations?
- Do they avoid eye contact with their partner?

If you use these strategies, your defender part flees the scene mentally, emotionally, or physically, effectively abandoning your partner until the coast is clear. Not to be confused with the freezer, the flight risk is not necessarily afraid. Instead, they are dodging the discomfort of the situation and the feelings it creates. This part focuses its attention on routes of escape in its attempt to protect you from the vulnerability of being present by not being present.

The Freezer

- Are they scared of their partner?
- Do they feel like they are walking on eggshells?
- Do they disassociate?
- Does their mind go into the clouds and disconnect from the moment?
- Do they feel light-headed or disoriented?
- Do they see their partner as a predator?
- Do they essentially lie flat or try playing dead until the threat is gone?
- Does their body freeze?
- Do they ever lose time or forget events during stressful periods?

- Do they lie to family and friends about their partner's behavior?
- Do they frequently make excuses for how their partner treats them?

If you employ any of these strategies, your defense is to freeze up and play dead. A freezer's nervous system shuts down until they feel safe enough to return to the present moment. People who freeze have often experienced severe trauma and may have symptoms of PTSD. If this is the case, you must seek the support of a trained therapist. Working with this traumatized defender without a professional's supervision could lead to retraumatization. I strongly urge anyone who falls into this category to get the support they need.

The Appeaser

- Do they always try to make peace?
- Do they try not to make their partner angry or upset?
- Are they continually putting their feelings aside to make room for their partner?
- Do they soothe or placate their partner?

Winston Churchill said the appeaser is someone who "feeds the crocodile—hoping it will eat him last." The appeaser is strongly related to and is sometimes considered an aspect of the freezer. I would argue that the appeaser is a more activated response to overbearing or abusive people. If your defense is to appease, it might be time to consider speaking with a therapist. As we saw earlier in the example of John, the appeaser defense often comes from trying to avoid abuse of some kind.

The Inner Critic

- Are they self-deprecating?
- Are they passive-aggressive?
- Do they continuously point out flaws in you or others?
- Are they always negative?
- Do they name-call?
- Do they shame you?

- Do they bully?
- Is nothing ever good enough?
- Do they guilt you into doing things you don't want to?

If the chief way you defend is through criticism of yourself or others, your defender is the inner critic. The critic does not want you to experience failure, loss, pain, or judgment from others. To keep you safe, it will point out your shortcomings in an effort to mitigate exposure to vulnerable situations. If you feel less confident, you are less likely to take risks. This part protects you by pointing out your faults before anyone else can. It draws attention to defects in others to keep them at a safe distance. The inner critic reaches its goals through a baneful narrative that spares few. This defender can take on many different faces. The problem comes when we fail to notice the critic, and we buy into the tales it tells.

Now that you have come to understand the primary way you defend and how this part of you behaves, let's take a moment to go a bit deeper with this side of self. Again, in your journal, answer these questions about your defender side of self. As best as you can, try to see this part from the observational perspective or the third person.

- What is their job in your life?
- Who are they protecting?
- What is their greatest concern?
- What is the positive outcome they are looking for?
- If they had a name, what would it be?

NAMING YOUR WOUNDED CHILD/CHILDREN

As I said earlier, our wounded child parts are frozen in trauma—subpersonalities caught at the time of wounding. Our wounded child parts are looking for the care and comfort they deserved but did not get. From the same observational position we used in the previous exercise, let's take a look at your wounded child side of self.

Set aside thirty to forty minutes to get to know the wounded child within you. Find a picture of you from childhood. Age does not necessarily matter. If a picture is not available, you can simply imagine an image or a memory of yourself as a kid. With respect to this image, ask the fundamental questions: Was this child loved? Was this child safe? Did this child matter? Did this child know they were enough? Do any of these questions create emotions in you? If the answer is no, there is probably a defender part standing in the way of your feelings. In this case, simply notice the defender, thank them for protecting you, and ask them to step aside so you can do this exercise. I will discuss in more detail how to negotiate with defenders later. For now, consider your wounded child and these questions from the observational position we used in the previous exercises.

Which of these questions resonates the most? At first, it might be confusing, but give each time to settle into your consciousness. The question that resonates is an apt way to describe the wounded child within you. Now from the observational, third-person position, say or write to your wounded child, "I see you. I know you were not loved, but I'm here now, and I love you" or "I see you, and I know you were not safe. I am here now and you are safe now" or "I see you, and I know you did not matter, but I am here now, and you matter to me" or "I see you. I know you never felt like you were enough, but you are enough for me."

What your inner child was missing, your adult self is now seeking in your love relationship, and this is true for your partner as well.

There is an old saying in therapy that goes something like, "Good couple's therapy ends with two individual therapists." In this process, one or both partners might discover significant inner work and healing that needs to take place. In this case, working individually with a therapist or embarking on your healing journey will be necessary. Relationships naturally trigger our wounded and unhealed parts. If we choose to see it, they offer us a rich opportunity to know and understand ourselves on a deeper level while healing what has been left unhealed.

CULTIVATING THE WISE SELF/ THE HEALTHY SELF/THE WITNESS

In his book *The Untethered Soul*, Michael Singer explains the inner witness. He says, "The process of seeing something requires a subject-object relationship. The subject is called 'The Witness' because it is the one who sees what is happening. The object is what you are seeing."[1] With this in mind, who in you is the one observing your parts? Take a moment and step back into the observer. What does it feel like to reside in your inner witness or wise self? This is the place where compassion, empathy, and understanding live.

Locating the wise self becomes problematic only when your defender, inner critic, or wounded child parts are triggered. The vulnerability of love will activate these sides of us and present themselves in our relationships. You will learn strategies for dealing with the defender, inner critic, and wounded child sides of you in the Negotiating and Reparenting exercises later in this book. For now, you want to become aware of your defender parts.

- Start by setting aside some quiet meditative time.
- Have your journal on hand for any notes you might want to make.
- Now consider how you typically feel about your partner and how you feel about being in this relationship.
- What happens in your body when you think of your partner?
- Consider who comes out to play when tensions run high or when you are stressed out or hurt.
- Begin to get a sense of your defender, inner critic, and wounded child.
- Now notice the one who witnesses.
- Who are you that sees these parts of self?

When you step back into your witness, there is a profound sense of calm and understanding. Inner wisdom rises to the surface as you uncouple from your other parts of self.

Part 3

PRACTICE 3: THE NARRATIVE

> Identification with your mind creates an opaque screen of
> concepts, labels, images, words, judgments, and definitions
> that blocks all true relationship.
>
> —Eckhart Tolle

"I don't know why I hate you anymore, Jeff, I just do." Tanya's words
were heavy with the burden of a long-held truth. They hung in the air
between the three of us, as if a tiny airplane had magically written them
in the space over our heads.

This was the fourth session for Jeff and Tanya. Jeff had made the
initial call, and while I don't like to paint with broad gender strokes, in
my experience, when a guy calls in for couple's therapy, it usually means
the relationship is in the ICU or, at the very least, in the ambulance on
the way there. Historically, men don't like to ask for help. We tend to
adhere to the persisting societal stigma, "Therapy is for people who are
not normal." The notion of divulging our deepest fears and vulnerabilities to a perfect stranger can feel akin to volunteering for a public
flogging. Needless to say, when Jeff called me, I knew his relationship
was in trouble.

After I'd heard Jeff and Tanya's individual stories, family histories,
and the arc of their courtship, I probed into what had changed. At first,
it had gone according to plan. Jeff got a job in sales for a large pack-
aging firm in the South that was quickly growing. His position made
it possible for Tanya to stop working when the kids came along. Her
willingness to make this choice surprised her. Tanya had a successful
career in public relations, but, in the end, the pull to stay home with

the children eclipsed her desire to help yet another company get their product placed in a magazine.

Jeff's chief complaint about the relationship was that something was missing. In our session, he said, "She's a great mom and is present for the kids, but it doesn't feel like she is present with me. When it comes to us, she's vacant. I have to admit that sometimes I don't know if she likes me anymore." As Jeff went further into his experience, his emotions and his volume began to crescendo. "Since Trevor was born, I mean, forget about sex. Our sex life has been nonexistent for three years!" Tears filled his eyes. "I mean, except for when she wanted another baby. Then she couldn't get enough of me. Now when we do it, I feel like she's doing me a goddamned favor. I feel like a fucking sperm bank." Tanya sat unresponsive in the face of Jeff's volley. My spidey sense told me she was holding something back.

Today, Jeff was determined to get answers. He shifted in his chair to face Tanya directly. She sat, head bowed, staring at the floor. "What's so wrong with me?" he asked. "Am I ugly? Is there someone else? What is it, Tanya? I want an answer. I deserve an answer. I did all the things you wanted, and I've tried to love you, but you won't let me in. I feel like an uninvited guest in my own fucking home."

Tanya stared Jeff directly in the eyes and coldly delivered the answer he'd been begging for: "I don't know why I hate you anymore, Jeff, I just do."

When the truth is spoken, even when painful, ugly, or riddled with shame, we begin to understand another person's experience more completely.

Unconscious agreements to hold back truth are prevalent in families and in relationships. When feelings go against familial, relational, or societal norms, we stop talking. Convinced that our honesty is more than anyone can handle, that it will hurt too many feelings or shatter too many lives, we bury it. It is common for people who are unhappy in their relationship to withhold their truth for the sake of the people around them. They say things like, "My parents, their parents, or our friends could never handle us not making it." And let's not forget the children. Understandably, the pull to keep our kids' lives happy and intact offers plenty of evidence that our truth is not fit for public consumption. The expectations of the people around us send the message that my honesty is not welcome here. The fear is that once I speak my truth, there is no coming back. That it might set off a catastrophic chain reaction that can lead only to the ruining of lives.

Jeff was both stunned and oddly relieved by Tanya's revelation. "I can't believe she said it. Don't get me wrong; it's hard to hear. But it validates everything I've been thinking and feeling."

Tanya looked at me. "You aren't supposed to hate your husband."

I didn't understand where Tanya's strong feelings came from. Jeff seemed to be a loving and loyal husband. He was a great father who spent the majority of his spare time with his children and family. He worked hard and did well, but he was far from a workaholic. He was a good communicator by most standards, and he genuinely wanted to connect with his wife. When pressed, Tanya admitted, "Jeff's great. I mean, he's a good man. No question." But where had it gone wrong for her?

I asked Tanya, "Do you remember a time when you didn't feel this way toward Jeff? Was there a time when it was good?"

"Sure, when we were dating and then when we got married. We took our time having kids, and we were really connected then. I think I noticed my feelings start to change around the time our first child was born."

Jeff jumped in. "*Everything* changed after Trevor was born. Suddenly I couldn't do anything right. She was constantly annoyed or pissed at me no matter what I did."

Tanya looked at him. "Well, you didn't do a lot right. You have to admit your head was in the clouds. For a long time, you weren't there."

Jeff immediately countered. "What are you talking about? I was there. I was more *there* than any father either of us knows. I was constantly asking to help and if I could take Trevor off your hands. You just didn't trust that I would do everything exactly the way you would do it."

"That's when it changed for me," Tanya said. "I noticed my feelings started to change then. I thought or hoped they would come back. As stupid and cliché as it might sound now, I hoped if we had another kid, things would change. But ultimately, it got worse, at least for me."

I asked, "Did you ever talk about how you were feeling with Jeff?"

"I tried, but I didn't know what to say. If I did talk about it, he would point to how hard he was trying and that he would do anything to make it better. I didn't know what to tell him to do. Ultimately, something was missing."

I replied, "But that 'something,' what was that something? What shifted for you?"

Tanya said, "Well, that's the million-dollar question, right? I'm not exactly sure. I don't know what happened to bring me here. I mean to the point where I don't even think I like him a lot of the time, and sometimes I think I hate him. It feels terrible."

Situations like Jeff and Tanya's are frustrating and perplexing for both the couple and therapist. In the beginning, we have a seemingly healthy and happy relationship. Quite naturally, with all evidence pointing in the direction that this is a love connection, the couple plan for the future. As the plan unfolds, suddenly, out of nowhere, something changes in one partner that causes the relationship to spiral. The partner points at nebulous and sometimes dubious reasons for why their feelings changed. The now "out of love" partner will say things like, "I'm not sure what's changed. I don't know what happened or what's broken. I just know that it has." Without an apparent suspect, many couples will simply chalk up their failing relationship to the vague argument that maybe "it" was never really there in the first place. Some couples simply don't have the connective tissue between them necessary to make it through the rigors and struggles of life together. But my question is, why? Why do some couples survive what we clinicians call the relational life cycle events[1] while others do not? Can we really say "it" was never there, or is something else at play?

In Practice 2: The Parts of Us, I said, "We are not the single organisms we see staring back at us in the mirror. We are made up of subpersonalities or parts of self that have their own beliefs, experiences, motivations, desires, and *narratives*." When I meet couples like Jeff and Tanya, beyond their level of mindfulness and the parts that show up, I check in with their narrative, or the story each partner has created about the other.

In Narrative therapy,[2] it is offered that clients don't have so many problems as they have problem-saturated stories. That people essentially curate the stories of their lives and then buy into them as fact. In my experience, this is undoubtedly true of romantic partners. After sitting with Jeff and Tanya, it was my theory that they had not lost some amorphous "it" as much as they had lost control of their narratives about each other.

9

WHAT IS THE NARRATIVE?

> Part of getting to know yourself is to unknow yourself—to
> let go of the limiting stories you've told yourself about
> who you are so that you aren't trapped by them, so you
> can live your life and not the story you've been telling
> about your life.
>
> —Lori Gottlieb

OUR STORIES MATTER

Their eyes gleamed as they gazed at each other. Her cheeks flushed as he laid a small peck on her forehead; she cuddled closer and rested her head on his shoulder. I tried not to stare as I stole curious looks at them from the other side of the subway car. Their connection was palpable, their love obvious. Their shared gaze was a mix of reverence and lust. I'm sure the thought "get a room" had crossed the minds of more than one of our fellow passengers. Surely this was the glow of a new relationship. As someone who works with couples who are often at odds, I was taken by the connective energy that emanated from these two. The puzzling part was neither of them looked to be a day younger than eighty, and I was convinced they must have met recently, maybe at a home for seniors or a retirement community. I'd read articles in school about the surprisingly robust sex lives of the aging. The sexual activity of nursing home residents and the increase in STDs in their populations had forced facilities to create policies and educational programs to handle the phenomenon.

The old man made eye contact with me, shaking me out of my daze with the knowledge I had been caught peeping into their public yet very private moment. He gave me a knowing smile, and his nod indicated they weren't from around here. Born here or otherwise, New Yorkers don't acknowledge each other on the subway. You just never know what you are getting yourself into. I assumed they were probably here visiting a son or daughter who lived in the city. My curiosity piqued, I broke with the unwritten subway code of conduct and struck up a conversation. Was what I witnessed the spark of a new relationship, or had this couple discovered a way to keep the energy and connection of new love alive across the expanse of time?

As it turned out, Jim and Kay were not in their eighties. They were both in their early nineties. The love that was so evident in this couple was not the glow of the shiny and new; it was a love that had been cultivated over sixty-three years. I told Jim that I was studying to be a therapist and that my passion was working with couples. That more than anything, I wanted to help couples create what I thought I saw in him and Kay. Beyond that, I wanted to create the same in my own marriage. I said, "Jim, I hope it's okay that I ask, but what's your secret? I see the way you two look at each other. It seems like you are still smitten. If I'm honest, it's not what we normally see, especially in couples who have been together this long." Kay looked at Jim with a knowing glance that said I was on to them. They knew they had something special, and I had witnessed it. Jim didn't launch into a lecture about their vows and the sanctity of marriage. He didn't talk about doing it for God or the kids. He paused for a moment, looked at Kay, and said, "No matter what was going on, no matter what we were going through or how hard things got—and they did from time to time, trust me—I always reminded myself of how lucky I was to be with this woman. You can buy into the problems and let them pull you apart, or you can keep your eye on what's important. For me, it was how fortunate I was to have her. I have always reminded myself of that." Kay nodded in agreement as Jim delivered his sage advice. Then she said, "And I did the same." With a wry grin, she winked at me as she added, "I admit that some times it was easier than others."

My takeaway from Kay was, this was not some magical elixir, but something they practiced, even when it was hard. We shared a laugh, and I gave them some solid advice on good restaurants if they made it down to the East Village. Then I was off to class, feeling enlightened and inspired by that ninety-year-old couple on a New York City train.

You never know when or where you will meet inspiration. I met one of mine that day in an elderly couple. Jim, of course, never talked about the story he told himself about Kay and their marriage. He never used the term "narrative" in any of what he shared that day. These are lines drawn by a budding clinician, but what I believed Jim and Kay were saying is, the story you tell about your partner matters. The narrative you create influences how you feel about the person you are with. That even when it's hard, you have to keep a sharp eye on how you think about the one you love and that practice, especially when it's hard, makes all the difference.

The narrative, as it pertains to couples, is that little story we tell in the back of our minds about our partner. One of my clients described her inner narrative well when she said, "It's like a little ticker tape in my mind, that constantly runs on loop about my husband." At the beginning of a romantic relationship, our narratives are colored by what I have called the "dopamine blast of the new." Dopamine is a type of neurotransmitter associated with feelings of pleasure, motivation, and reward. When a stimulus triggers a rush of dopamine, the brain assigns importance to that stimulus, and we are pulled to reach for more of the same. Dopamine levels are at an all-time high when we're first pursuing a relationship. This, coupled with our evolutionary and biological need to procreate, lowers our defensive measures and perception of negative attributes of our prospective partner, creating what has been called "love-blindness" or "limerence,"[1] the hallmark of a new romance.

However, dopamine is not sustainable in the brain, and typically, after six months to a year, levels taper off. Pair this dopamine drop with the stressors that challenge couples, and the rose-colored glasses quickly come off, inviting a decided shift in the stories we tell about our mates.

This is a pivotal time for couples where ways of interacting and habits of thought take shape. No longer inebriated by the elixir of new love, defender parts of self surface to protect us from the vulnerability love now offers. Our parts then tell stories about who our mates are and who they are not. These dialogues start with the quiet whispers that say something like, *You've never understood me. I think you think you would be better off with someone else. I've never been able to trust you. I don't really matter to you, never have. I don't think I'm attracted to you. You always disappoint me.* These are just a few examples of the globalized language as well as the tone and tenor of our inner monologues when they turn negative. It's the fleeting thoughts or judgments we give little weight to in the moment that when left to proliferate become the predominant way we see our mates.

However, when we use the skills offered in our first two practices, we can mindfully observe our narratives and the parts of self who author them. In this mindful space, we have a choice about the narratives we buy into and the directions they take. In Practice 3: The Narrative, we will discover that when told from the wise, healthy self, our narratives can become loving and compassionate aspects of our relationships that strengthen our bond and bring us closer together. However, when left on autopilot, they can spread like a virus and infect our connection to our partners.

This is where I found Jeff and Tanya. My questions were: When did their stories about each other turn? How did Jeff move from seeing Tanya as his best friend to feeling utterly abandoned by her? And how did Tanya move away from loving Jeff and wanting to spend her life with him, to, "I don't know why I hate you, I just do"?

Both agreed that everything changed after the birth of their first son. This is not surprising. As much as we like to say that the birth of a child is amazing and wonderful, the truth is, it's also tough, draining, and exhausting. The hospital hands you this helpless creature, who you've just met but somehow love more than you can possibly put into words, and says, "Good luck." When our first son was born, we were shocked to find out there was no user manual or directions. Somehow the midwife trusted that Ashley and I would figure it all out. I, however, spent the first few weeks looking out the window, wondering when his real parents were going to show up.

A stock phrase in marriage and family therapy is, "When you add or subtract a member of a family, you double the stress." Cue the cascade of well-documented couple's issues that include less time together, more fighting, and less sex. The turbulent waters that couples face after introducing a child into the mix caused best-selling author Jancee Dunn to pen a book on the subject called *How Not to Hate Your Husband after*

Kids, a funny yet candid account of her quest to bring her post-baby marriage back from the brink.

Jeff and Tanya reported many of the stressors common to this life cycle; however, their behavior said there was something else driving a wedge between them. Couples who experience normative struggles associated with having a child manage to find their rhythm again either through self-intervention or therapy. However, for this couple, even with these interventions, the space between them remained distant and cold, with seemingly few points that brought them closer. Their physical connection was nonexistent, Jeff was desperate, and Tanya's words were stark, her demeanor bleak.

Using the strategies offered in Practices 1 and 2, I asked Jeff and Tanya's defender parts to step aside and invited their kinder, wiser sides of self to the table. This exercise gave both of them the ability to talk about their feelings surrounding their son's birth for the first time.

Jeff said, "As soon as Trevor was born, I lost her. I lost my best friend, and I lost my partner. Listen, I know things had to change and that being a new mom is hard, but we entered this thing as a team. When Trev came along, it was all over for me."

Tanya shared that while the experience of becoming a new mom was hard, those difficulties were only made worse by what happened with Jeff. "I know he thinks he was there, but he wasn't, at least not in the way I needed him to be. Yes, he helped with the baby, yes, he cooked and cleaned and worked, but I had no connection to him. He stopped talking to me, and I felt alone in this place filled with so many unknowns. It was like he was there, but his heart was not. He says he felt like he lost his best friend. Well, that's exactly how I felt. My person was gone when I needed him the most, and frankly, I didn't have the stamina to chase after him. That's when the resentment set in."

At this stage of their work, the verdict on whether Jeff and Tanya's relationship would survive was still out. I had to admit from my vantage point, things didn't look promising. Tanya seemed like a wife that might not be walking out the door yet, but she definitely had her hand on the doorknob, and Jeff was doing little to change her mind. Jeff had gotten caught up in his narrative about being left out, abandoned by his person, and passed over for their son. This left little to no room in his mind or heart for the fact that Tanya had actually needed and wanted him there.

The story he concocted left out the possibility that his wife wanted to experience their new family together.

Consequently, while Jeff thought he was being "there" by doing his punch list of fatherly duties, Tanya sensed the perfunctory nature of his efforts. She began creating story lines of her own that included the idea that Jeff didn't really want this anymore, that he had abandoned her, or that he was emotionally incapable of understanding her needs. Compounding this experience for Tanya was the disappointment she felt as she watched her dream and vision of her new family disintegrate before her eyes. Tanya's narrative about her husband was now dangerously close to malignant while Jeff's bordered on hopeless.

So the question becomes: Is that my sweetheart who stumbled, who is struggling to understand me, who made a mistake, or are they the selfish, emotionally stunted dolt who only thinks about themselves? I am not suggesting that the only thing that counts is the story we tell or that if we could simply muster up enough positive affirmations, then all will be okay. Of course, couples have real experiences; people make mistakes and are, at times, thoughtless, selfish, cold, and even harsh. In relationships, feelings do get hurt and old wounds resurface. What I am saying is that the stories we tell resonate throughout our lives and influence our thoughts, feelings, and beliefs. They inform our decisions and directly affect how we relate to the people we work with, live with, and love. Once the narratives about our partners sour, our feelings are soon to follow. Accordingly, the narrative is a key and fundamental marker of the health of romantic relationships. Once clients are made aware of their narratives and the roles they play, the natural question is "why?" Why are those little stories so impactful? How is it that something as simple as a thought could be so vital to making a heart-centered connection?

10

WHY OUR NARRATIVES
ARE SO IMPORTANT

Although the body is very intelligent, it cannot tell the difference between an actual situation and a thought. It reacts to every thought as if it were reality. It doesn't know it's just a thought.

—Eckhart Tolle

OUR THOUGHTS BECOME OUR
FEELINGS BECOME OUR BELIEFS

Think for a moment about your favorite food. Imagine how it smells, how it tastes, and how good it would be to eat it right now. As you get deeper into this narrative about your dish, you will begin to feel the rumblings of hunger pains. Even if you've just eaten, if you think these thoughts long enough, you will land on "Sure, I could have a bite," even though you are not actually hungry. Now try this with sexual fantasy. If you think sexual thoughts long enough, the body will, in turn, fire off feelings to support this experience, saying in effect, "Yeah! Let's do that," and you will experience all of the reactions in your body that accompany those thoughts.

The brain is inexorably linked to the body. They are in a constant biochemical conversation through the transmission of neuropeptides, neurotransmitters, and hormones, the specifics of which are interesting but not necessarily germane to this subject. Suffice it to say, when we have a thought, the brain sends a chemical signal to the body, and the body matches that chemical signal and creates a state of being, like with the examples, either hungry or horny.[1] Said even more simply: Our

103

thoughts become our feelings. If we put enough of these thoughts and feelings together, we create a belief or, for our purposes, a narrative. This understanding makes those little "one-off" thoughts we have about our partners, the ones that seem rather insignificant and unimportant, now seem very important. In this light, they can no longer be written off as not how we really feel or as an expression of some petty, in-the-moment frustration. The thoughts we have are not inconsequential little scripts. They kick-start a chemical tide in the body that ultimately affects how we see our world and the people in it.

As an example, have you ever had the experience of being short, frustrated, angry, or even resentful of your partner, but you are not exactly sure why? Have you ever experienced your partner acting this way toward you?

Imagine a friend or coworker who does or says something that hurts your feelings. A bit stunned, you don't say anything about it at the time. You are left thinking about the interaction for the rest of the day. Your thoughts become feelings. These feelings then create more thoughts that, in turn, become a narrative. "How dare they say that to me?" "Who the hell do they think they are?" You take that narrative to a friend and ask, "Can you believe the nerve?" Your brain fires off chemical signals to the body that say you are pissed, and the body sends signals in support of this experience. You then wake up in the middle of the night, and you think about it again in the shower the next morning. To some degree, your feelings about this person have changed. Your story about them has been compromised and will affect the way you speak to them and treat them, but, in truth, not a lot has actually happened. Most of what went on happened in your head, but the feelings are very real. What this amounts to is a form of mental rehearsal. Because of our large prefrontal cortex, we are the only animals on the planet that have the ability to imagine circumstances that have yet to occur and experience them as if they have.

For many years athletes and performers at the highest levels have used mental rehearsal to their advantage. By just picturing how they will perform, they increase the likelihood of recreating similar reactions, both mentally and physically, in the future. Research in the area suggests that the brain learns how to respond even in the absence of real-world stimuli. To a large degree, the body and the mind do not know the difference between an event that is happening in real life or just in the imagination. Brain imagery shows that when we imagine ourselves in situations, we stimulate the same brain regions when we physically perform that same action.[2] This has far-reaching implications with respect to success in sports, on the stage, or at the big presentation, but also in our relationships. This is yet another compelling reason why we must be mindful of the stories we create about our partners. If we are on autopilot, we will continually have thoughts that become feelings, that then become our narratives. In essence, we are rehearsing to fall out of love. When we continue to cast our mates in the role of the villain, our brains and bodies conspire to create the state of being necessary to support that experience. This research suggests that through our narratives, we train ourselves to respond negatively to our mates.

On the contrary, when we mindfully change our narratives and choose love and compassion, and when we remind ourselves to bring gracious consideration to our mates, we take advantage of Hebb's Law. Hebb's Law is the neuro postulate I mentioned in part 1, which says that neurons that consistently fire together will eventually wire together, thus creating new habits of thought that support connection. When couples practice retelling newer, more positive stories about each other, they rewire their brains for love.

"PRUNING" THE NARRATIVE

I was leaving the nest, so to speak, about to be launched into the world as a newly minted therapist. As per the departure ritual at my internship site, my colleagues gathered in a room and wrote down on pieces of parchment the effect I'd had on them both personally and professionally. As part of the ritual, they read them aloud. One by one, my fellow therapists spoke kindly and generously of my work and of me. A few said they admired my courage and dedication. One woman said that, for her, I represented the embodiment of husband and father. Still another said she hoped her two boys might grow up to be like me. After reading from their bits of parchment, they folded them up and placed them in the specially chosen container: a chrome-plated vessel, about the size of a large coffee cup with a wooden top. The metal was chosen for its reflection and sturdiness, the wood for its warmth. My coworkers said the container was an apt representation of me and what I'd brought to the practice.

As I listened, I was dumbfounded.

I had spent the better part of those two and a half years waiting for my pink slip, silently wondering when they would get wise to their mistake. Although I had done exceedingly well with my clients, that part was pruned from my inner monologue about my internship. My fear and vulnerabilities had gotten the better of me, and I created a prevailing story line that said I would never be accepted in this world of learned professionals. After all, I was the son of a fifteen-year-old mother who grew up in abject poverty and would forever be the kid from the wrong side of the tracks. The idea that I was now an intern at an upscale Madison Avenue private therapy practice did not fit my narrative. It seemed the stuff of movies, and some parts of me, the protective parts, would not believe a bit of it. So I wrapped myself in the protective armor of my inner narrative, and while that story kept me from getting hurt, it also meant I missed out on a number of deep and connective relationships. I had been unable to see the truth of those people, that place, and that experience. I missed all of it.

In his book *The Art of Stillness: Adventures in Going Nowhere*, author Pico Iyer gives a simple but profoundly accurate description of the interplay between our thoughts/narratives and our reality: "So much of our lives takes place in our heads—in memory or imagination, in speculation or interpretation—that sometimes I feel I can best change my life by changing the way I look at it."[3]

We are often the misguided, unconscious, and unreliable editors of our inner monologues. A central theme in Narrative therapy is the concept of "pruning the narrative"—that humans have a tendency to focus on and include information that supports our prevailing narratives while de-selecting or omitting details that do not. In those two-plus years, I had done a lot of selecting and de-selecting, a lot of including some information about my colleagues and my experiences while excluding a host of other details. As I pruned my narrative about my internship, I changed how I felt about it and the people there. Rather than seeing them as the kind, supportive group they were, I often saw them as people to guard myself against.

In my experience, couples do not spare each other from this penchant. Whether through memory or imagination, speculation or interpretation, we create story lines about our partners and cast them somewhere between conquering hero or nefarious villain, between sexy and alluring or dull and boring. With this in mind, we can no longer see our passing thoughts about our partners as unimportant, as factless fairy tales, or mind-made fables with no merit. Indeed, our narratives affect all aspects of how we connect, and that includes how we connect physically. Much of our sexual attraction starts in the mind, but, as we will see, sexual attraction or lack thereof is only part of a story we tell.

HOW THE NARRATIVE AFFECTS OUR SEX LIVES

"Are you asking me if I'm having sex with a pregnant woman? Because if that's what you're asking, the answer is yes, I am. I'm having sex with my pregnant wife. And if you must know, I'm doing it as often as I can."

My annoyance at my friend's question was apparent, and he began to stammer, "Well, yeah. I mean, how is that? How, how do you do that?"

"Well, I started by growing the fuck up," I replied.

I probably didn't need to be so harsh. My friend was considering how he might feel if or when his girlfriend became pregnant. He was asking a genuine, though clumsy question. At the time, Ashley was about eight months pregnant with our first son. If I'm honest, when she became pregnant similar questions lingered in my mind. "What *was* that going to be like?" "Would it be weird?" The last thing I wanted was not to be attracted to my wife, especially during this incredibly vulnerable time, but what if those thoughts crept in? I'd heard of men who became suddenly repulsed by their wives' pregnant bodies, throwing their relationships into peril. Oprah had even done a show about it. Later in my career, I would treat the pain, wounding, and rage of the women whose partners had treated them this way. I was struck with the fear of "What if that happens to me?" In the end, I decided to take what would later become my own advice, and I grew the fuck up. Growing the fuck up meant turning toward love and consciously creating a narrative based on compassion and understanding. Ashley's body was going to do what it naturally needed to do to create our child; it was going to become full and fleshy as it should. She was going to carry our baby, and that was not repulsive. As a matter of fact, it was amazing, and it was beautiful, and yes, it was sexy. At the beginning of her pregnancy, I bought her a pair of "boy cut" panties with a pistol pattern on them. We joked that by the time Jake was born, those little pistols looked more like muskets. In the end, Ashley carried our boy like a goddess, and because I slew the demons of selfishness and stupidity, I didn't miss it. I could be present for it all, but to a large degree, that was a story—one I fed consciously—a narrative I chose to tell and one that made all the difference.

Sex for most couples is a big deal. In relationships where it is good and healthy, it seems sex makes up about 20 to 25 percent of a relationship. In relationships where it is inadequate or nonexistent, sex seems to occupy about 75 to 80 percent of the mental and emotional space in a relationship. The stories we tell about ourselves and each other as sexual beings carry a lot of weight. As we saw with our couple, Tanya's lack of sexual attraction to her husband was in lockstep with her narrative about him. As her story about Jeff began to degrade, so did her pull to connect with him physically. As a therapist who deals with these issues almost daily, I don't think enough attention is paid to how our narratives affect us in the bedroom. These inner monologues are the backdrop of our sexual attraction. The sexual attraction between long-term partners is notoriously difficult to maintain, especially after the time of limerence in a relationship that I spoke of earlier. This is a period when love and lust can disappear, as couples tend to argue more and communicate less. This is when the sexy story about your mate shifts from "I want you to jump my bones" to "I want you to leave me alone." As our stories shift, we see imperfections in each other's bodies more readily, and we dis-compassionately focus on what is wrong rather than what is right. Perhaps we start to compare our spouses to other people in real life or on social media, further diverting our narratives in the wrong direction.

Accompanying the removal of our rose-colored glasses is the factor of familiarity that also impacts the stories we tell about our partners and our sexual attraction to them. In the beginning, we strive for familiarity. We want to know our partners and for our partners to know us. There is both safety and a sense of intimacy in knowing someone and being known. Psychotherapist and author Esther Perel said in her book *Mating in Captivity* that "love enjoys to know everything about you," it grows through repetition and familiarity. However, it is through these same elements of repetition and familiarity that "eroticism is numbed." She says that desire "thrives on the mysterious, the novel, and the unexpected."[4] There is a slippery slope with respect to familiarity between romantic partners. If we get lazy in the telling of our tales and if we let our inner monologues slide down that slippery slope into the mundane, we run the risk of smothering our sexual fire. I say that it is impossible for desire to thrive in an environment where the prevailing narrative is something like, "Been there, done that."

If passion is numbed by familiarity, we must consciously create stories about our partners where they are an ever-evolving puzzle to be solved. Whenever possible, we must make them objects of our desire by constructing inner monologues and fantasies that ignite a craving and a longing for their touch. Studies support the idea that creating passionate sexual narratives or fantasizing about our partners has positive effects on our sex lives and on our love relationships as a whole. Four separate studies on the subject show that fantasizing about one's partner heightens the sexual desire for that partner and increases engagement in relationship-promoting behaviors.[5] One crucial detail from these studies was that the fantasies did not have to be spontaneous to achieve these effects. In fact, "artificial fantasies," or erotic narratives that we intentionally construct, worked just as well. In this, we see the impact and importance of our thoughts that become feelings that, in this case, become what we believe about our partners and ourselves in the bedroom.

It should be said at this point that human sexuality is a broad and complex topic. By no means have I figured out everyone's sexual issues by asking them to tell new and sexy stories. Sex is complicated, and despite the wonders and potential of prescriptions like Viagra and Addyi, there is no magic pill when it comes to creating a better physical connection. Having said that, becoming mindful of our narratives and telling a new and healthier story is more than a superficial reframing of our plotlines. Narrative work in this area asks us to not only cast our partners as the object of our desire; it reminds us to claim the sexual narratives we hold about ourselves. Sex is often overcoupled with familial, cultural, and generational mores that influence our ability to connect physically. Couples who work consciously on their stories together have the opportunity to bring kindness, compassion as well as empathy, and reverence to what is a vulnerable and often shame-based aspect of being human. This creates trust, and trust is the foundational building block of deep and abiding intimacy on every level.

JEFF AND TANYA

My days are usually a long series of fifty-minute sessions. In the hoped-for ten-minute break between patients, I will run to the bathroom, make coffee, field a message or two, and/or schedule another client. The pause between sessions is often capped by my next appointment's muffled conversations as they sit in the waiting room. Today, however, there was no muffled conversation. It seemed Jeff and Tanya were running late. This was supposed to be their fifth session. We had spent our first few sessions unpacking their histories, learning about mindfulness, and dabbling in parts of self. The thought floated into my mind that there could have been an abrupt decision to discontinue therapy. They were a couple on the fault line, and anything was possible. Their interactions had de-escalated, but a chill had replaced the emotional volatility, and it was palpable. So I was surprised when I opened my door to see they had arrived on time. The two entered my office in silence. After the obligatory greetings, the silence continued for four full minutes. Their eyes met mine from time to time, only to dart away in the discomfort of prolonged eye contact. It seemed no one was willing to break the quiet.

Whenever these long silences occur, I am reminded of when actor Sacha Baron Cohen, posing as his character Borat, infiltrated the Pima County Republican Club and held a long silence for the people who died in the fictitious "Tishnik massacre." Cohen let the camera run for ten minutes that seemed like hours, and the discomfort felt by the members of the club was obvious. Silences in the therapy room can feel just as long and just as uncomfortable, but not nearly as funny. It is often difficult for even seasoned therapists to allow space for them. I think humans have a compelling need to fill the void. In my training program at Helix, we learned to get comfortable with silence in our monthly process group. These sessions were two hours in length, and they often started with long pauses in conversation that could last for an hour or more, no one willing to be the first to speak. The longer the word embargo, the harder it seemed to finally break it. It was in these process group experiences that I not only got comfortable with the discomfort of silence; I also learned to read the quiet between people. Sometimes the silence at the beginning of these process groups was merely shyness, however, more often than not, the quiet was pregnant with something more. Someone was usually holding on to a thought, a feeling, or an experience, that when finally shared, would begin the inevitable argument. From what I could surmise, this was the case for Jeff and Tanya. Neither wanted to break the tentative peace, perhaps knowing what lay around the corner once people got talking.

Finally, Jeff asks, "Do you want to start?"

"No, you go," Tanya replies.

Frustrated, Jeff shifts in his chair, takes a deep breath, and says, "Well, I guess things this week were better?" He looks to Tanya for some confirmation that he's on the right track.

Noticing his inherent question, Tanya finally speaks. "Yeah, it was better. I mean, we didn't argue as much. As a matter of fact, we didn't argue at all."

Jeff adds, "Right, we would have to actually interact for an argument to happen. She still wants nothing to do with me. The only thing I'm good for in her eyes is to make money and to fix stuff around the house. Oh, and give her a kid when she wants one."

Tanya, now angry, retorts, "Really? Really, Jeff? That's what you think?"

"Well, what the hell am I supposed to think?" Jeff replies.

They both stop, and the silence returns.

Tanya takes a breath and speaks carefully. "You checked out, Jeff. You checked out. And I know you think you did all the stuff, but you didn't. When you're not at the office, you're on your phone. But more than anything, you stopped talking. You forgot one key part, me! Emotionally you are nowhere to be found. You've been gone. You think you lost me, but I lost *you* in this. You don't want to be here. Admit it. I'm not saying you don't love the kids, but this life, I don't believe you want this. It's obvious."

"Really, then why am I here in this room? Why did I make the call? Why am I working so hard to keep us together?"

Tanya answers, "I don't know. I've been thinking about that. Maybe the money, divorce is expensive? Maybe you don't want the label of 'divorced'? Or maybe you're here looking for the doctor's note out—I don't know, maybe you just want to be the 'good one,' the one that tried."

Jeff shakes his head. "That's what you think of me? I'm here because I love you and the kids. Because I won't give up on you the way you gave up on me. You think I quit, but you are the one who quit. You had a kid, and then it was curtains for me—marriage over."

Tanya turned to me with a sarcastic grin. "As you can see, not much has changed since you saw us last."

I replied, "To be honest, I wasn't expecting much in the way of change for you yet. You are still on autopilot with each other, still reacting pretty mindlessly. You are, from what I can see, still trying to communicate from your defender parts of self. But what's really jumping out at me is the story each of you tells about the other. If your narrative doesn't change, your feelings won't change. As long as your story about Jeff and your marriage remain as they are, he has no opportunity to be anything other than the husband who doesn't show up for you and the guy who doesn't understand you. And Jeff, this goes for you too. You are holding on to this idea that Tanya left you out in the cold, doesn't need you anymore, has gotten what she wants from you, and is done."

I continued. "Here are my concerns: right now some of that story you're telling about each other is true, and a lot of it is not; some of it's fair, and some of it's not. You have to decide if you want to end your relationship based on what might add up to some half-truths. It will be up to you how the story ends—which narrative you buy into. Look, you have some issues to surmount, and there is scar tissue—you've both been hurt. However, I think in a very real sense, you do have a choice, and it's one you should make consciously."

My wife likes to say, "When the communication stops that's when our relationships begin to wither." When the narratives start, the communication stops. We cease being curious about our partner's actual experience as we dive headfirst into our assumptions. Jeff and Tanya had their fair share of what might be considered obvious relational issues, such as anger, trust, resentment, and communication problems as well as an inability to connect physically. However, through the lens of our Five

Practices, I saw two people who had become mindless, mindless to the parts of self that were showing up in their relationship, but also mindless to the narratives they had created about each other. Both accused the other of purposefully and maliciously abandoning the marriage. Jeff's story centered on Tanya giving up on him and needing him only for financial security. Tanya, on the other hand, had fabricated a narrative where Jeff no longer wanted family life and only stayed to save money or because he didn't like the optics of divorce.

This couple is a near-perfect example of how our thoughts can proliferate into negative narratives. In their acute need to protect themselves, both pruned their narratives, gripping onto any information that supported their prevailing stories while ignoring evidence that might change the plot, all the while mentally rehearsing over and over, day by day, to fall out of love.

My task with Tanya and Jeff wasn't to save their marriage at all costs. Therapy focused on saving marriages for marriage's sake is pointless, shortsighted, and frankly doesn't work. People ask me all of the time, "How many relationships have you saved? What's your record?" To their surprise, I say, "I have no idea. That's not my job." I have just as many people writing to me years later saying, "Thank you for helping me get out of that relationship, I'm finally happy," as I do people thanking me for helping their relationship survive. I am not what you would call a "pro-marriage therapist." I am a pro-happiness therapist, and if two people are far healthier apart than they are together, I'll be damned if I am going to try to "therapize" them into staying. When we boil it down, I help people uncover information, information about themselves, their partners, and their relationships. That is what this book is geared to do, and that was my focus with Jeff and Tanya—to get them the information they needed and to help them make an informed decision about the course of their lives. The question remained: How? How to get two hurt and angry people to let their guard down long enough to see the cycle of thoughts, becoming feelings, becoming narratives that were ultimately creating their beliefs about each other.

11

HOW TO USE THE NARRATIVE

Stories become transformative only in their performance.

—E. Bruner

A TALE OF TWO WOLVES

A young woman went to her grandmother looking for advice. She said, "Grandma, I need your help. It seems there is a terrible battle raging inside of me. It's like two wolves fighting it out. One wolf is filled with fear. It's angry, prideful, jealous, superior, and resentful. The other wolf, however, is full of love. It is kind, compassionate, benevolent, generous, and empathetic. My question for you is, how do I know which of the wolves inside of me will win?"

The grandmother smiled and said, "That's easy, my dear, the wolf that wins is the one you choose to feed."[1]

This story has been told over the years in many different versions. It is usually told from the perspective of the masculine. I take some artistic license in my telling of it by using female characters.

This simple fable illustrates how we can let our negative thinking rule our minds. It also shows how becoming aware of the narratives is the first step in taking control of them. The story offers that we have power over our inner monologues and an ability to change them through mindful choice. Like the young woman in the story, we must become aware of our narratives. If we want our relationships to thrive, we must actively feed the wolf of love and compassion.

115

This is not to say that we should blindly feed the wolf of naivete and gullibility. To adopt a mindset of guilelessness and unbridled loyalty where we mindlessly gloss over serious problems with saccharin-sweet smiles and positive affirmations is nothing short of magical thinking and is, frankly, unhealthy.

The power and influence of our narratives should not be underestimated. However, neither should our ability to sway the direction of the plotline. In his book *Buried Treasures: The Journey from Where You Are to Who You Are*, author Guru Singh captured the strength of our stories as well as our authority to change them: "I have a choice in every moment—I always have a choice. When the attitude of my thoughts changes, the entire outlook changes simultaneously—an identical scene can become glorious or hideous. With every moment a choice is born, and with every choice, a moment is born."[2]

Before we can choose our narratives, we must first become aware of the stories we tell. We do this by turning up the volume on those quiet little thoughts that we might not want anyone else to hear. We have to be bold enough to say them aloud or to write them down, if only for ourselves, in order to experience the weight and profundity of the beliefs we are building about our partners. After turning up the volume, we need to assess our narratives for validity and ask if they are compassionate, empathetic, fair, and understanding, or if they are true.

TURNING UP THE VOLUME

In that same session with Jeff and Tanya discussed in the previous chapter, I said, "I'd like you to try something that might seem rather counter to our goals. I'd like for each of you to say out loud the little thoughts, feelings, and judgments that you have about each other."

Both Jeff and Tanya shot each other uneasy looks.

I continued. "Are you aware of the inner dialogue I'm referring to? You know the thoughts you have that you might not say out loud unless you are really hurt or really angry?"

Both gave a nod of agreement.

Jeff added, "Well, this oughta be interesting. I guess we're gonna get our money's worth today."

I replied, "I'm not going to lie, this can be hard, but if you hang in there with me to the end, there is a good chance some healing may occur before the day is out."

I turned to Tanya. "I'm going to start with you if that's okay?"

She gave another nod of silent agreement.

"In our last session, you said, 'I don't know why I hate you anymore, I just do.' Now I believe that there are some very real feelings behind what you said, and I don't want to discount how you feel. Hate, however, is a strong word, and I want to know if you actually hate Jeff? Because if you are walking around silently telling yourself that you hate him and building a story about him that includes your utter disdain for this man, well then, I don't know where we go from there. I want to be sure that's what you actually feel. Before you answer, I'd like you to become aware of the part of you that's here. If there is a defended side here, just ask it to step aside and speak as best as you can from the wise self."

Tanya takes a deep breath, and she rubs her hands together in her lap. She looks away as she contemplates my question. I get the sense that she knows where I am going. She knows that I will ask her to take "hate" off the table if she can, and that might make her more vulnerable to Jeff.

Reluctantly, she turns to Jeff and says, "I don't hate you." She then runs down my narrative checklist.

"Saying I hated you was not fair, compassionate, or understanding. I admit I shouldn't have said it. *And,* I don't necessarily think you stay because of the money or because you don't want a divorce."

I interjected, "If it wasn't hate, what were you feeling?"

"I am hurt, really hurt, and really angry. I do feel abandoned by you. I guess those feelings built up, and my parts started telling me things."

Jeff reaches for Tanya's hand, and she accepts it. It's subtle, but I notice what I think is a reluctance in her receipt of his touch.

"That's a great point, Tanya," I said. "Our protective parts create narratives in an attempt to keep us safe. Your narratives about each other derived from these places, and I think that's a big part of what has derailed your connection."

I turn to Jeff. "Now, let's talk a little about your narratives." Jeff shifts in his chair as if to ready himself. Tanya uses the opportunity to recover her hand.

As per the practice, I ask Jeff to check in with the part of him present and to invite the wise self to the table. Seeing his wife go through this process made letting go of his defender and accessing his wiser parts that much easier.

Jeff says, "Well, where should I start? I've told myself a lot about Tanya, some of it you've heard. I've told myself that she abandoned me, that once the kids came, I was done. That I was just an ATM and a sperm bank to her. I've entertained the idea that there was someone else, and I even thought about snooping her phone a few times but didn't."

I said, "Let's check your narratives for validity. When you consider them now, are the stories you tell about Tanya compassionate, empathetic, or understanding—are they fair, or are they true?"

Jeff replied, "I think we all know my narratives are not compassionate, empathetic, or understanding. Sometimes they felt fair and true, but if I really look at it, I know that's not who she is or who she has ever been. I know how much she wanted a family, and if I'm honest, I'm sure I was always a part of that equation. I'm just not sure that's true now. There is a part of me that still feels hurt and left out. I think that's real."

Turning up the volume allows couples to assess their relationship and their partners from a macro perspective. In this process, they ask, "Has this been true of this person historically?" "Is this who they are, or are they having difficulty during this time or with this life event?" This exercise begs that we consider the continuity of the relationship and how any one challenging experience fits into that context. Further, turning up the volume acts as a centrifugal force, effectively deconstructing our narratives. It separates our unhelpful and often damaging stories from our actual feelings. When we boiled it down, Tanya felt hurt, angry, and abandoned while Jeff felt hurt and left out. These are emotions and experiences we can talk about and process. The often globalized language of our inner monologues traps our partners and us, as there is simply nowhere to go from "He always . . ." or "She never . . ."

At first, the difference between our narratives and our core feelings can be murky. If we take the step to move our defender parts aside and ask if our stories are compassionate, empathetic, true, and fair, our actual feelings are revealed. Parsing a feeling from the narrative is made even more straightforward by allowing yourself as few words as possible to describe your experiences. An example of this might be, "I'm so pissed off.

He is an emotionless asshole who doesn't care about me at all." Another way to express this is, "I'm hurt and angry, and I don't feel cared for." The latter is arguably less dramatic, less incendiary, far more accurate, and decidedly easier to discuss and process.

Jeff and Tanya left this session closer to understanding each other's perspectives. Their homework was to turn up the volume on their inner monologues and to be mindful of negative stories they tended to tell about each other. When a story surfaced, they were to stop, push pause, and assess it for validity as we did in session. While this can all seem cumbersome in the explanation, the application can happen in just a few seconds with a little effort.

As this practice takes shape, we are effectively interrupting the progression of thoughts becoming feelings becoming beliefs. This kickstarts the process of repatterning the brain. Pushing pause and turning up the volume gets us out of our knee-jerk responses of thinking. By interrupting this cycle and bringing awareness to the cognitions related to our partners, we take advantage of the brain's natural ability to change and adapt. Later, the step of re-authoring new, more positive, and often more accurate narratives will be added to the practice. However, before re-authoring, I help my clients remember why they chose their partners in the first place. Often buried under years of negative storytelling are the loving and compassionate experiences they have forgotten about. This is important information that has been pruned from the narrative. We rediscover these understandings through gratitude, loving-kindness meditations, appreciation, and compassion practices, all of which have been scientifically proven to lead to positive change for couples.

GRATITUDE JOURNALS, LOVING-KINDNESS MEDITATIONS, AND THANK-YOU'S

Exercises such as gratitude journals have become such a regular part of the therapeutic arsenal that they border on the obligatory. Usually one to avoid the cliché, I often gravitate toward the new and the different since it awakens the brain and tends to be more interesting. However, sometimes the old standards offer so much benefit to clients that they cannot be ignored and, for me, practicing gratitude falls into this category.

As the currents of life roll on, couples focus on the annoying, the frustrating, and the painful and forget what once drew them close. Left to fester, these thoughts become feelings that become a prevailing narrative that sounds something like, "Maybe the person I chose wasn't so great after all" or "I love him, but I'm not sure I'm *in* love with him."

To combat these negative story lines and to aid in the effort of forging a new narrative, I ask couples to practice gratitude for each other. Often, this takes the form of gratitude journaling; however, gratitude meditation can work as well. In this practice, I have clients set aside a few minutes every day to write down or meditate on four or five things they are grateful for in their partner. It can be anything, big or small, that creates positive thoughts or emotions about their spouse. Sometimes when I assign gratitude journals, I hear something like, "Yeah, I've done that before. It was okay. I mean, I don't know how well it really worked." To that, I say you probably did it wrong. Whether you are writing your thankful points down or meditating on them, you have to remember that this is not an exercise in fact recording. If what you write down is an unemotional laundry list, it will, of course, fail. This is an exercise designed to touch into emotion—specifically positive emotions in the direction of your partner. I have my clients sit with their list and feel into the emotions that each point on their list creates in them. I want my couples to steep themselves in the good feelings that those thoughts produce. I ask that they not move on to the next item on their list until they feel a positive, chemical shift in their bodies.

Studies show that practicing gratitude is a fundamental and necessary component of a healthy relationship. These studies also show that couples who create a relational culture based on an appreciation of each other experience more trust, respect, and physical connection and feel a greater sense of commitment.[3]

LOVING-KINDNESS/METTA MEDITATIONS

In conjunction with gratitude practice, I also assign "Loving-kindness" or what's also known as "Metta Meditations." Metta means kindness and positive energy towards others, and the practice of Metta[4] is meant to engender a sense of benevolence, kindness, and compassion in the practitioner, who sits and intentionally wishes peace, goodwill, and overall health and wellness for specific people in their lives. The benefits of this type of meditation have been known for centuries; however, science has only recently caught up. Loving-kindness meditations have been proven to increase a host of mental, emotional, and even physical issues, including chronic pain, PTSD, stress, depression, and anxiety.[5] This practice's effectiveness with couples is found in its now proven ability to enhance relationships by increasing empathy and compassion. Empathy and compassion are the lifeblood of a loving and connected relationship. My clients make their partners the focus of their Metta Meditations, thereby creating a more loving inner monologue about their spouse. This practice changes the record, so to speak, for couples with negative inner monologues about each other. Those that suffer from negative narratives are caught in a "thoughts feelings feedback loop." In this cycle, negative thoughts about one's partner, in turn, become negative feelings, which then supports more negative thoughts. These thoughts cause a release of negative emotions and feelings in the body, which foments negative narratives. The practice of Metta Meditation reverse engineers this process. With Metta, the creation of positive thoughts about one's partner then creates positive feelings.[6]

Thoughts Feelings Feedback Loop

Thoughts   **Thoughts**

Feelings   **Feelings**

Figure 11.1. In the "thoughts feelings feedback loop," our thoughts create a chemical response in the body we call feelings. Those feelings create more thoughts that again create more feelings, and so on and so on.
Courtesy of the author

THANK-YOU'S AND APPRECIATION PRACTICE

In our house, we say "thank you." If you are drinking a cup of coffee you did not brew, it's "Thank you." If you see a made bed that you did not make, a clean kitchen you did not clean, or a fed kid you did not feed, it's "Thank you." Almost every day of my life for the last twenty years, my wife has taken a second, looked at me lovingly, and said, "Thank you for working so hard for us." And I have to tell you it never gets old. I never take it for granted, and I try never to miss a chance to return the sentiment. When someone expresses gratitude for us or for something we've done, we feel seen, appreciated, and understood. This is a part of our familial/relational culture, and, though seemingly small, it is a powerful part of what makes us work as a couple and family.

Gratitude journals and loving-kindness meditations create positive feelings that lead to more loving narratives in couples, but it is imperative those warm feelings have a means of expression. Time and again, clients tell me of the loving sentiments that lie dormant and unexpressed to their significant others. As time goes on and that dopamine haze subsides along with an uptick in life stress, we cut corners, we stop saying thank you, and we miss the incredible effects that studies show appreciation practices can bring to a relationship. Expressing gratitude for your spouse not only shows that you love and respect them but that you are aware of their inherent worth and value. On both sides of this didactic experience, appreciative feelings change the narrative for partners and remind them that they are in a relationship with a good person and someone worth investing in.[7]

Clients who are in challenging relationships often report that while they can see the benefits of my menu of gratitude exercises, loving-kindness meditations, and appreciation practices, something inside them doesn't want to do it. They will find themselves avoiding the task in its entirety or unable to complete it as though something is blocking them. To that, I ask, "Is *something* or *someone* blocking you?" referring to the inner someone or a part of self who is pushing back on opening to gratitude and ultimately opening to their partner. As we saw in the session with Jeff and Tanya, there is often a natural defensive response to vulnerability in the form of a defender part that tries to hijack the process by holding on to their negative stories. For these couples, practicing gratitude is problematic because it is a tidal shift in the flow and the tenor of their usual back-and-forth. In situations like this, where partners experience what might be considered normative anger or frustration not linked to mental, emotional, or physical abuse, we refer to Practice 2 and negotiate with the part that is avoiding feelings of love or appreciation for their partner. Once that part has been negotiated with, most clients report an ability to complete the exercises with relative comfort and ease.

RE-AUTHORING AND INTOLERANT COMPASSION

Gratitude for each other did not come with relative comfort or ease for Tanya and Jeff. Both tried to shift their inner narratives through mindfulness, gratitude, and loving-kindness practices, and both experienced only minor changes. Though their combative cycle had de-escalated and they had taken ownership of their negative narratives, this couple continued to struggle for connection and intimacy.

No one story can encapsulate the totality of one person's experience of their partner. This is especially true of a couple like Tanya and Jeff, two people who have been together for many years and have logged several life cycle events. There will always be inconsistencies and moments that challenge a prevailing negative narrative, moments that have been forgotten, but moments that, nonetheless, a therapist can utilize for healing and reconnection. This is the process of re-authoring, searching a client's history for what narrative therapists call "unique outcomes," experiences that run counter to the current and problematic plotlines. Aiding clients in re-authoring these difficult stories means helping them rediscover their unique outcomes and then reintegrating those more positive experiences into their current narratives.

For our couple, this meant finding those times when Jeff did show up for Tanya and searching for instances when Tanya felt love and respect for Jeff. In this exercise, I ask clients to remember the "good times," to find those moments in their shared history when they felt connected. This can take the form of journaling your memories or merely sitting in meditative contemplation of those experiences. In-office I will actively search for my client's unique outcomes by encouraging partners to share fond memories of their happier times. I then juxtapose the current negative narrative with the more connective memory and ask clients to notice how it feels to remember their partner and their relationship this way.

Highlighting these experiences and seasoning their current narratives with the information culled from our gratitude and loving-kindness exercises help clients to externalize the problem and to see their struggles as perhaps a difficult time, rather than as a defining aspect of their partner or their relationship. Once a narrative has been re-authored, couples can see each other in a more compassionate and loving light. They often feel safer and more available to make a heart-centered connection.[8]

Throughout the re-authoring process with Jeff and Tanya, I uncovered many unique outcomes in their relationship. The time before children was loving and connective. From time to time, they would smile and laugh with each other as they reminisced. However, when the state of their current relationship inevitably came up, they would immediately go weapons hot, shut down, and go back to their negative story lines.

When gratitude and loving-kindness fall short, when re-authoring proves difficult and romantic partners adhere to their negative inner dialogue, I will then offer intolerant compassion. Intolerant compassion might seem like an oxymoron, but it is a powerful practice on the road toward healing. The concept provides, for example, that while I am intolerant to the things you said, the way you treated me, or that thing you did, I am at the same time compassionate to the fact that you made a mistake, are fallible, were in a difficult position, and are an imperfect human being. The power of intolerant compassion is that it gives us the ability to hold the duality of our experiences, especially when someone we love hurts us. In this practice, we can entertain both the good and the not so good without having to deny either, and that gets us closer to our truth.

Applied to Tanya's narrative, intolerant compassion meant holding both truths about Jeff. At the same time, she could be intolerant of his abandonment of her while still being compassionate to the fact that he made a mistake and was shortsighted in his consideration of her experience. For Jeff, this practice meant he could be intolerant of Tanya's treatment of him after the children were born while still being compassionate to the fact that she struggled as a new mom.

Intolerant compassion leaves the door on hope open if only a crack. It says that while I am hurt, I can still hold the light of my love for you in my heart while I reconcile what happened. For me, intolerant compassion is the midpoint between wounding and forgiveness. People come through my door almost daily looking for that ever-elusive sense of forgiveness. Often they are surprised that they don't know how to find grace or pardon and will instead embark on a campaign that amounts to "fake it till you make it," only to be disappointed when their negative feelings persist.

Intolerant compassion, like re-authoring and gratitude, can change our narratives and help us to remember the good in our partners. These exercises have the potential to remind us why we love who we love and why we entered into a relationship with them in the first place. Excluding situations of extreme toxicity and abuse, our narratives come down to our willingness to turn up the volume on our problematic stories, to practice gratitude and loving-kindness, to show appreciation, and ultimately to re-author a new and more loving inner monologue. The question that remained for Jeff and Tanya was which wolf would get fed and which wolf would finally prevail.

TANYA

I'm pouring what should be my last cup of coffee of the day during my Indy-car-like pit stop between clients when I notice there isn't any muffled conversation in the waiting room. The familiar thoughts come; maybe Tanya and Jeff are late, or maybe something happened. Maybe they are sitting in my waiting room in icy silence again, hoping the process of therapy might untangle the mess and reconnect them. Speaking plainly, it had not been going well with this couple, and I hadn't managed to untangle or reconnect them at all. Lately, it felt like I was doing just enough to get them through their week and to our next session. We had not been able to find our traction, and my interventions seemed ineffectual. I feared Tanya and Jeff might be facing an inconvenient truth that there was too much scar tissue between them, and their relationship might not make it.

I opened my office door to find Tanya sitting alone. This was a decided departure from the norm. Tanya looked up from her magazine and said, "Hi." With a brief smile and a look that acknowledged the inconsistency, she moved through the door and took her usual seat across from my chair.

Something was different in Tanya's energy. I talked in part 1 about attuning to your partner—trying to perceive and understand their emotions in an attempt to fully grasp the depth of their experience. As therapists, we attune to our clients for much the same reason. Beyond what they say, I give special consideration to their nonverbal messages such as eye contact, physical spacing, gestures, facial expressions, body movements, and posture. In poker, these messages are referred to as your "tell" and essentially indicate the information you are not verbalizing.

Today Tanya looked radiant. Gone was the familiar stoic mask, and in its place was a soft, warm smile. Beyond the nonverbal transmissions, attuning to a client means reading their energy. Our emotions create energy in our bodies, and that energy resonates as a frequency in the field around us. From the time it took for her to walk from my waiting room to her seat in my office, Tanya's energy and her "tell" told me something had changed, and it was big.

I sat down, and we both took each other in for a beat. "Jeff's not coming, is he?" I asked.

Tanya replied, "No, he's not. He said he's done with therapy."

"I'm sorry to hear that." I made a mental note to reach out to Jeff to encourage him to come in for a closing session.

Tanya said, "I think we all knew there was a good chance we were headed here. I think you've been thinking it for a while. You know I really did want it to work, but at the end of the day, something broke in me, and I just don't feel the same about him. I'd hoped we could build it back but I realized I don't hate him. I'm just not in love with him anymore. We've decided to separate. We are going to try not to involve lawyers, but we'll see how that goes."

Former lead singer of the band Black Flag and alt-icon Henry Rollins is one of my favorite thinkers/speakers. He said, "It's sad when someone you know becomes someone you knew." Unfortunately, often what is sad is also what is necessary. I found Tanya that day caught between the sadness of her marriage ending and the relief and freedom one experiences in finally making a decision they know has to be made.

Tanya paused briefly, pondering the floor, then changed tracks. "Why do you suppose I couldn't change my feelings, my 'narrative' as you say, about Jeff? I mean, he *is* a good man, a great dad, and there is no doubt how he feels about me. Am I really that much of a cold, heartless bitch?"

"No," I replied.

"Well, that's not what Jeff thinks. Trust me," Tanya said as her eyes filled with tears.

"Tanya, I see this kind of thing happen a lot. We armor up when we get hurt. We start telling ourselves stories about our partners that are often only partially true and maybe not particularly fair. As I've said before when the narratives start, the communication stops, and that's precisely what happened for you and Jeff. You guys stopped talking— you stopped being curious about the other's experience. You assumed you knew each other's intentions. Making matters worse, you let it simmer over time. That's when the resentment set in. If there is not some awareness or someone like me, perhaps, who points out that you have created a negative story about your partner, you will buy into it, again and again. That story will concretize and become a belief. Before you know it, you end up at 'I don't know why I hate you, I just do.' At that point, feelings have changed, and they are really, *really* hard to get back."

Tanya nodded in silent agreement.

As mentioned in chapter 7, I have always disliked self-help books or therapy texts that sum up the often messy and complicated experience of love, relationships, or life in neat and tidy anecdotes. These are the stories where a therapist or a self-help guru says something profound or offers *an* intervention that the client immediately and without hesitation employs, and all is saved. My professors in school would use some of these anecdotes as teaching pieces. I would argue vehemently that therapy didn't always end so tidily. I knew for sure mine never did. Authors, teachers, and self-help gurus who offer us these immaculate stories are teaching us to expect the Hollywood ending and are, in my estimation, practicing irresponsibly. Books like these should come with the same small-print disclaimers as infomercials, which say, "These outcomes are not necessarily typical." What we find out in life is what you will find in this book; not everyone gets their Hollywood ending. Like Tanya and Jeff, sometimes couples wait too long to seek help, and sometimes there is simply too much scar tissue between romantic partners, and feelings have irrevocably changed.

In his book *A New Earth*, author and spiritual teacher Eckhart Tolle writes, "The voice in the head tells a story that the body believes and reacts to. Those reactions are the emotions. The emotions, in turn, feed energy back to the thoughts that created the emotion in the first place. This is the vicious circle between unexamined thoughts and emotions, giving rise to emotional thinking and emotional story-making."[9] Our thoughts don't exist in the vacuum of our minds, and there is an ongoing conversation between our brains and our bodies that ultimately forms what we believe to be true about everyone and everything. The mistake we have made is thinking that we are doomed to be the unconscious, passive passengers on our "trains of thought."

Tanya and Jeff began the process of divorce shortly after this last session. They report still using this book's techniques to nurture their ongoing relationship as co-parents and hopefully one day as friends. For our purposes, Jeff and Tanya live as a cautionary tale reminding us of the importance and gravity of those little thoughts that become our feelings that become our beliefs. Their story says, no, things won't just get better with time, that time is in fact of the essence, and if we are to continue to souse our minds and hearts with our partner's failures, our relationships are destined to also fail. With every thought, we make a choice that affects the direction our relationship takes. The question is, will your path resemble Tanya's and Jeff's, or will you one day be like that old couple on that train, staring longingly into the eyes of the person you hope to take your last breath with?

12

NARRATIVE EXERCISES

> In countering the effects of a problem-saturated story, it
> is important to develop as rich, detailed, and meaningful a
> counter-story as possible.
>
> —Jill Freedman and Gene Combs

The narrative is the cure or the cancer to ailing relationships. Paying close attention to our inner monologues allows us to turn up the volume on any problem-saturated stories we tell about our partners and gives us the opportunity to mindfully re-author the narrative with kindness, love, understanding, and compassion.

In this chapter, you will learn to hear and understand your own inner dialogue, while cultivating the ability to bring compassion practices to your partner. Practice these exercises and notice how your thoughts and feelings about your partner change.

NARRATIVE EXERCISES

1. Turn Up the Volume Exercise
2. Gratitude for Your Partner Journal
3. Loving-Kindness Meditation
4. Thank You and Appreciation
5. Continue to monitor the part of self frequently present with your partner, especially around times of stress or turmoil. Record in your journal.
6. Re-authoring Exercise

TURN UP THE VOLUME EXERCISE

For the next three to four days, reflect on your partner and your relationship. This reflection can happen whenever they come into your mind, or it can be a planned event. For example, use the three-minute breathing space we learned in Practice 1 as your reflective time. You might also choose to sit with a journal and consider how you feel about your partner. Turn up the volume on the story you tell about your partner by paying close attention to your thoughts, feelings, and the narrative you've created about him/her.

Questions:

- What are the stories you tell consistently about your partner?
- Do you notice any global language, such as, "*He always . . .*" or "*She never . . .*"?
- Is your narrative positive or negative?
- How does it make you feel in your body to think of your partner or the story you tell?
- What part of self tells the story?

Remember, this is an exercise in information gathering. At this point, we are not trying to change anything; just notice what is there. Honesty is a crucial aspect of this exercise so, as best as you can, try not to tell the story you think you should be telling.

GRATITUDE FOR YOUR PARTNER JOURNAL

Gratitude is not a thought; it is a feeling. Over the next three to four days, please take a few minutes and make a list of four to five things you are genuinely grateful for, like, or admire about your partner. This exercise can be done whenever you have a few moments to reflect and write in your journal. The critical aspect of this exercise is not to merely think of the item on the list and cross it off but to let the items on your list create a feeling within you. At the end of your three to four days of gratitude practice, stop and notice how you feel about your partner and your relationship. Has anything changed?

LOVING-KINDNESS, OR METTA MEDITATION

The Metta Prayer is designed to bestow a sense of benevolence, compassion, love, and goodwill for oneself and others. The idea is to wish good things; first for yourself, then for a close loved one, then to someone you don't have an attachment to, such as your mail person, a store clerk, the guy down the street, and finally, to someone with whom you are having a difficult time. We will focus at least one of these parts of the exercise on your partner for our purposes. The instructions are simple. First, find a few quiet moments. Then bring the object of your meditation to mind. As you consider your partner, repeat the meditation, as shown below. Like gratitude practice, this exercise is to be a visceral experience. As best as you can, feel into your good wishes for your partner and all the goodness you hope to bring them. Try this as often as you like for the next week, taking just a few moments to practice.

> *May I/he/she/they be safe.*
> *May I/he/she/they be healthy.*
> *May I/he/she/they be happy.*
> *May I/he/she/they be free of afflictions.*
> *May I/he/she/they be at peace.*

APPRECIATION PRACTICE

As I said earlier, appreciative feelings change the narrative for romantic partners and remind them that they are in a relationship with someone worth investing in. As time passes in a relationship, we become familiar, and we begin to cut corners. Quickly things like word choice, tone, and appreciation for our partners are forgotten. This practice is designed to help you remember some of the reasons why you partnered with this person in the first place. For the next four or five days, practice saying thank you to your partner for the little things they do for you or the relationship. Notice how they reach and stretch in your direction, and let them know you see it. Beyond thank you's, practice noticing two or three new things about your spouse every day this week. It could be a haircut, how hard they work, a new outfit, or the time they spent with the kids; whatever it is, take a moment to let them know you see their effort.

RE-AUTHORING

Re-authoring is a Narrative therapy approach where the goal is to help individuals reframe how they see situations. Re-authoring offers us an opportunity to reclaim information and experiences pruned or edited out of our narratives. I'd like you to look back at our "Turn Up the Volume" exercise. Read over your narrative from that time. With the information you have gathered in this section, rewrite a new narrative about your partner and your relationship. Notice how your story has changed. Whenever you recognize aspects of your old story line creeping in, ask, is this true? Is this fair? Is this compassionate? Over the next week, take the time to revisit your new narrative. Repeat it to yourself and allow it to create emotion in your body.

Part 4

PRACTICE 4: CHOOSING

We all share the same fear: Will you be there when I need you? Knowing we are chosen offers shelter in an otherwise perilous situation.

—Sue Johnson, *Hold Me Tight*

"Okay fine, fine. Just tell me what it is you want me to do, and I'll do it. Anything to stop this fucking merry-go-round conversation. Give me a list of shit, and I'll just do it. That way, there is no guessing game. I'll know what's required."

Imka turns to me and says, "Ya see, that's what I'm dealing with."

Jumping on her words, Mitchell replies, "What, what exactly are you dealing with?"

"You," Imka states flatly. "You, Mitchell. I'm dealing with you and your unwillingness to hear what I'm saying."

"What are you talking about? I heard you, and I said I'll do whatever you want. Just tell me what it is."

"Don't you see, Mitchell? I don't want to have to ask you! I don't want to have to ask you to clean up around the house, to know we need toilet paper, or to take *some* initiative. I'm not your fucking parent. I don't want to have to ask you to do nice things for me, to plan a date night—or God forbid, take me to a Broadway show. I'd take anything at this point that I didn't have to do all of the legwork on."

Mitchell, trying to appease his wife, says, "Look, if it's helping around the house, we can hire someone. As far as a show is concerned, you know I hate the theater—I'm asleep before the second act starts, and don't even get me started about the train ride in and out of the city."

Imka tries to keep her cool. "No, Mitchell, it's not about more help. It's about you *wanting* to help out, to help *me* out, to do your part, so I'm not left doing everything. It's about you wanting to take *me* to a show, not because *you* like it, but because *I* like it. Because you care about me and what I like so much that you would be willing to stretch yourself past the discomfort of an extra train ride."

Mitchell rolls his eyes. "Are you kidding me? We just went to dinner a couple of weeks ago, and *I* planned it."

Imka shakes her head. "You're right. You did suggest dinner out. You said you wanted to try the new restaurant up the street, but that was over a month ago, and *I* made the reservation because I knew you wouldn't. I'd like to do something fun for once—something you plan."

A brief quiet sets in.

Mitchell breaks the silence and says, "What about Spankies? We go to Spankies all the time. That's fun."

"That's for you. I do that for you. Those are your friends, time for you with your buddies so you can watch sports together and get shit-faced. Half the time, I think you ask me to go so you don't have to Uber home."

Mitchell turns to me. "Well, Doc, what's the verdict?" He shrugs his shoulders and raises his eyebrows in Imka's direction in a manner that suggests I obviously see things as he does. He continues. "What are we dealing with here?"

"Well, one of the major issues I see, the issue I think Imka is trying to get you to see, is that you don't choose her."

Mitchell's face tells me he is confused by my answer. It's an answer not in keeping with any of the top-of-mind couple's issues we've grown accustomed to hearing. He squints his eyes and says, "What do you mean I don't choose her? I chose her the day we got married. She's literally the one I chose."

"Right," I reply. "You did. You chose her then. But you said 'chose,' 'I *chose* her.' You might think I am being too literal here, but you used the past tense, indicating that perhaps you've stopped. That's essentially the point Imka is trying to get across. For my money, if we want to keep the flames of romance burning, we have to keep choosing each other every day—all of the time. We have to remind ourselves that the someone we are with is someone we don't want to lose. If we don't, we'll find ourselves in an office like this one."

Mitchell pauses, his demeanor now more severe. I'm betting he can sense that his fears about couple's therapy are going to be realized. I am going to challenge him in a way he doesn't want to be challenged. Eventually, I will ask him to put down his mammalian bravado and be vulnerable to this woman. However, today is too soon. I haven't gained his trust yet. Mitchell looks me dead in the eye and says, "I'm a good husband."

With that statement, Mitchell set the boundary. For him, it was an indisputable fact and something not up for discussion. Boundary aside, I would have to challenge him on this point if the therapy was to go anywhere. I would have to push on his notion of what it is to be a good husband and partner if he was ever going to be able to meet Imka emotionally. Make no mistake, this was a wrestling match for control of the therapy, and it was a match I had to win. If I didn't win this match, Mitchell would lose all respect for me and the process, and Imka would lose an advocate for her and her marriage.

Carl Whitaker was part of the first generation of family therapists and broke the rules of psychotherapeutic orthodoxy and convention. At various points in his long career, he was known to purposefully fall asleep during sessions, to metaphorically bottle-feed clients, as well as refuse to let them speak at all. He was also known to arm wrestle some of his more challenging patients. He famously explained that if he was going to have to struggle with someone to help them to change, he might as well bring this right out on the table.[1]

Some clients come ready and willing to do the work even if it is hard. Then there are clients like Mitchell, clients who would prefer to dictate where the therapy can go and where it can't go. They build fences around specific topics and put signs up that say in effect "Off Limits." With clients like Mitchell, I like to bring the struggle right out on the table. Instead of arm wrestling, I name the issue the client is protecting and let them know that I might have to lean into them from time to time. The issue or feelings they are protecting is where the therapy needs to go. Speaking plainly and directly to clients like Mitchell builds a modicum of trust in the beginning stages of therapy and prepares them to meet their growing edge.

I point to the clock and say, "Look, Mitchell, I've known you all of about thirty minutes, so I haven't built up a ton of trust with either of you yet. Having said that, you strike me as a person who likes to cut to the chase and let's face it; you aren't paying me to beat around the bush. I might as well let you guys know that I don't believe in mincing words or wasting your time or your money, so from time to time, I'm going to lean into one or both of you. That's part of my job, and I would be remiss in my duties if I didn't do that. Having said all of this, Mitchell, I have no doubt you love Imka and that your intention is to be a good husband. However, as partners, we don't get to write our own reviews. It has to matter to you that Imka feels the way she does despite your good intentions."

Mitchell ponders my statement for a beat and then says, "So, you're saying I'm not a good husband?"

I gesture toward Imka, indicating a need for her input. Imka replies, "No, Mitch, no one is saying you're a bad husband."

Dovetailing on her response, I add, "Right, 'not a good husband' feels loaded, it feels out of scope, and starting from there would only shut you down, and we would lose you in this process. I said I don't think she feels chosen. 'Bad husband' feels like a referendum on you, like a label or a diagnosis. Choosing, on the other hand, is a skill you can build."

13

WHAT IS CHOOSING?

Real living is living for others.

—Bruce Lee

WILD FLOWERS

One afternoon, I sat among a few other men in the waiting area of a New York clothing store while Ashley tried on clothes in a dressing room in the back of the store. I'm convinced waiting areas like the one I sat in are explicitly designed for the bored partners of potential buyers. Centrally located, this area usually consists of a group of small couches or chairs arranged in a circle or square. I remember getting out my phone and starting to scroll, not because there was anything specific I was looking for but because that was what the other guys sitting next to me were doing. From what I could tell, they were busy looking at football scores. It was a Sunday afternoon during football season, after all, so periodically, someone in the group would break the silence by yelling "Yes!" or "No!" That man would then look up sheepishly as if he had shouted in church or in a library, only to see that the other men were not put out by the interruption; they merely wanted to know what game was being yelled about. The "yeller" would then say something like, "Miami" or "Vike's just beat the Pat's." Heads would nod, and it was back to the play-by-play. I like football enough, don't get me wrong, but as time has worn on and I have grown emotionally, it has somehow lost its luster. Now, I describe myself as someone who is smart enough to understand the game but not dumb enough to think it's in any way important. To those who ask why I don't make it a priority to watch college or pro ball, I say, I'm someone who likes to do cool shit, not sit around all weekend and watch other people do cool shit. Obviously, this ideology has not made me the popular husband in Charleston, South Carolina (my new home) social circles where football sits on the mantel next to God and country.

As the men watched, scrolled, and checked, I looked around and wondered when I became this guy. It was like our partners had "put us on screens" the way you might a child to buy time and keep the child from complaining or throwing a tantrum in a store. It dawned on me that I was actually missing something. While Ash shopped and I sat there with my new friends, I was missing time with my girl. I had just started grad school, and time together was limited. I had to admit when she asked me to make a "quick stop," I was less than enthused, but as I considered the situation, I decided to try to make the best of it. We were together, after all, so why not get involved and make this time spent rather than time wasted. I jumped up and began looking around the store for things I thought might look good on her. I had no idea if my choices were even in the ballpark, but I was going to give it a try. When I knocked on her dressing room, she opened the door to see me standing there, smiling proudly with arms full of clothes. Needless to say, she was shocked, not only at some of my choices but at my effort in her direction.

The fashion show began. We laughed as she tried on all of the outfits, many of which were complete busts, but I have to say a few were a hit. The time together flew by, and, as silly as it sounds, we grew closer that day in the Fifth Avenue H&M.

Later Ash would say that when I showed up to her dressing room door carrying clothing, I might as well have been carrying a bouquet of wildflowers. My effort and the fact that I would go out of my way and get involved in something as mundane as clothes shopping made her feel reached for.

CHOOSING? DON'T YOU MEAN LOVE LANGUAGES?

In the Narrative, I said you never know where you will find inspiration. It's often found in the most unlikely places, such as in a pile of dresses, skirts, and blouses. Ashley's face that Sunday afternoon reflected that something beautiful had transpired between us. As we walked home that day, I knew I'd stumbled upon something that would profoundly affect not only the way I loved but also the way I worked. It was simple; when we do things for our partners that register in them as acts of kindness, consideration, thoughtfulness, or benevolence, they feel chosen, and when we feel chosen, we feel loved. If I could help my couples to actively choose each other in ways that spoke to their individual hearts, then I could help them connect more deeply.

Emboldened, I began researching, reading anything I could find that supported these ideas. I stumbled onto Emotionally Focused Therapy (EFT) and the work of Sue Johnson, who essentially coined the phrase "choosing,"[1] as well as John Bowlby's Attachment theory.[2] Wondering if the notion of choosing would resonate with romantic partners, I wrote an article outlining my ideas and the research. I called the article "Why Would I Want to Do Dishes? The Importance of 'Choosing' Your Partner in Relationships."[3] I assumed a few friends, family, colleagues, and clients would read it. When the readership topped out at more than 624,000 reads, I knew choosing was a concept that resonated with people.

In the article, I offered that choosing your partner does not have to happen in the "big moments" or on the "big day" in the pretty dress and the fancy suit; it does not happen when everyone is watching. Choosing your partner occurs in the ordinary, often mundane moments of life—in the dead of night when a crying baby rouses an already exhausted couple, and one partner says, "Go back to sleep. I got this one." It happens in the heat of an argument, where everything in you wants to win and to fight dirty, but instead, you say: "Help me understand how I hurt you."

This kind of choosing is essential to the formation of a healthy bond, found in something as simple as a few outfits I thought Ashley might look good in or, in Imka and Mitchell's case, toilet paper bought or a date night planned. It registers in us when we see our partner reaching beyond their own comfort zone to connect to us. Too often, the small moments in a relationship can be written off as unimportant or inconsequential. But it is precisely these "small" moments that carry the biggest message of I love you and I choose you.

The notion of choosing your partner is relatively accessible. As opposed to Mindfulness, Parts of Self, or even our Narratives, concepts that can feel a bit esoteric or abstruse, Choosing lands firmly in the province of the conventional. We tend to get it, and when I mention the idea of choosing to clients, invariably, someone will say, "Oh, you mean our love language." To a degree, the act of choosing *is* akin to speaking each other's love language. The term "love languages" has seeped into our vernacular. It's an idea so popular and universally understood that it has become a part of the parlance of our time. Evangelical pastor and author Gary Chapman hit a nerve with couples when he penned his book *The 5 Love Languages*. Chapman was able to synthesize this concept into five categories of how we express and experience love. They are acts of service, gift-giving, physical touch, quality time, and words of affirmation.[4]

Having said all that, there is a crucial difference between acts of choosing and love languages. Choosing is not a stand-alone practice. It's part of a larger system and therefore not limited to its own merits. In fact, choosing takes advantage of and is bolstered by all of the other Practices within this modality. For now, let's look at how Practice 1, Mindfulness, supports and reinforces the practice of choosing.

Research suggests that merely trying to speak your partner's love languages does not work. That the effectiveness of the practice hinges on each partner's ability to "emotionally self-regulate."[5] Emotional self-regulation is our ability to manage our thoughts and feelings with consideration for their long-term effects, which is another term for mindfulness. Packaged within the Five Practices, mindfulness and choosing are both indivisible and supplementary practices.

Human beings are not fixed. We are ever-changing. Consequently, what makes us feel loved often changes over time and is dependent on the shifting tides of life. Decades of empirical research shows that part of what leads to long-term happiness and satisfaction is being responsive to your partner's changing needs.[6] Rather than holding fast to a fixed idea of how they need to be loved, mindfulness and mindful attunement to our mates used in conjunction with choosing gives us the ability to be aware of when our partner's love language shifts. When it registers that you are keeping up and staying current with your mate's changing needs, they in turn experience a felt sense of being profoundly seen, heard, understood, and met where they are on their life's journey.

As Practice 4 unfolds, you will come to understand the practice of choosing is not limited to knowing what makes our partners feel loved and then robotically doing those things. Indeed, choosing our partners is about tuning in to what touches our partner's heart. It is elemental to building trust, with far-reaching implications that dive into the very fiber of our oldest wounding, calling into question why we love who we love and the spiritual nature of romantic relationships.

14

WHY CHOOSING IS SO IMPORTANT TO CONNECTION

> I love you, in a really, really big, pretend to like your taste in music, let you eat the last piece of cheesecake, hold a radio over my head outside your window, unfortunate way that makes me hate you, love you. So pick me, choose me, love me.
>
> —Meredith Grey, Season 2, Episode 5 of *Grey's Anatomy*

TRUST

Going to my bartending job had become a rather rote process. I would come through the door and say hi to the patrons and the waitstaff as I made my way to the manager's office located in the restaurant's basement, where I would retrieve my drawer of money and any marching orders for the evening. This day, however, was quite different, and, as it turned out, it would be a day that changed my life forever. As I entered the office, I was struck by the unmitigated beauty of the young woman sitting in the chair opposite our manager's desk. She was being interviewed for a job as a waitress. We said hello to each other, and when our eyes met, I was dumbstruck. I did all I could to look casual and close my mouth that now hung agape, collect myself and my things, and leave. When I closed the office door, I leaned back against it. I looked up at the dingy basement ceiling and, though I am not a religious sort, said, "Really, God? Really?" That was the day I met Ashley, and that was the day I knew I had met my girl, the person I was supposed to spend my life with. It felt like a lightning bolt hit me dead center in the chest. I was mesmerized by her. I spent the next few days making equal attempts at trying to get her out of my head while also trying to find out when she was working next. As it turned out, the timing couldn't have been more inconvenient as I was actually engaged to someone else. This, however, is a story for another time.

Now, when I tell the story of how I met Ashley, I jokingly say, "It was love at first sight, at least it was for me." While most of this is a true story, one aspect of it might not be. If I am honest, I don't think the lightning bolt was love. In retrospect, what I felt was a mix of lust, dopamine, limerence, and an intuitive understanding that I just met someone who would be pivotal in my life. Real love doesn't happen in a moment. Popular culture tells us that love hits us like a flash in those thunderstruck movie romance moments. I say real love builds and develops; it crescendos and is maintained over time in the small things that say I pick you—I choose you.

Author and speaker Simon Sinek made a similar observation about how love tends to grow in the seemingly inconsequential instances between partners when he said, "She didn't fall in love with you because you remembered her birthday and bought her flowers on Valentine's Day. She fell in love with you because when you woke up in the morning, you said good morning to her before you checked your phone. She fell in love with you because when you went to the fridge to get yourself a drink, you got her one without even asking. She fell in love with you because when you had an amazing day at work, and she had a terrible day at work, you didn't say, 'Yeah yeah yeah, but let me tell you about my day.' You sat and listened to her awful day and didn't say a thing about your amazing day. This is why she fell in love with you. I can't tell you exactly what day, and it was no specific thing you did. It was the accumulation of all of those little things that she woke up one day and it was as if she just pushed the button and said 'I love him.'"[1]

Acts of choosing your partner are the secret formula and the essential component to romantic love. It's what Sinek was pointing out in this quote, it's what I discovered in that H&M dressing room, and it's what Imka was asking for from Mitchell. However, beyond all of the warm and fuzzy feelings we get when our partners make us feel picked, the practice of choosing also tells us it's safe enough to trust.

Like love, trust doesn't suddenly or magically appear. It is cultivated over time through acts of choosing. Acts that say, in essence, you can count on me, I will be there for you, and that I am concerned about you and your well-being even when you are not here. I tell my clients that we all have "Love Banks" attached to our hearts. Our partners can make deposits, or they can make withdrawals. Deposits into these accounts are usually acts of choosing. When we have made enough deposits, then and only then will couples experience deep and abiding trust in each other. This is a place where real intimacy on all levels can be shared. However, couples who dawn my doorstep have usually made too many withdrawals on their partner's bank. It might come in the form of a series of small drafts over time like Mitchell, or it could come by way of one major breach that essentially cashes the account. Either way, if we are not making deposits through choosing, we will most certainly find ourselves upside down and overdrawn, as it were, in our relational banks.

THE DOPAMINE BLAST VS. THE OXYTOCIN FEEDBACK LOOP

I have described what happens to the human brain during budding romance as "the dopamine blast of new love." It's the time when everything our partner does is amazing, and everything they say could be put to song. As I said earlier, dopamine is not sustainable in the brain, and when the dopamine runs out, panic often sets in. Couples and individual clients alike come running to session wondering, What went wrong? Have their feelings changed? or Have they made a huge mistake? In lieu of the dopamine blast, I offer them the oxytocin feedback loop.

Produced in the hypothalamus and secreted by the pituitary gland, oxytocin is a hormone that plays a vital role in reproduction, initiating contractions before childbirth and the release of breast milk, as well as early infant/parent attachment. Not only is it thought to be involved in early bonding between mother and baby, but oxytocin has also been implicated in the bonding of romantic partners. It has been called the "cuddle hormone" or the "love hormone" interchangeably because it is produced when we connect socially, snuggle up, or engage in sex. Early studies billed oxytocin as a kind of naturally occurring love potion. However, the latest research offers that its effects on romance are far less straightforward than originally believed. Oxytocin doesn't suddenly change a person's behavior or magically make you trust or fall in love with a perfect stranger. However, it does boost feelings of love, contentment, and security toward someone you already care for. Most researchers agree that oxytocin is responsible for lowering blood pressure and anxiety while promoting feelings of generosity, compassion, empathy, trust, and well-being. In short, it helps create the "warm and fuzzy feelings" of closeness we experience with a partner.[2,3,4,5]

I wondered if there was a way for couples to take advantage of this powerful hormone. If oxytocin is so pivotal to attachment, was there a way for couples like Imka and Mitchell to regularly and reliably produce it, especially after the dopamine of new love wore off? While lovemaking and cuddling seemed like fairly dependable means of producing oxytocin, those methods are not always convenient or available. As it turns out, acts of kindness also boost oxytocin levels in the brain. When partners act kindly, benevolently, and lovingly toward each other or the relationship, love hormone levels increase. This research has far-reaching implications for our practice of choosing each other. As we know, choosing one's partner is essentially performing random acts of kindness in their direction. Choosing is defined as reaching and stretching for your partner. It's doing things that say I love you. It's speaking their love language and, in essence, investing in the relationship. In two separate studies, researchers found that "participants who felt a strong personal investment in their relationship demonstrated an increase in oxytocin levels."[6] This may be due to its influence over the reward pathways of the brain, meaning the more we choose our partners and the more our partners, in turn, choose us, the more we produce brain chemicals that support those warm and fuzzy feelings. This implies that couples who practice choosing, who intentionally create a loving-kindness feedback loop within their relationship where they are regularly doing nice things for each other, will experience more love, trust, and intimacy. The trick is to practice regularly. Oxytocin levels cannot be maintained by a single act here or there. In order for couples to take advantage of the benefits oxytocin offers, especially after the glow of new love wears off, they must make regular investments in their partners and in their relationships.[7] They can make those investments through acts of choosing. I ask couples to consider the time of their courtship regularly, a time typically marked by would-be partners going the extra mile to secure their prospective mate's heart. It's a time that is often characterized by copious messages of choosing when we don't cut corners with each other and will leave little to the imagination. I encourage my clients, whenever possible, to adopt that energy and focus.

CHOOSING MAKES US FEEL UNDERSTOOD

While studying to be a therapist, it's natural to find yourself, as well as your friends and family, in the pages of your textbooks. Professors will warn against diagnosing yourself or your loved ones as you move through your coursework. Even with those warnings, we still do it. I know I did it, and that's precisely what I was doing one afternoon sitting at our kitchen table catching up on some light reading on core wounding. I began drawing parallels between Ashley's experience and a core wound explained in my book. I felt like I had been inadvertently handed the teacher's edition to my relationship. There in big, bold print, it said something akin to: The prevailing experience of a person with this core wound is that the world can seem to be a dangerous place.

When she came through the door of our tiny East Village apartment later that afternoon, I knew her day had gone badly. Almost in tears, she reached out for a hug, and, rather than try to fix whatever was ailing her, I squeezed her a little tighter and said, "I know, sweetie, sometimes the world just seems like a dangerous place." Ashley's tears stopped as she pulled back from our embrace to look at me. Through bloodshot eyes, she scanned my face as if to check and make sure I was the person she had been living with for the past two years. When she finished her analysis, she buried her face in my neck and pulled me even closer. Later she would say that she had had rare occasion to feel so loved and understood by another human.

This was the moment I realized that understanding is fundamental to making someone feel chosen. Found somewhere between "Esteem Needs" and "Love and Belonging Needs," the need to be known or understood makes the list of Maslow's *Extended* Hierarchy of Needs, needs that are basic to human survival and development.[8] When we attempt to know a person more deeply, when we try to comprehend another's experience, it endorses their sense of self and beingness while sending the message that I choose you. It validates us when we feel truly gotten, and few things prompt us to be more vulnerable or more open to connection than being understood.[9] Studies support the importance of feeling understood, offering that people actually reported higher life satisfaction on days when they felt more understood by others. Research also suggests that fluctuations in daily well-being actually correspond to daily experiences of felt understanding or misunderstanding.[10] Further quantitative support for the importance of choosing your partner through understanding your partner was a study using brain imaging. The scans showed that feeling understood activated areas of the brain linked with reward and social bonding while feeling misunderstood activated brain regions that correspond with negative affect.[11] These findings are bolstered by even more research that suggests feeling understood, especially during conflict, buffers against feelings of dissatisfaction in relationships. Researchers believe this is because understanding strengthens the relationship by signaling that one's partner is invested.[12]

There again, in the evidentiary analysis of why choosing our partners is so important to making a heart-centered connection, we find the word "invested." We want to know that we are worth investing in and that our partners are compelled to make efforts to secure our hearts. Acts of choosing are the best way to send those messages.

LOVE INERT

Feelings of love without conveyance is love inert. It is love that lies dormant, still, or inactive. Choosing acts as a means of conveyance for our inner feelings. It is a tool for expressing our love for each other. I know it is not necessarily a new idea, but I believe love is not so much an emotion or even a noun. I believe love is also a verb. Love is not only what you feel but what those loving feelings compel you to do. Those acts of choosing are the translation of our emotions and are the only tangible way our partners can experience how we feel about them. My client Zach was unable to understand the importance of choosing. He thought his inner feelings of love for his wife were sufficient. For him, they were a given—something she should simply understand as fact because he married her. Finally, in a desperate attempt to help Zach understand why choosing is so essential to a relationship, I asked, "Zach, do you love your wife?"

He replied, "Yes, of course" in a tone that suggested my question was ridiculous.

"How would she know that?" I asked.

He responded again as if I were daft. "Well, because of all the *feelings* of love I have for her."

I said, "Well, that's great for you, isn't it? But how is she going to have any experience of your love for her if it stays bottled up inside of you? If it is not expressed in a way that she can see, feel, or understand it?"

CHOOSING, OUR DEEPEST WOUNDS, AND OUR CORE QUESTIONS

It might not be immediately obvious, but the things that make us feel loved are actually requests for healing. These requests come from the most wounded parts of ourselves. They call out and ask for their injuries, those suffered in childhood or in past relationships, to be soothed in our present-day relationships. The entreaty comes in the form of those familiar and fundamental questions I offered in chapter 5: Am I safe? Am I loved? Do I matter? Am I enough? These questions are basic to the human experience, and their answers define who we are and who we are not. For example, am I a person who is safe, or am I a person who is not safe? Or am I a person who is worthy of love, or am I not? When any one or more of these questions is not affirmed, we experience a foundational wound. Those core questions and our oldest hurts are undeniably linked to how we want and need to be loved. The practice of choosing is the answer to our core questions and the salve to our deepest injuries.

It was with this concept in mind that I began the work with Mitchell and Imka. In our first session, I told Mitchell that Imka didn't feel chosen by him. That it was not necessarily about picking up around the house or Broadway show tickets, as it was about making her feel like she was a priority. As we dug a little deeper into Imka's youth, we found that her father was a man who was physically there but never truly emotionally present. He worked hard, and they had nice things, but he never made his children a priority.

Consequently, Imka got the message that she was not worthy of her father's love. She went forth in her life unconsciously asking the world and the people in it to affirm that she was of value. Imka's core question was, Do I matter? Mitchell was recapitulating the wounds of his wife's childhood. He was unwittingly sending the message that she didn't matter when he failed to plan those date nights, to pick up around the house, or to take her to a show.

As I unpacked the intricacies of choosing, our work progressed, and Mitchell seemed to understand. He said in one session, "Now I see why these 'little things' seemed to carry so much weight with her. I was treating her like her dad treated her—acting like her dad did—and trust me, I don't want to be like that guy."

From this point, the course of action seemed obvious; Mitchell would simply have to attune to his wife's actual needs, begin to listen to her requests, and fulfill them through small acts of choosing her. But as sessions passed, it became obvious that while Mitchell understood choosing and how he might make Imka feel like she mattered, he was failing to execute outside of therapy. Time and again, Imka was frustrated with her husband's efforts or lack thereof. Finally, she stated in one meeting, "Mitchell, I'm starting to think you just don't want to do the things I need you to do." It was becoming increasingly apparent that Mitchell and Imka were experiencing a "love embargo."

THE LOVE EMBARGO

An embargo is a term that typically refers to a ban on the trade of goods between two countries. A love embargo is a term I coined to describe a ban on "goods" traded between romantic partners. The goods that get traded in a relationship tend to be acts of choosing, things like kind words, benefit of the doubt, understanding, loving touch, attention, compassion, and empathy. While I don't like to boil love down to such transactional terms, it is human nature to keep score. An occasional imbalance between partners tends to be fine enough, as long as there is an understanding that the imbalance will eventually be rectified. However, in couples where the scales remain uneven, where one partner feels that they are constantly paying love forward but rarely receiving love in return, a love embargo will often set in. Walled off and armored up, partners will wage their war of attrition, communicating, in essence, I will choose you once you have chosen me.

This was where I found Mitchell and Imka. They were stalemated in a love embargo. It was not immediately apparent, but there it was, buried under Mitchell's bravado and his inability to share his true feelings. When asked, Mitchell would say, "I'm good. I'm not sure why we are even here. I'm happy in my marriage. She seems to have the problem."

As therapists, we not only consider what is said, we have to also consider what is not said. We must pull back, reassess, and ask again some of the same questions we may have asked at the beginning of the therapy. Often couples are not ready to divulge everything the first time their butts hit the seats. As time goes on, hopefully, trust builds between client and clinician. This is the time to notice what has been notably not present. These are topics that typically carry vulnerability or shame, things like addiction, anger issues, finances, and sex.

We had only briefly touched on their sex life, and since sex is such an important part of a healthy relationship, I thought it merited a second look. Because it was not a part of the presenting complaint, I assumed their sexual connection was okay enough for the two of them, box checked. However, it now seemed as if it was conspicuously omitted from the conversation. When I circled back around to the subject of sex, I found the source of their embargo.

I said, "Mitchell, we've talked a lot about Imka's needs and how you might not be fulfilling them. I'm wondering if we can change track and look at what makes *you* feel loved and cared for? What makes you feel chosen?"

He shook his head, searching for the right words. "You know, like I said, I'm pretty good. I—"

Imka cut him off mid-sentence and said, "Sex. It's sex. Sex is what makes him feel 'chosen,' and maybe when I say nice things to him. He likes that too. I'd bet, if he were really honest right now, he'd say we don't have enough of sex. *And* that I don't initiate it enough. He's right I don't—I don't initiate that often."

Mitchell smiled a wry grin at her candor, candor he was loath to find on this subject, and offered, "It's fine, baby."

To which I answered, "Is it? Is it 'fine'?" My tone was purposefully abrupt and a little pushy. "Are you happy with your sex life and her participation in it? Because you said 'fine' and fine often—not always—but often means, we are protecting something, keeping up a facade or trying not to go there, as it were."

Mitchell took a beat. It was as if he were trying to decide whether to answer honestly or continue his ruse. "No, I'm not happy with it. I haven't been happy with it for a while. It sucks to feel like your wife isn't attracted to you anymore."

"What's that like for you?" I asked. "To feel like your wife is no longer attracted to you?" I mirrored his words to get beyond his protective measures. Often hearing our words repeated back to us can lend a sort of weight to them and deepen the experience.

"Well, what do you think it does to me? It fucking pisses me off."

I asked, "Does it make you feel anything else other than pissed? I'm wondering what else is in there?"

For the first time, Mitchell's face softened. "It fucks me up. It fucking hurts, man. It hurts a lot." Mitchell's chin dimpled as he tried to hold back his feelings.

I asked, "Where do you feel it in your body?"

Mitchell pointed to his heart center.

"What does the pain make you want to do?" I inquired.

"I don't know. It shuts me down."

"Walls you off?" I asked.

"Sure. It sure doesn't make me want to do all the shit she wants me to do."

And there we had it, the love embargo. When it started and who started it could be argued. Insight is not always curative, and the excavation of its origins would offer little to this couple. What we now knew was, the embargo was on. Both partners were standing behind their walls of protection, saying, in effect, I'll choose you when you start choosing me.

Like his wife, Mitchell was facing the wounding of his childhood in his present-day relationship. As a boy, he didn't feel like he was ever enough for his father. Whether it was his grades, athletics, or the kids he chose as friends, Mitchell never received his father's approval. Consequently, he went forth into his life unconsciously hoping every person and situation would answer yes to his core question, Am I enough? Sex and adoration for his achievements became the ultimate means to assuage his need for approval in his adult life. Again, where it started, we may never know, but when Imka failed to fulfill his needs, Mitchell acted in kind and would not fulfill hers.

WHY WE LOVE WHO WE LOVE

In his book *Making Marriage Simple*, author Harville Hendrix said it best when he wrote, "Romantic Love delivers us into the passionate arms of someone who will ultimately trigger the same frustrations we had with our parents, but for the best possible reason! Doing so brings our childhood wounds to the surface so they can be healed."[13] This healing takes place when we perform acts of choosing that speak directly to our partner's core wounding—when we dive beneath the surface and answer their core question.

My graduate work and much of the foundation of Practice 4 is founded in Emotionally Focused Therapy (EFT) and the work of Dr. Sue Johnson and Les Greenberg. In her book *Hold Me Tight*, Johnson says, "Counselors, too, are missing the crux of the issue. They just work their way down the iceberg to the waterline. We have to dive below to discover the basic problem."[14]

I believe there are always two conversations happening between romantic partners, conversations on the surface and conversations below the surface. The on-the-surface conversations focus on the typical top-of-mind couple's issues. These topics can include everything from sex, money, and how to raise the kids all the way down to what we are having for dinner tonight.

The below-the-surface conversations are the discussions that happen between our wounded parts of self. This is where the wounding of our childhood comes into play. This is the conversation where we ask, Are you going to choose me? Are you going to show me that I am loved, that I am safe, that I matter to you, or that I am enough? Are you going to love me the way I need to be loved?

When couples come to me, they are caught up in the surface issues and in the noise of those details. They are often shocked when

I tell them that the issues and the details they argue about are largely unimportant, or, at the very least, they pale in comparison to the dialogue going on below.

The on-the-surface conversation, the noise that Mitchell and Imka were caught in, centered around menial household chores and sex. While these issues are not insignificant, they are not nearly as important as the communication happening beneath the surface. This is the place where Mitchell was asking Imka to tell him he was enough and the place where Imka was desperately asking Mitchell to show her that she mattered.

As we go through life, we try on different romantic relationships looking for a good fit. We search not only for the person uniquely designed, able, and equipped to bring our childhood wounds to the surface, as Hendrix pointed out, but the person who can help us heal those wounds. For Imka and Mitchell, the former was certainly true. They had, in fact, brought out each other's childhood injuries. However, the question remained: Would they be willing to drop their respective love embargoes and choose each other?

We *are* seeking the love we've known in the hope that we will find a love we have never known. This is why we are drawn to who we are drawn to. This is why we love who we love. We are desperately looking for that person who will answer our core question, someone who will hold and heal the most injured and broken parts of us. That profound healing happens through the practice of choosing and speaks to the spiritual nature of romantic relationships.

THE SPIRITUAL NATURE OF RELATIONSHIPS

There is a spiritual aspect to romantic relationships that can be accessed through the healing properties of choosing. Choosing is a liniment to our oldest injuries. When we choose our partners and they, in turn, choose us, we receive the message that we are loved, that we are safe, that we matter and are enough. Answering these questions through choosing helps to catalyze healing on a soul level because healing like this brings us closer to wholeness. When our wounded parts finally get the love and sustenance they have been seeking, many will come back to the fold of the self. Now our protective parts can stand down because we have at last had our deepest needs met. While it is true that these parts of self may always be with us at some level, we will be less reactive because we have become a more integrated, more unified being. Now we are able to spend more of our time in our higher consciousness, the wise or healthy self. Here there is more ease in life. Less rocked by our fear, anxiety, depression, or anger, we experience more internal harmony and inner peace.

I know some therapists who don't include spirituality in their work. They will sit and listen to what a client believes, but their duties seem to stop at the energetic, religious, and/or meta-physical door. In my training, I was taught that what affords us deeper meaning has to be integrated into the work of therapy. We have to treat clients from a mind, body, and spirit perspective if we are to treat them holistically. It is incumbent upon us as practitioners to be able to speak to those spiritual aspects with some authority, or at the very least be able to resource clients within those facets. It is vital to be able to discuss with clients that which brings them "something more" to their lives. One of my greatest teachers as a clinician and in my life has been Julie Winter. Julie is the author of the book *Dancing Home* and cofounder of the Helix Training Program. Julie says, "Spiritual awareness adds a crucial element to life. It enhances the depth of consciousness, brings an opening to joy and the experiences of compassion, mindfulness, and the power of living as an active co-creator with Spirit. A relationship with Spirit taps open the gateway to the sacred nature of the ordinary."[15]

There are experiences in life that offer us value and significance beyond the physical act of performing them. A walk in the woods, for example, can be considered nothing particularly special, or it can be inspirational if one were open to seeing it that way. Author Lou Kavar in his book *The Integrated Self: A Holistic Approach to Spirituality and Mental Health Practice* offers that spirituality is evident "when working is transformed from routine and drudgery to something meaningful" that the spiritual dimension is accessed, "when the tedium of hobbies like gardening or needlepoint are experienced as valuable and enjoyable," or "when pain, as in childbirth, is a source of joy; when physical exhaustion from dancing at someone's wedding or from exercise and bodybuilding become purposeful because there is something more than just exhaustion taking place." He says we find meaning and purpose that reaches into this realm when "cultural customs, foods, and icons take on particular value as national anthems, the raising of a flag, singing a Christmas carol, or gathering for a holiday meal become something more than songs or routine habits."[16] I see spirituality made manifest in the Broadway dancers in my practice who leap and jump across the stage in what only can be described as a transcendent experience, inspired by something supernatural. In this place, a dance is not simply someone flailing their bodies about, a song is not merely a mob of words set to music, and a flag is not just some colorful cloth. This is a place where the everyday is anointed with meaning. This is the space where magic happens, and our relationships can live here too.

My wife has been my constant guide and teacher in all things mystical. She lives in a world of meaning, purpose, and magic. Once when I cynically questioned her otherworldly experiences, she said, "If I have the choice whether to live a life in magic or a life in the mundane, I choose magic." For her, all things hold the possibility of deeper significance; nothing happens without reason; there is no such thing as coincidence.

I know there is something more, something that lives beyond our physical world when I am on my surfboard, as I open my heart center to the vastness of the ocean and of the universe. I experience deeper meaning through the vulnerability I feel when I hug or play with my children, and when I touch into the sacredness of two souls connecting when I choose Ashley.

Poet, philosopher, and scholar John O'Donohue's words were ever-present in my training as a therapist. One of my first supervisors and mentors, Elena Hull, was a friend and mentee of O'Donohue's. An extremely gifted clinician and teacher, she seamlessly blended O'Donohue's work, the importance of the divine and of the spiritual in life and into the therapy room. In his book *Anam Cara: A Book of Celtic Wisdom*, O'Donohue wrote, "When you learn to love and to let yourself be loved, you come home to the hearth of your own spirit. You are warm and sheltered. You are completely at one in the house of your own longing and belonging. In that growth and homecoming is the unlooked-for bonus in the act of loving another. Love begins with paying attention to others, with an act of gracious self-forgetting. This is the condition in which we grow. Once the soul awakens, the search begins, and you can never go back. From then on, you are inflamed with a special longing that will never again let you linger in the lowlands of complacency and partial fulfillment."[17]

Indeed, there is a spiritual aspect to loving our partners, and the practice of choosing connects us to that experience. However, in order for us to tap into this realm, doing and saying the things that comprise our partner's love languages cannot be perfunctory. That would relegate us to, as O'Donohue put it, "linger in the lowlands of complacency and partial fulfillment."

As I said, when I tell clients about the practice of choosing, they very often bring up *The 5 Love Languages*. Those same clients are often unable to remember if their partners are a 1, a 4, a 5, or a 2, or a 3. What makes us feel loved and chosen cannot be a punch list of things to do that sit next to walking the dog, taking out the trash, and bathing the kids. The practice of choosing requires us to love our partners with intentionality, to imbue each act of choosing with kindness, compassion, concern, and reverence for the one we love. In short, choosing in this way asks that we assign significance and meaning to whatever we do that speaks to our partner's heart. For me, this is the stuff that inspires the movies, poems, and songs that move us, and this is the essence of romantic love. Whatever is given from the heart comes from the soul, and in this way, choosing our partners becomes a spiritual practice that holds us, heals us, and binds us together on our journey toward a heart-centered connection.

Let this be fair warning; there is much at stake with respect to the practice of choosing. We can pick either a life where we dare to love wholeheartedly or a life of banal contrivance, a life lived in the mundane or a life lived in magic.

15

HOW TO CHOOSE

Love is absolutely vital for a human life. For love alone can awaken what is divine within you. In love, you grow and come home to yourself.

—John O'Donohue

IMKA AND MITCHELL

"Do you trust each other?"

Both Mitchell and Imka looked at each other, chuckled, and then looked back at me.

"I'm serious." This time I said it with more inflection. "*Do you* trust each other?"

Imka answered first, as if my question was silly. "Yes, Lair, I trust my husband."

Mitchell followed. "Of course I trust Im."

I nodded and said, "I don't believe you."

This couple had been around me long enough at this point to know my style of therapy. They knew not to take me so seriously as to be offended and that I was making a point.

"I mean, I think you trust each other with the big things. Imka, I think you are pretty sure he's not cheating on you, so you *trust* he's not going to run off with someone else, right? And Mitchell, you trust her enough that she's not hiding some terrible gambling problem or that she's not going to run off with the family fortune."

Both nodded in agreement.

I continued. "But, I'm not convinced you actually trust each other with your hearts. The truth is, I think the vulnerability has drained out of this relationship, and it's because neither of you is willing to choose the other. Every moment this happens adds another brick to the wall that separates you."

By their stunned looks, I could tell two things: Both knew I was right and both understood the gravity of what I was saying.

If practiced, choosing could unblock the flow of love by eradicating the love embargo. By reestablishing the give-and-take of kind words and loving acts, Mitchell and Imka could begin the process of rebuilding trust and fortify their bond through the production of oxytocin. Furthermore, choosing would make their inert love active and offer both Mitchell and Imka an opportunity to heal their deepest wounds. However, before all that could happen, we would have to go back to the beginning and start with Practices 1, 2, and 3. Going directly to choosing would not work for this couple or couples like them. For relationships where there is resentment and little warmth left, where both partners are armored up and walled off in a love embargo, acts of choosing would ultimately prove to be empty and meaningless. Choosing would be discarded at the first possible opportunity, using an excuse akin to "Life got too busy" or "I forgot."

Over the course of the next few weeks, Mitchell and Imka used Practices 1 through 3, Mindfulness, Parts Work, and Narrative. Using mindfulness, each began to take notice of their own thoughts and feelings. They were able to get out of their knee-jerk reactions toward each other. As they cultivated an ability to witness their own inner experiences, I then had them turn that focus on attuning to each other. As John O'Donohue said, "Love begins with paying attention to others, with an act of gracious self-forgetting."[1] Mindful attunement to our mates is an integral part of making them feel chosen. When Imka and Mitchell paid more attention to each other in this way, they became less focused on what they were not getting and more considerate of what they might be able to provide. This is where I will try out my best John F. Kennedy impression as I tell my couples, "Ask not what your relationship can do for you, ask what you can do for your relationship."

Building on this practice, they began mapping the parts of them that showed up in their relationship. Both were surprised how often their inner defenders were present. These sides of self tended the wall that stood between them, nurtured the embargo, and kept them safe from the vulnerability of connecting.

Mitchell reported his defender part stepped forward whenever Imka asked him to do anything or whenever he felt "required of." He said, "I notice my body tenses, and I just want to say 'no.' *And,* I recognize it's 'no' to stuff I actually don't mind doing. I mean, there is a part of me in there that really wants to make her happy. He just doesn't get a lot of airtime."

Imka, on the other hand, became aware of how remote and icy her defender side of self could be. She said, "There is a penalty for Mitchell when he doesn't do the things I want him to do. If I don't get my needs met, I become cold. He will tell me about something really great that happened to him at work, and I won't react. I give him nothing when I'm like that, no supportive words, no encouragement. None of the stuff that fills him up. When I'm in this part of myself, you can forget about sex. This side of me doesn't even know sex is a thing. It's a big 'Fuck you,' is what it is."

In concert with parts work, we turned up the volume on Mitchell and Imka's narratives about each other. Mitchell found he was telling a story about Imka that was riddled with anger and resentment. He said, "If I'm really honest, I found myself saying things to myself like, 'I fucking hate you.' In truth, I don't hate her, I love her, but there were times when she would ice over. I felt alone and left, and like nothing I ever did was good enough. That no matter what I tried to do, she would always point out the thing I'd missed."

Like Mitchell, Imka's prevailing narrative about her husband came from her defended side of self. She said, "When I did the exercise, I heard myself say, 'You don't matter to him. He doesn't really love you. Sooner or later, he's going to leave because you don't mean enough to him to stay.' I was shocked by the story I was telling myself."

Using the first three practices, Mitchell and Imka began to slow down. They took the time to tease out their thoughts and feelings and to recognize their parts and narratives, all of which were natural deterrents to choosing. As our work progressed, they gradually learned to step out of the noise and drama so many couples get caught up in, and they landed in parts of themselves that were open to connection, compassion, empathy, and vulnerability. This was the pivot point that turned each of their needs from a list of obligatory tasks into opportunities to create love and meaning for their partner.

Mitchell said, "Before *if* I did what she needed me to do, I did it begrudgingly at best. I did it because I either knew I had to or I didn't want to piss her off. Now I can say there is love in what I do for her."

I asked, "Okay, so what's different? If her needs haven't changed and you are essentially doing the same things, what's different now?"

He replied, "The feeling behind the act. I'm not gonna lie, I thought it was corny as hell when you first said it, but it's true, everything, every little thing can be a message of I pick you. Now I don't do anything because I have to. I do it because I want to see that light in her eyes."

Imka added, "This work—this practice, in particular, woke something up in us. It woke up our romance. I feel more open to doing the things that I know make him feel loved. Look, we are humans, and shitty thoughts and feelings still creep in. I know they do for me. When they do, I remind myself that I can choose him and I choose him over those thoughts. He deserves that from me." With a chuckle, she continued. "I'll admit it's made a hell of a lot easier when he does things to support those thoughts and feelings."

Mitchell and Imka were learning to choose each other—to love and to let themselves be loved, and in doing so, they were connecting to "something more." Dropping out of the noise of their surface conversations, both could finally see each other not as the sharp-tongued critic or angry defender but as the wounded child asking "Am I enough?" and "Do I matter?" They discovered that choosing each other offers the possibility of magic and that at its most basic level, "love requires curiosity." It requires a curiosity about our partner's pain, about what they did not get in their upbringing, and about their core question. Loving in this way invites selflessness, grace, and benevolence. All of these are the rewards reaped through choosing each other, but choosing is not a "one-off." It is a mindset and a way of living. So for now, I invite you to practice. Use the following exercises to integrate choosing into your life and your relationship.

16

CHOOSING EXERCISES

> Wholeness is not achieved by cutting off a portion of one's being, but by integration of the contraries.
>
> —Carl Jung

These exercises beg a couple of questions: If you know what makes your partner feel loved and you are not doing those things, why? And, if you don't know what makes your partner feel loved . . . why do you not know what makes your partner feel loved?

THE LOVE LIST EXERCISE

The purpose of this exercise is to get clear about the actions that make both you and your partner feel cared about. Each of you will need one sheet of paper and a pen or pencil. You will be making two lists. List 1 will consist of four actions that make you feel loved, cared about, or chosen when your partner performs them. List 2 will consist of four actions that you are sure, when you perform them, make your partner feel loved, cared about, or chosen.

Steps

- Set aside about forty-five minutes to an hour to do this exercise with your partner.
- Make a list of four actions that make you feel loved, cared about, or chosen.

Example:

List 1: For Me

I feel loved, cared about, and chosen by my partner when:

1. He/she makes the bed.
2. He/she plans a date night.
3. He/she takes the kids so I can have some quiet time.
4. He/she reaches out first after an argument.

List 2: For My Partner

My partner feels loved, cared about, and chosen by me when:

1. I seek out physical contact.
2. I tell them how proud I am of them.
3. I surprise him/her with a gift.
4. I fold the laundry without having to be asked.

- Now compare your List 1 with your partner's List 2. Here you are comparing your list of actions that make you feel loved and cared about to your partner's list of what *they think* makes you feel loved and cared about. How did your partner do?
- Now compare your List 2 with your partner's List 1.
- Assess how you did:

  Did you get most or all of your partner's list correct?

  Are you currently doing some or all of the actions on your partner's list regularly?

  Did your partner agree with your answers to how they feel loved, chosen, and cared for?

  If you know what actions make your partner feel chosen and you are not doing those things, what is standing in your way?

  If you did not get many or any of the actions on your partner's list correct, do you know why you don't know this information?

MINDFULNESS OF PARTS AND CHOOSING

As you finished the Love List Exercise, you may have found that you know what makes your partner feel chosen, but you are not doing those things. Or you might have found that you did not know many or any of the things that make your partner feel chosen.

In either case, there is a very good chance that a part of you is standing in the way, an inner critic or defender side of self that is prohibiting your ability to choose your partner. This is compartmentalization of the mind, and being able to engage in Practice 4 means recognizing that this side of self is present and the effect it is having on your relationship. After bringing awareness to the defended part, we then follow the same steps as we did in Practice 2, Parts of Self, and negotiate with this aspect of self, asking them to step aside.

Steps

- Take a few moments to reflect on how you felt during the Love List Exercise or around the notion of choosing your partner. Stop and mindfully notice what comes up for you. Ask yourself the following:
- How do you feel in your body?

  ○ Is there tension?
  ○ Is there anxiety?
  ○ Is there pressure anywhere?
  ○ Do you feel a sense of "No" come up?

- Where do you feel those feelings in your body? Do you feel like:

  ○ Something is caught in your throat?
  ○ Someone is standing on your chest?
  ○ There is a pit in your stomach?

- What do these feelings around choosing make you want to do?

  ○ Do they make you angry?
  ○ Do they make you ice over, go cold, or vacant?
  ○ Do they make you want to run and hide?
  ○ Do they make you become critical of your partner?

- If you were to physicalize these feelings through body language or hand gestures, what do you notice? Is your body language or gestures:

  ○ Defensive?
  ○ Protective?
  ○ An effort to cover up?
  ○ Boundaried, as with hands up to push back?

If you experience any of these, we can assume that there is a protector part of you present that is standing in the way of you choosing your partner. Now it will be important to name and negotiate with this part of self.

NAMING AND NEGOTIATING

This step may seem a bit redundant and merely a repeat of the previous step. However, it is not. Naming is more than simply becoming aware that your defender part is present. It is about formally announcing to yourself that this phenomenon is occurring. Again, naming is a simple but powerful practice that calls out what is happening in the moment while also offering room, as it were, between you and the protective part. The idea is, the moment we can name an experience, we cease to be overcoupled with that experience, we have space from it, and with that space, we find a new perspective.

Steps

- Take some time to consider the part of you that keeps you from choosing your partner.
- As best as you can, imagine that side of yourself. Perhaps see them sitting across from you in your mind.
- Now say to yourself or write in your journal, "I see you, you are my defender part of self, or you are my inner critic, and I know what you've been doing."

From here, we can move directly into the negotiation phase.

NEGOTIATING

Having brought the presence of this part to mind and naming it, it is now time to negotiate with this side of self, to get that part to step aside so you can engage in the practice of choosing your partner.

Steps

- After naming, say to yourself or write in your journal something like, "I know how hard you have been working to keep me safe. I see all that you've done for me. You have done an amazing job, but I need to connect to _____ (your partner's name) in order to make this relationship work. I need you to step aside. I need you to let me love and to let me be loved." You can tailor your dialogue as you like. You know what your part needs to hear in order to do what you are asking of it. What is important here is that this side of you is acknowledged for what it has tried to do and that you formally request that it stop thwarting your efforts to love your partner fully.

THE LOVE EMBARGO

Are you in a love embargo? Do you notice that there is a decided ban on the flow of loving acts, kind words, or physical affection between you and your partner? Is there a sense or a feeling in you, for example, that you will only choose them when they start choosing you? Does the space between you and your mate feel stark, chilly, or unfriendly? If you are experiencing any of these, there is a good chance that a love embargo has set in. An embargo between romantic partners offers one of two options for your relationship: Either it will stagnate and stay the same, relegating you to a life that lacks love, compassion, empathy, or understanding, or it will rot your relationship from the inside out, and it will eventually fall apart.

Some embargoes between partners can be "partial embargoes," meaning it does not pervade the entire relationship. This type of ban might exist only in one area of the relationship, such as in physical affection or emotional connection. I see couples in both my personal and professional life who seem to live in these embargoes. These couples rarely touch each other. They spend time together because it is expected. There is perhaps little warmth, and their connection is tenuous at best.

Steps

- Take some time to consider how you feel in your relationship about your partner and the concept of choosing. As in the previous exercise, become mindful and aware of what comes up in your body. Is there a sense of:
  - Withholding?
  - I don't want to?
  - I'll choose you when you choose me?
  - I'm tired of being the one who does all the work?

Essentially, anteing up means breaking the embargo and choosing your partner. It means finally doing the things that you both have agreed to put a freeze on. I am not suggesting that anyone do anything that makes them uncomfortable. I ask my clients to mindfully decide if they are willing to break the embargo by leading through example. When I suggest this, I often hear, "Yes, tried that, and it didn't work. There was no 'choosing' done in my direction." Sometimes anteing up is just calling it out. This means saying in no uncertain words we are in a love embargo, or we are withholding love in this area of our relationship, and I want it to stop. Anteing up in this way might mean saying, "I see what we are doing to each other, and I think we need to seek professional help." All of these can break the love embargo.

Steps

- Bring mindfulness and awareness that there is an embargo.
- Name it for your partner.
- Decide if you can or are willing to break it through example.
- Seek the help of a therapist to help reconnect you.

YOUR NARRATIVE AND CHOOSING

As you now know, the stories we tell ourselves become our feelings, which ultimately become our beliefs about who our partners are and who they are not. As with our parts of self, our narratives can also get in the way of our ability to love, pick, and ultimately choose our partners. As you might recall with our couple Imka and Mitchell, both had constructed narratives that shut them down to loving and being loved. Once the story you tell about your partner sours, so does your empathy and compassion. When the narrative sounds like "He always . . ." or "She never . . ." our ability to think and act from generosity and kindness is severely compromised. In this exercise, the goal is to discover any problematic narratives, to turn up the volume on them, and to re-author them into a more positive story line that paves the way toward choosing.

TURN UP THE VOLUME EXERCISE

For the next three to four days, pay close attention to the narratives you hold when the opportunity to choose your partner presents itself.

Steps

- Read over your partner's "Love List" or simply think of what makes them feel loved and cared for. Try doing or imagine doing some of those things.
- Either write down or say out loud the thoughts or narratives that come to mind. For example, "I don't want to . . .," "Why should I . . .," "They never . . ."
- Do you notice any global language, such as, "*He always* . . ." or "*She never* . . ."?
- Does your narrative breed feelings of love and generosity or defensiveness and contraction?
- What does it make you feel in your body to think of choosing your partner?
- Notice if these narratives are kind, compassionate, fair, or understanding.

- What are some of the consistent themes?
- Make a list of any negative narratives.

RE-AUTHORING AND CHOOSING

When we initially construct a narrative, we often do it mindlessly. Our inner dialogues tend to come from a defended part of self, and we omit or prune important information from our story line. The feelings these narratives create can keep us from acting from our heart centers. As we re-author our stories, we open our formerly closed hearts and are able to choose our partners.

Steps

- Consider the negative narrative list you have just created.
- Invite a kinder, more wise part of you to this exercise.
- If you are experiencing difficulty, practice the Gratitude Exercise or Loving-Kindness Exercise from Practice 2 to help bring this side of self out.
- As best as you can, rewrite your narratives from kindness, compassion, empathy, and understanding.
- How have your narratives changed?
- Reconsider your partner's Love List from this new narrative and a new perspective. Notice if you feel more open to doing the things on their list.

Note: If there is deep-seated resentment or mental, emotional, or physical abuse, these exercises will not work and are not recommended.

DISCOVERING SOMETHING
MORE EXERCISE, SENSE MEMORY

Sense memory exercises are used by actors to trigger truthful emotional responses when they need them, either on stage or in front of the camera. Recalling a memory and then feeling into the sensations associated with that memory unlocks emotion. Think of a time when you have heard a song, smelled a familiar scent, or seen an old movie and said, "Man, that brings back memories." These experiences tend to bring back more than memories. They also bring back feelings. The following is a technique I have borrowed from my acting days that helps couples remember the magic.

Steps

- Make a list of any movies, poems, songs, memories, or places that create warm, loving feelings in you for your partner. We will refer to this as your "object."
- Take some time to listen, read, watch, or visit in your mind the objects you've chosen.
- Notice your thoughts and feelings.
- Allow yourself to delve into the memories. Feel deeply and fully into the emotions that come to you.
- With these feelings now present, pick something from your partner's Love List and perform that action or imagine performing that action.
- How does it make you feel to choose your partner from this place?
- How do the feelings from your object inform your effort?
- Notice your partner's reaction as you perform this task from this heart-centered place.

Part 5

PRACTICE 5:
PERSONAL RESPONSIBILITY

> Most of us are like children or young adolescents; we be-
> lieve that the freedom and power of adulthood is our due,
> but we have little taste for adult responsibility.
>
> —M. Scott Peck

"I think you love me. I'm just not always sure how *in love* you are with me. And I don't think you like me very much sometimes." May spoke as if she were reading the daily specials off of a lunch menu.

Keisha responds in kind. "Well, I don't think you like me very much either. You seem frustrated or annoyed with me most of the time. I can't ever seem to get it right. If you would just try and connect with me—"

May, cutting her off in mid-sentence, says, "Well, I would if *you* would just give me a signal that you were even open to that."

I break into the conversation and point one finger at each of them. "*There* it is! There it is, you both finally said it."

Both women look confused. May asks, "There what is? What did we say?"

"'*If you would just* . . .' Your relationship has fallen into the 'If *you* would justs . . .'" Now speaking directly to May, I continue. "By Keisha's account, if *you* would just try to connect to her, then everything would be just fine." I shift my focus to Keisha to further emphasize my point. "And Keisha, if *you* would just give May a signal that you were open, then everything would be unicorns and rainbows."

Both women sit in silence. I continue. "Here's the thing, neither of you is uniquely broken, and you are not necessarily with the wrong person. What I think you have is a *personal responsibility* issue. Both of you are guilty of trying to shirk your responsibility to your relationship and each other. I've watched you both for a while now, and you're constantly pointing the finger at each other, and neither of you wants to own anything. Both of you are waiting for the other to do it better. Let me ask you a question. How many times have we been to this place?"

"What do you mean?" May asks.

"This place right here." Both women look perplexed.

"Don't you see the pattern? This is what, our third go-round together?" I could see they were still confused by the looks on their faces.

Giving them the answer, I say, "You call me when the shit hits the fan. I help you calm things down and deal with whatever the problem seems to be. We de-escalate the cycle, as it were. And *now*, if history tells us anything, you will walk out that door at the end of this session, and I won't see you *until* things boil over again. And trust me, they will boil over again because neither of you is willing to own your shit and take responsibility for making this relationship better."

17

WHAT IS PERSONAL
RESPONSIBILITY?

> Karma means that all actions have consequences. Grace
> means that in a moment of atonement—taking responsi-
> bility, making amends, asking for forgiveness—all karma
> is burned.
>
> —Marianne Williamson

Sometimes I get what I call "drive-thru therapy" clients. Clients who
come to patch the holes in the raft or put out the flames. Clients
who are looking for brief, strategically oriented interventions. There is
usually a central, very acute problem that has brought them in the door.
Once they have gotten the requisite insights or skills, they vanish into
their lives only to be seen again if the problem persists or if another issue crops up. I am by no means suggesting that "brief therapy" is bad.
Brief therapy is an umbrella term used to describe a number of viable
and well-researched therapeutic approaches that are both short-term and
solution-oriented. For me, the difference between drive-thru and brief
therapy is clients who are in the market for the drive-thru version either
know for sure or have some sense that there is a larger issue on the table.
This is an issue beyond the one they came to work on. It is an issue that
both partners are afraid to confront, and there is an implicit agreement
to go only so deep. These clients are "comfortable" skimming over the
top for fear of disturbing whatever might lie beneath.

Keisha and May were skimming. They were an upwardly mobile,
gay/interracial couple whose families were both loving and supportive
of their union. Having successfully navigated the often turbulent waters of coming out, these women were now faced with the everyday
rigors of life in a long-term relationship. As I said, this was the third

time we had all done this dance, fourth if you count my couple's workshop where we first met. They initially sought professional help for cyclical fighting that never seemed to find resolution. They then came in for "communication issues." This latest problem had to do with Keisha having a questionable text relationship with a coworker. For me, all of these issues were symptomatic of another much larger problem, personal responsibility.

It was evident in the caustic and unrelenting manner in which they argued. It was apparent in their inability to communicate effectively. It was present in Keisha's need to seek outside attention from another woman. It was visible in their failure to connect on a deeper level and be truly vulnerable to each other. Like so many couples, Keisha and May could go only so far in that department.

When they were not displacing their responsibility onto each other by using the dreaded "If you would just"s they were displacing it onto me. Keisha and May would come to see me when they were "in the ditch." I was like the Triple-A membership for their relationship. They would come in the door and quite literally say "Time for a tune-up," or "Okay, Lair, do your magic and fix us." Once the crisis was averted, the therapy would stop, never going far enough to touch onto the more significant issue at hand, their avoidance of personal responsibility.

For therapy geeks like me, Irvin Yalom's book *Existential Psycho-therapy* is a treasure trove of therapeutic profundities, and, for my money, it should be a part of every clinician's library. In it, he discusses at length the importance of a client's responsibility for their own lives, their therapy, as well as the role of accountability in healing. He said, "The assumption of responsibility is a precondition of therapeutic change. As long as one believes that one's situation and dysmorphia are produced by someone else or by some external force, then what sense is there in committing oneself to personal change?"[1] Like so many couples I see, Keisha and May were all for making positive changes in their relation-ship as long as the vast majority of the responsibility for those changes lived in their partner's camp.

At large, personal responsibility has many different meanings, con-notations, and implications. When we say someone is a responsible person, they are principled, trustworthy, and reliable. It can also imply a level of ethical, legal, or fiscal responsibility. In the corporate world, someone who is deemed responsible is someone who can get the job done and is a leader and a person we should emulate.

In theory, most of us can accept the idea that we are responsible for our actions. This is especially true for the good things that happen. For example, we are happy to take responsibility for the pitch at work that went well, the family trip that created so many great memories, or the act of kindness that made someone's day a little bit brighter. However, there is another side to personal responsibility. It is a term that elicits a variety of feelings, not all of which are particularly positive. This is undoubtedly the case when it comes to couples. Personal responsibility in romantic relationships tends to feel more like blame or getting caught. Less than a virtue to be aspired to, this brand of accountability is something to be skirted, dodged, and otherwise avoided at all costs. It seems antithetical to accept responsibility for hurt feelings, as an example, especially when we intended to create precisely the opposite experience for our partner.

Most people do not understand that learning to accept personal responsibility in your life and your relationship is an extraordinary strength if you are open to seeing it that way. When we finally learn to take 100 percent responsibility for ourselves in every situation, we harness our power as well as the power of compassion, empathy, and validation. In addition to our own experience, we find a deep and abiding understanding for our partner's. In this practice, we stop giving our power away, and we see the situations of our lives as manifestations of the choices we have made and as opportunities for radical growth and learning. Personal responsibility is a maturation, a passing from childhood to adulthood. Journalist and author Sydney J. Harris said, "We have not passed the subtle line between childhood and adulthood until we move from the passive voice—that is, until *we* have stopped saying, 'It got lost,' and say, 'I lost it.'"[2] For me, this is the essence of personal responsibility. However, beyond owning the things we have done or said and learning to apologize skillfully, personal responsibility lives in this model as the key and foundational practice, the one the other four sit atop of and rely upon.

When I first created this way of working, there were only four practices: Mindfulness, Parts of Self, Narrative, and Choosing. In that first iteration, it felt like something was missing. These were all exceptional practices, but, as they stood, they were no different from so many other forms of therapy already out there. What those initial strategies needed was an impetus to act, something to catalyze them into action. Personal responsibility is that spur to action, a stated call or an oath to yourself and your partner to use the first four practices in the moments when they are truly needed. It's a push to not only use these skills when it's easy, but to employ them when you least want to and when everything inside you is telling you to point the finger, to place blame, or to play the victim.

As we move from this chapter on what personal responsibility is, notice how this concept lands on you. What does it make you think? How does it make you feel? What, if anything, does it make you want to do? For some, the idea of being personally responsible on this level in your relationship is daunting, even scary. However, as we move through the next section of this book, you will come to understand how vital personal responsibility is to the health of romantic relationships.

18

WHY PERSONAL RESPONSIBILITY IS INTEGRAL TO RELATIONSHIPS

> As long as you fight a symptom, it will become worse. If you take responsibility for what you were doing to yourself, how you produce your symptoms, how you produce your illness, how you produce your existence—the very moment you get in touch with yourself—growth begins, integration begins.
>
> —Fritz Perls

A BOILING POT

I had been a parent long enough to become a connoisseur of screams. Meaning, I could tell by the pitch, tone, and emotional tenor of my son's wails, his level of actual pain, danger, or duress. The current screams emanating from our house to my ears in the back lawn told me that no one had lost a limb and no one was bleeding out, at least not yet anyway. Yep, I was good to stay right here, to finish my beer and my conversation with my friend who had stopped by. I was free and clear to let the little lady inside handle this one. Whatever had happened, I was convinced *it* was fine—*I* was fine. And then, just like that, the howling and the crying stopped. *See, I was right,* or so I thought.

When I finally came through the back door, that night's dinner was not the only thing simmering in the kitchen. Ashley looked at me in a manner I was not used to. It was a manner that said she was angry and maybe a little disappointed. "So I'm guessing you must not have heard any of that?" Her tone was stern and a bit cold, again not something I was particularly used to. Typically, no matter the situation,

Ashley affords me the benefit of the doubt. I could tell she was trying hard not to blast me, and, immediately, my defender parts came rushing in. My inner fighter took over, and that's when I said it—"Last time I checked, you had a voice." As the words left my mouth, it was as if an alternate part of me came to life, a part that could see the folly of trying to defend my position. It was as if someone had hit the slow-motion button, like in a movie where everything slows down, the words and the voice in my head elongated and oddly deep: "Noooooo! Whaaaat arrre youuuuu dooooinggg?" As the words left my mouth, I wanted nothing more than to shove them back down the gaping hole from whence they came.

Ashley's back stiffened, and her eyes narrowed. On the surface, she was ready to fight; underneath, she was hurt. And why shouldn't she be hurt and angry? In our fifteen years together, we'd had our share of arguments, but, throughout our relationship, we had created a culture between us forged in love and respect for each other. My words were a decided departure from our agreements, spoken and otherwise.

Then she did something I had few occasions to see her do. She turned and was now about to exit the room. She was not leaving the room because she had lost the fight or because she was so angry. She was leaving the room because she was the only adult standing in that kitchen that night. She didn't want to say or do anything that she would have to apologize for later. She was taking personal responsibility.

As she took her first steps out of the kitchen, I finally came to my senses. *What the fuck are you doing*, I thought. At that moment, I threw my hands up in the air and said, "Wait!" She wasn't stopping, so I repeated it. "Wait! Please wait." Her forward momentum finally stopped, but she didn't turn back to face me. Not yet committed to continuing the discourse, she was going to see if my words would be enough to bridge the gap between us. "I'm so sorry. I *did* hear him screaming. I should have come in to help you, and I didn't. I didn't want to deal with it, and I left you hanging. But more than anything, I never, *never* should have spoken to you that way. You don't deserve that."

I saw something in her energy shift, a softening as she reluctantly turned to face me. With a skeptical grin, she said, "I know what you're doing. You're doing that thing you do." I knew what she meant. That "thing" was holding myself fully accountable. I didn't make any excuses or try to justify my behavior. Simultaneously, I made the space safe enough for her to lower her defenses and open to me and my apology. She did know what I was doing, and I knew she found it irresistible. I said, "You're damn right I'm doing it, and I bet you're glad I am."[1]

MORE THAN AN APOLOGY

"Never apologize, mister, it's a sign of weakness." Actor John Wayne delivered that line in the western movie classic *She Wore a Yellow Ribbon*. Though Wayne delivered this line back in 1949, for me, it is emblematic of how our society holds apologies. For this reason and many others I will discuss later, most of us do not like to take personal responsibility, and we certainly don't like to take it in the form of an apology. Admitting to a transgression can go against our vision of who we are. It can temporarily reduce self-esteem, making us feel what John Wayne said, weak.[2] You don't have to be a therapist to understand the damage done to relationships when the "I'm sorry" step is skipped or the apology is insincere. If amends have not been made and personal responsibility has not been truly claimed, the wound remains open, and the experience is incomplete. In these scenarios, family members are cut off, former friends are left estranged, and romantic partners cannot connect at the heart center.

When apologies are real, when they are sincere and from the heart, they play a decisive role in healing. "I'm sorry" is validating; it says I see you and that something I have done or said has hurt you.

When we think of apologies, we usually think first of the person receiving the olive branch, how nice it must be to finally have their experience considered. The contrite person also gets a boon, as the act of apologizing relieves shame and guilt for the transgressor.[3]

As important as it is to express regret, apologies are only a small component in taking personal responsibility and the execution of this fifth and final practice. Taking personal responsibility gives us the genuine opportunity to turn a formerly polarizing experience into a galvanizing one. When we show our mates compassion, empathy, respect, and understanding, it affords us the ability to resolve our conflicts and rebuild trust. This practice asks more of us. It reaches deeper into our lives and into our relationships than merely expressing regret. Time and again, I have witnessed partners who are willing to say "I am sorry," but they fall short of taking responsibility for real change. Real change means treating each other in such a way that apologies are rendered almost unnecessary or even obsolete because each partner acts and speaks from kindness, compassion, and reverence for the other. Personal responsibility on this level breeds trust, enhances our ability to communicate, and makes our relationships a safe-enough place to learn and grow. Practiced in this way, personal responsibility in relationships, especially romantic ones, is a game-changer.

The Road Less Traveled, by M. Scott Peck, was the first self-help book I ever read. It was the book that tipped off my curiosity about the mind and how we work as humans. In it, Peck talks a lot about responsibility, saying that those who are brave enough to accept it "find themselves living in a new and different world. What they once perceived as problems they now perceive as opportunities. What were once loathsome barriers are now welcome challenges. Thoughts previously unwanted become helpful insights; feelings previously disowned become sources of energy and guidance."[4] What Peck is saying is that personal responsibility is, in fact, a game-changer. Those who are willing to accept it will experience a profound shift within themselves, affecting how they see their world and the people in it. I say anyone willing to bring this practice to bear on their relationships grants themselves the opportunity to expand into a fuller potential of romantic connection. I have seen it firsthand in my own marriage and in the relationships of the couples I have worked with. When romantic partners agree that personal responsibility will be a crucial component of their relational culture, they experience this "expansion," this "fuller potential." They see it as a dramatic increase in their ability to be intimate and vulnerable, to trust, to communicate, to express love, and in their ability to handle difficult times.

COMMUNICATION

I experience this expansion in relationship, this leveling up that personal responsibility provides, in my communication with my wife. Ashley and I communicate very kindly and respectfully with each other. We take care to do this even in our everyday or routine communications. Truthfully, some of our friends make fun of us. It's not that we do it annoyingly so or falsely. It's that the way we speak to each other is a decided departure from how many other couples communicate. If I could define it, I would say that there is care taken, a consideration of our words, and how those words will make the other feel. I try to talk to her as someone I not only love but someone I like and respect. I take responsibility for speaking to her as someone I value. I'm not saying that we don't joke with each other either, because humor is a big part of who we are and our connection; we take responsibility for what we say and how we say it. In my experience, couples can become complacent in their speech. Corners get cut, as it were, and sooner than later, partners take unfortunate liberties in the way they talk to their mates. These liberties come out as snide little back-and-forths that, on the surface, are explained away as just a little humor or "having some fun," however, to the careless couple, these jibes carry a deeper meaning and are the expressions of feelings unprocessed. Have you ever been out to dinner or at a party where another couple fires off little barbs at each other guised as humor? "Oh look, is that another chardonnay, Sharon? Would you like to save some for the rest of the guests?"

"Oh no, don't worry, Todd, I bought plenty. I knew I'd need it to get through your stories, sweetie."

We can take jokes made at our expense when there is trust that the other person has our backs. With trust, we know they do not mean what they are saying. When couples are too "jokey" or what I call "chippy" with each other, there is a carelessness present. There is a lack of trust because there is a lack of ownership over the emotions behind the snide remarks. When feelings get hurt, we often stand on the faulty ground of "plausible deniability." Plausible deniability comes out in "Oh come on, I was kidding," or "Oh relax, it was just a little joke." All the while, what has happened is we've touched a sore spot. Feelings have been hurt because we've been careless and gotten too close to the truth. The bottom line is, we know when we are being shitty. There is an erosion of trust between couples who don't take responsibility for how they communicate.

Responsibility is not only crucial in the daily or routine correspondences between partners, it's also vital in the bigger-ticket communications couples have. Of course, I am referring to the conversations about the often activating topics of sex, money, kids, or the in-laws, to name a few. It might sound too obvious to mention, but with problems in communication topping the list of reasons couples seek therapy or divorce, I thought it a topic worth unpacking. I said in chapter 6 that people don't have communication problems so much as they have a parts-of-self problem. I said our communication's health is not dependent on some device or technique but rather hinges on the part of self that shows up to that conversation. The topics that matter tend to trigger us into our most protective parts of self. Once that part has taken hold, we see the world from that part's perspective. This is where communication goes off the rails, this is where higher-level discourse can turn quickly into stone-throwing, and this is where personal responsibility has the most significant impact on our ability to communicate well.

In some therapy sessions, there is an understanding either stated or implied that today is the day we are going to have the big conversation about the big topic. Then again, therapy is also where the big topic can suddenly materialize seemingly out of nowhere. Couples are often surprised and say things like, "Well, I didn't think we'd go here today, but I guess this is why we came in." Whenever situations like this present themselves, I make everyone stop and take a mindful breath. I have each partner take an inner inventory of what parts of them are present. I'll say, "As we enter this conversation, a conversation that has perhaps been difficult in the past, can each of you notice what parts of you are here, and can you take responsibility for the part of you that gets to speak today?" Here is where we ask our inner defenders, critics, and wounded children to step aside. It is also where we take responsibility for showing up in our wisest and most compassionate parts, and this again is where personal responsibility becomes a game-changer. The same feelings expressed from a different part land differently. Instead of being imbued with our defender's bitterness and anger, our wise self can express the love, compassion, and concern that may also be there. This does not happen without personal responsibility. It is one thing to be mindful and aware of the negative feelings and defended parts that often accompany difficult conversations. It is another thing to take responsibility for not allowing those parts to steer the ship. I know for me when my partner has done or said something that hurts my feelings or makes me angry,

I have to do more than just notice what I am feeling or the part of me that is present. I have to take an extra step and take responsibility for the part of me I speak through and the way I express myself. Couples who don't take ownership in this manner will forever suffer from poor communication, cyclical arguments, and topics that they simply agree not to talk about.

PERSONAL RESPONSIBILITY IS A LANGUAGE OF LOVE

Personal responsibility is a language of love. When we hold ourselves accountable for our shortcomings and take ownership of the way we treat and speak to our partners, it registers as acts of love, benevolence, selflessness, and altruism. Placing the onus of more mature and more connective behavior firmly on ourselves is critical in preventing the recurrent and sometimes perpetual disputes many couples find themselves in.

When Sara and Ben landed in my office, they were at their wits' end with each other. They married immediately after finding out Sara was pregnant, which shortened their courtship considerably. On the heels of their first child's birth, they quickly had another, and their second son was born with special needs. As the pressures of life mounted, so, too, did their list of grievances with each other. At one point, they had instituted a policy of being allowed to converse only about the weather. All other topics were deemed far too inflammatory. Sara said, "It feels like we've been fighting nonstop for four straight years." Ben said, "I want it to work out, especially for the kids, but we can't live like this anymore. If something doesn't change soon, I'm done." Like Keisha and May, Sara and Ben were caught in the "If you would just . . ."'s with neither willing to own any part of their responsibility for making their relationship a better and safer place. Both were convinced that the lion's share of the responsibility for the relational breakdown lived in the other's camp, and so, too, did the duty to fix it. I put Ben and Sara on a strict personal responsibility program. Rather than pointing fingers and diving into the "If you would just . . ."'s I had them practice asking themselves, "If I were taking personal responsibility in this moment, what would I do differently?" They then, to the best of their ability, had to do that thing. The first leg of their journey wasn't easy. For reasons I will cover later, personal responsibility is rarely the easiest of the Five Practices. However, after some stops and starts, Ben and Sara began taking ownership of how they showed up in their relationship, how they spoke to and treated each other. Sara said, "My son's doctor's appointments are often difficult—overwhelming and hard. I usually fall completely apart afterward, and Ben usually stares off into space as I cry. No hugs, no comfort, only silence." Ben reported going through his version of falling apart after those doctor's visits, but he kept it all inside, not wanting to make it worse for Sara. When he started practicing personal responsibility, something changed. He said, "It was like a light bulb went off in my head. When I asked your question, 'What would I do differently?' I realized I would stop acting like it was all about me and see how hard this is for her. There was a mom, my wife, sitting next to me that needed my support. Suddenly I felt something that I hadn't felt in a long time, compassion for her. That's when I reached out and held her, told her it was going to be alright and that we got this." Over time, Ben and Sara learned to take turns being strong for each other. They learned to hold their mate's feelings and care for them.

In rock climbing and rappelling, there is a safety protocol called being "on belay," and it is a term I have co-opted in my work with couples. When you are on belay in climbing, you are the person responsible for holding the safety rope; if there is a mishap or a climber gets in trouble, the belayer will make sure the climber falls only so far. I've always thought this was an apt analogy for taking personal responsibility in relationships. It might not always be our first choice, and it might not always feel fair, but taking responsibility in our relationships means that we are on belay for our partners, holding the rope, as it were, only letting them fall so far. Being on belay is a practice that should be shared. The same person cannot always be the one holding the safety rope. Practiced in this way, accountability becomes a communication of love. This is the often unforeseen and added bonus to personal responsibility. It sends the message to our mates that they are worth showing up for. It is a sacrifice in their direction that lets them know that they are loved, that they are safe, that they matter, that they are enough, and, in this way, personal responsibility is a language of love.

IT'S JUST PLAIN SEXY

A few years back, there was a rash of funny memes, videos, and commercials depicting women ogling men. They were comically objectifying these men and seeing them as sex objects. However, the guys in the videos were not doing any sort of cliché sexy activities. They were not depicted as hard bodies, sweatily working out or doing some heavy lifting. No, these men were diapering a kid, making dinner, doing laundry, and cleaning up around the house. They performed what might be considered menial household chores, but they were owning their share of the work. They were proactive, and they showed up for their partners and family by taking personal responsibility for what needed to get done. These commercials depicted accountability on even the most mundane level as sexy. I said earlier that personal responsibility is not just a good apology. In fact, there are a myriad of situations and opportunities where taking responsibility is a turn-on.

Monica and Jerry came in for several reasons, not the least of which was Jerry's lack of inspiration at work and in his life. He made great money, but he was not living out any of his dreams. Monica hated seeing her husband unhappy but became increasingly tired and frustrated at his lack of drive. In one session, Monica said, "I don't care what you do, and I don't care about the money. I just want to see you inspired. But if I'm honest, Jer, this isn't sexy, and I don't really want to sleep with this." Monica was delivering a difficult but necessary truth. Jerry's inactivity and borderline depression had been affecting them in the bedroom. For many of us, when we observe our partners turned on by something, we are turned on. It is infinitely more exciting and arousing for your mate if you are someone who is unafraid to carry some weight. When our mates are inspired, in flow, and taking responsibility for their lives, it is attractive and helps keep things sexually exciting. I told Jerry, "Your main problem is personal responsibility. At this point, it's not what you're doing or not doing. You haven't owned your fear. You haven't taken responsibility for the fact that you're stuck. You own that shit by cracking a book, getting a coach, going to a seminar, or by getting active. Energy in *a* direction—*any* direction at this point would be forward momentum. That would be taking responsibility for your life and for your dreams. *And* if I'm hearing your wife correctly, it would be just plain sexy." Monica and Jerry laughed a laugh that said it was funny because it was true.

However, what is not sexy is always having to beg, plead, and ride your mate to own their accountability. Whether it's routine household chores, choosing a path in life, or taking responsibility for missed steps and hurt feelings, if your partner has to continuously beseech you to own it, it becomes unsexy really fast.

When we have to convince our person of our pain, it creates frustration and resentment. In this dynamic, one partner is cast in the role of police and governing body. They are forever the "heavy," always coming down on their mate. What is more, they rarely, if ever, get the support they need, as they are, in effect, parentified by their mate's inability or unwillingness to accept personal responsibility. Consequently, the partner who takes no ownership of themselves is infantilized. The symptomatic pieces in relationships like these are a one-up, one-down power dynamic and feelings of love but not necessarily being in love. The connection for the parentified partner becomes more caretaker and custodian than lover. The infantilized partner feels as if they are always trying to get away with something. This, of course, leads to overt lying and lying by omission. From here, a game of cat and mouse ensues where the parent-partner is left trying to spoon-feed their mate accountability. By its very nature, this relationship leads to sexual disconnection as sex with someone who is seen as childlike can feel "icky," bordering on incestual.

GASLIGHTING

In the most extreme cases, lack of personal responsibility becomes "gaslighting." Gaslighting is a form of psychological abuse in relationships where one partner makes the other question their memories, perception of reality, and even their sanity. Someone who uses this tactic does so by dismissing their partner's feelings or their entire experience by explaining it away as an overreaction or due to being overly sensitive. All of this is an effort to dodge accountability and demonstrates that I would rather you suffer than take responsibility for my actions and experience the consequences. As a result, the gaslit partner's reality is stolen through lies, manipulation, and denial, which can leave them feeling crazy, confused, anxious, and unable to trust their own perceptions. Needless to say, gaslighting drains a relationship of its vulnerability and trust and, in most cases, leaves sex off the table.

On the other hand, when your partner comes to you with an honest and sincere apology and validates your experience, that apology can act as its own kind of aphrodisiac. Personal responsibility is sexy. When someone does not deny your feelings or experiences, when your partner is willing to stand in the mess they have made and says "I'm so sorry I hurt you," when they don't ask you to qualify your pain when they own their stuff and share some of the weight, it is nothing short of hot. Jerry found that out firsthand. He began taking the initiative. Not only did he get proactive around the house, he found momentum in his life. He stopped playing the victim in his golden cage and owned the choices he'd made that brought him to this point. He understood that he would have to be the one who made an effort to forge a new path. When the couple returned for another session, Monica talked about how good it felt to see her husband this way. She winked at Jerry and said, "I can't lie, when I see you like this, it turns me on, and my clothes come off."

"ME" TO "WE" AND 200 PERCENT RESPONSIBILITY

This practice represents a paradigm shift for most couples because it's a change in mindset from a "me" centered way of thinking to a "we" centered way of thinking. It's an internal pledge that I am going to consider my partner's feelings and needs as well as the needs of the relationship at least as much and sometimes more than I consider my own. Though the argument rages on as to whether humans are innately selfish or selfless, I find that generosity of heart and a perspective of abundance is often a learned skill in long-term relationships. When resentments form, partners become increasingly more contracted. As the space between them cools, our defended parts of self become more prevalent, while narratives globalize and become negative. Personal responsibility ends when mates resort to tactics like the "If you would just . . ."s the "love embargoes," plausible deniability, and finger-pointing. Employing these strategies ushers in a "me" centered way of thinking. Here, romantic partners tend to languish, fighting over almost anything and surprised when they are made aware that what they have been fighting over is the "victim position." In Gay Hendricks's book *The Big Leap*, he says that arguments are caused by two people or countries, "racing to occupy the victim position in a relationship. That once the race for the victim position is underway, each person must find some way to out-victim the other. In other words, each person must present an escalating series of 'proofs' that he or she is the real victim." Hendricks goes further to say that the only path to resolution is for each person to accept 100 percent of the responsibility for ending the conflict. Anything less will not work.[5] What Hendricks is suggesting is radical personal responsibility. A scenario where we are not competing to out-victim one another but instead accept full accountability for our part in creating the problem and its solution. It might feel natural to argue for the victim position. It might seem easier in the moment to foist blame onto others. It might even seem prudent to call penalties on our mates rather than calling them on ourselves. However, ultimately, it's not. One of my clients who struggled but eventually gave himself over to the practice of personal responsibility put it simply: "It's just easier this way." I have to say he's correct, and though it may be hard to believe in the beginning, attempting to get someone to accept that your suffering is entirely their fault is a far more difficult prospect. Being considerate of how your behavior is affecting the overall health of the relationship and owning your accountability marks a shift into a "we" mindset that sends our mates the message they are loved and that it is safe enough for them to do the same.

A ZERO-SUM GAME AND TRUST

We were about to put ourselves back into the food chain. Over the course of the last few thousand years, humans have successfully removed themselves from the menu, and we were consciously deciding to jump right back onto it by taking our first surf lesson. This thought hit me dead in the face as Ashley and I drove past the marshlands and then over the two bridges connecting the mainland of South Carolina to the barrier island of Folly Beach. It struck me as odd that the vision of facing man-eating sharks was actually not the scariest prospect in my day. What was more terrifying than sharks, you ask? Funnily enough, it was the thought of my wife besting me at surfing.

Up until that moment, I had simply assumed, having been a pretty good athlete all my life, that I would be good at surfing and, of course, better at it than Ashley. Admittedly this was my unconscious bias playing out. After all, she had always been good at sports too. Athletic prowess aside, there was something more in my assumption, a tiny vestige of male prejudice, yes, but also competition. As the thoughts and images of her getting up on her board or even finding some proficiency at the sport rushed past, I felt my body contract. I could almost hear the laughter of friends as we retold the tales of Ash riding down the line while I "kooked" it up and ponderously flopped around in the water. No, absolutely not, I thought. I'm going to crush this sport, and I *will* be better than her. My mind then went to an alternate version of our car ride home. In this image, the car was silent. Ashley felt dejected and disappointed in her first surfing experience. Perhaps there would be the simmering level of resentment that often accompanies competition in couples, that might turn into a fight. I, of course, did not want her to do poorly. I suppose I just didn't want her to do better than me. I certainly never wanted her to feel beaten by me or that she somehow lost to me. It was clear I had a choice in how the day would go. I could take responsibility for my ego, my unconscious bias, and my competitive side of self. I could choose to have fun in this new endeavor. I could, if I decided to, show up in my more mature parts, and no matter how good or bad a surfer I turned out to be, I could be my partner's biggest supporter. In fact, isn't that what a "partner" is supposed to do?

When the day was done, we both got up on the board a bunch, and, if I'm honest, we both flopped around a fair bit too. We had a great time and were each other's biggest cheerleaders. It was an experience that brought us closer together. To this day, we are avid surfers; however, the biggest takeaway from that experience had little to do with what I learned about surfing and everything to do with what I learned about competition and its corrosive effect on love relationships.

In America, we compete. We are capitalists, after all, so competition is in our blood. Even if you don't consider yourself a particularly competitive person, it is still there. Competition is a part of who we are.

It feels as if it is woven into the small fiber of our beings to be the best, to strive, and to triumph over the other, no matter who that other might be. To lose anything is humbling and humiliating. It induces shame and strikes at the very core of our self-esteem. Who are we if we are not number one? What are we if we are not the winner? Vince Lombardi, one of the winningest coaches in NFL history, famously said, "Winning isn't everything, it's the only thing." There is no second place, after all; there is the winner and the losers who came after. These are only a small sampling of the sentiments we hold about competition in our culture. It is a way of thinking so prevalent in our country that we see it as a natural law, a virtue to be aspired to, a skill worthy of listing on a resume. It is an idea so fundamental to who we are it seems almost an act of sedition to speak out against it.

It is for all these reasons that I believe competition at large but especially in love relationships to be cancerous. It is one of the most pervasive and undoubtedly one of the most immature and pernicious mindsets a couple can adopt. Competition is sneaky. It creeps up on you and presents itself as a false friend. What is wrong with a little friendly competition? In Willard and Marguerite Beecher's book *Beyond Success and Failure*, they outline the pitfalls of competition as they eviscerate this most time-honored of American principles. In it, the Beechers say, "One of the basic, emotional attitudes that underlie competition is the feeling of hostility: there is no such thing as friendly competition. All competition is hostile. It grows out of a desire to achieve a position of dominance and to enforce submission over others."[6] Cue the "Yeah but . . ."'s and the "What about . . ."'s Can we not play with our spouses? Are board games and playful wrestling matches a thing of the past? Are we regulated to lives where we can converse only about the weather because spirited discourse on politics, art, music, and the like are deemed too dangerous as they might incite competition? To this, the Beechers offer, "The spirit of competition is the opposite of the spirit of play. The competitive person is incapable of play for the sake of play because he must win or make a good impression."[7] I say competition in romantic relationships breeds insecurities and petty jealousies, where the face of our romantic partners, if only for a moment, becomes the face of our enemy, where vulnerability and compassion are subverted by rivalry and contention and connection is replaced by one-upmanship.

If you think this is a bridge too far in your beliefs about couples and competition, let us look at the various ways competition seeps into relationships and undermines connectivity. I routinely work with couples who fall prey to endemic rivalry and take no responsibility for it. These are couples who cannot be happy for the other's successes, cannot compromise, use ultimatums, belittle each other, lie by omission, and fight to win at all costs.

A woman once asked my wife, who is also an aspiring writer, how she felt about my book deal. "Isn't that hard for you? I think I would be jealous if it were my husband." Ashley's response was simple but to the point: "Jealousy never even occurred to me." It had never occurred to her because we both take responsibility for not competing with each other in our relationship and being genuinely happy for each of our achievements.

Two men in my practice recently adopted a baby. As if child-rearing wasn't hard enough, these partners could not compromise on anything. Whether it was feedings, type of food, diapers, childcare, or sleep schedules, you name it, and they fought over it. They used ultimatums to force the other's hand, and there was rarely, if ever, a clear victor. I let them know, however, there were very clear losers in this equation, both of them and their child.

The place where most couples experience the negative effects of competition is in the way they fight or argue. When we fight, we fight to win, even in our romantic relationships. When couples first come in, they fight like it's a sport where the prize isn't a closer connection or resolution but victory over the other, dominance, and power. What couples don't seem to understand is this is a victor-less win. Obviously, couples are going to argue and, frankly, when couples tell me they never fight, my spidey sense kicks on. It lets me know that someone is unable, unwilling, or simply afraid to share their thoughts and feelings or they have tried and their partner has proven unable to hear it. The question is not if you fight but how you fight. Fighting to win in romantic relationships simply does not work for the long term. It builds resentment and is fueled by hostility and fear. I tell couples, "If your partner loses, guess what? *You* lose, and if you truly love this person, why would you want them to lose at anything?" Can you imagine a scenario where romantic partners actually fought for each other and the relationship? A situation where the goal of a squabble was to bring partners closer to connection? Truth be told, romantic relationships should be thought of as a zero-sum game, a situation where if partners come to loggerheads, both leave the experience feeling like they gave as much as they received. The goal achieved cannot be mayhem and destruction but must be mutual respect and connection. When we are able to do this, the space between romantic partners becomes a safer place because trust is built as our mates feel profoundly seen and chosen. The only way to achieve this is to root out the endemic competition by owning it, holding ourselves accountable for it, and taking personal responsibility for when we slide into it.

The real byproduct of taking personal responsibility is trust. When we stop fighting against our partners and start fighting for them, it engenders faith and assurance. If I am not constantly looking to, in some manner, undermine or defeat my spouse, but rather build them up, I send the message that they can rely on me and they can trust me. One of the best ways to convey that message is through accountability in all its forms.

However, this is easier said than done. When I ask partners to drop the fight and pick up their responsibility, most recoil at the suggestion; they armor up and push back against me and this process. One conversation about accountability with a client went like this:

Client: "So you're asking me to take responsibility?"

Me: "Yes."

Client: "You're asking me to 'own my shit,' as you say?"

Me: "Yes."

Client: "You want me to stop trying to win the fight and accept responsibility?"

Me: "Yes."

Client: "So you want me to surrender?"

Me: "No."

Personal responsibility is not a surrender. The fear is that with the acceptance of responsibility, we lose something, that we become too permissive and open ourselves to bad behavior. It must be made clear;

personal responsibility is not about giving up ground. It is about taking the higher ground or the road less traveled. It's what Robert Frost said in his poem "The Road Not Taken": "Two roads diverged in a wood, and I took the one less traveled by, and that has made all the difference."[8] Having said this, no one can make you take responsibility. What we hold ourselves accountable for and the manner in which we do it is up to each individual. To try to make someone responsible is, in effect, taking their autonomy and their responsibility away. In every moment of our lives, we are faced with choices, two roads, as Frost says. The road of fear, or the road of love, the road of blame, or the road of responsibility. Personal responsibility is the road less traveled by, and it is also the road that will make all the difference.

19

HOW TO TAKE
PERSONAL RESPONSIBILITY

The concept of responsibility is crucial to psychotherapy—
and is pragmatically true, it "works": acceptance of it
enables the individual to achieve autonomy and his or her
full potential.

—Irvin Yalom

KEISHA AND MAY (SAME SESSION)

Both May and Keisha had the look of two people who had been caught. They now knew I was wise to their game, a game of which they perhaps were only vaguely aware. Both partners were displacing their responsibility onto the other and often onto me. Avoidance of responsibility is a common tactic in psychotherapy and relationships. However, a relationship without personal responsibility is a relationship without trust or intimacy. My comments about them doing "drive-thru" therapy had hit a nerve

"You know, Lair, I appreciate your no-bullshit approach most of the time, but this time I feel like you're just 'mansplaining' our relationship to us."

I had to admit, that one hurt. I go to great lengths to make sure I avoid the pitfalls of being a middle-aged, white, male therapist working with a diverse population. As a clinician, one of our responsibilities is to check for blind spots and unconscious bias. It is a myth that we can somehow be blind to our differences. It is one of the first things the brain acknowledges. In order for white, male, heterosexual therapists to build trust with diverse clients, we have to acknowledge the existence of our differences and name them, while at the same time be skilled enough to avoid stereotyping. All that considered, I had to ask myself: Had I inadvertently missed a blind spot with Keisha and May? Had I stepped in it with these clients and resorted to "mansplaining" to them? The mere thought of it made my skin crawl. The idea of being some tone-deaf dude holding forth with women in a condescending or patronizing manner made me shudder. Was it possible? Sure it was possible, but it was not probable, especially considering my training, my sensitivity to the issue, and the fact that I was raised in a house full of powerful women. No, this time the more probable explanation was that Keisha knew where I was going, and she was avoiding it by putting her responsibility onto me. I said, "Look, If I was in any way disrespectful or condescending, I'm deeply sorry, and I stand by what I said. I don't think you two are taking enough personal responsibility in this relationship. I would be remiss in my duty to you if I didn't say what I think. Now it may feel like I'm leaning into one or both of you from time to time, but that's part of my job." Keisha and May both shifted in their chairs at the discomfort of the situation. Sometimes you have to stand your ground with a client when they push back on you. At times they can feel like you are standing up to them when you are actually standing up for them and their relationship.

"I don't think you were mansplaining anything, Lair," May said. "I think you hit a nerve, maybe some truth?" The last part of her statement was directed toward Keisha.

May began to speak again, but I interrupted her. "I'm sorry, May, I want to hear what you're saying, but I want to make sure Keisha and I are okay."

Keisha looks up from the seam she is fiddling with on her jeans and says, "We're good." She smiles a no-nonsense grin and says, "So what part of my 'shit' am I not owning?"

I smile back at her. Two no-nonsense people had come to an understanding. I was going to say some difficult things from time to time, and she was going to give me and this process the benefit of the doubt, at least for now.

"Well, let's start with those texts to your colleague. What are your thoughts about those?" I ask.

Keisha rolls her eyes. "Oh boy, we have to start there? I don't think there is anything there to talk about. I don't have feelings for this woman!"

On the heels of Keisha's words, May quickly says, "Keisha, I saw the damn texts!"

"Well, it didn't mean anything. It was harmless flirting, May. Like you don't flirt when you're out at a bar? I've been there, and I've seen you dancing and flirting. Those women have their hands all over you, and do I say anything?"

Now a bit more reserved, May replies, "No. No, you don't, but that's because you like to see me flirting with other people—you've said it turns you on to see it. But that is precisely the difference. You are *there* to see it. It all happens in front of *you*, and in large part, it's *for you*. This stuff at work I have no experience of. I don't know this woman, and I don't know her intentions. I just know that she texts my girlfriend sexy pictures at all hours of the night."

Keisha turns to me. "And that's about as far as we get on this one. The fact is I didn't do anything. Yes, we flirted a little bit, but it was no big deal. We talk at work, and she was becoming a friend. There were no feelings on my part, and then she sent me some pictures. We didn't do anything physical."

"Well, Keisha," I reply, "I'm sorry, but I gotta push back on you with this one. You see, I'm sure everything you're saying is true; it's just not particularly helpful."

Some things between romantic partners fall under the tent of being true but not helpful, and Keisha's account of her involvement with the woman at work was one of them. It was factually true that Keisha hadn't been physically intimate with her work friend. It was true that she hadn't technically done anything wrong. However, standing on that hill of plausible deniability was a disaster waiting to happen. From there, she was denying all of May's feelings and validating none of her experience. Keisha could try to prove herself right, but it would be at the cost of alienating the person she professed to love most in the world.

"Okay, what would you have me do?" Keisha asks. "Admit to something I didn't do? I simply don't agree with her or you." May is silent but obviously frustrated with her partner. She inhales deeply in an obvious attempt to keep herself calm.

"You could try owning something," I tell Keisha. "You could try a little personal responsibility. I'd bet it would go a long way. Okay, maybe you don't feel like you cheated, but you didn't do anything to put this woman off. In fact, I'll go as far as to say you led her on a bit. Is any of that in the ballpark? Ask yourself, if you were to take responsibility for something in this, anything, what would it be?"

Keisha takes in a deep breath and looks at May. "Okay, if I'm honest, I knew she had feelings for me that went beyond friends. I knew it, and you're right; I didn't do anything to stop her. I hate to admit it, but it felt good to get the attention. I was never going to do anything. I would never cheat on you. But things between us have not been great, especially physically. It felt good feeling desired—feeling wanted. I'm sorry I hurt you."

As Keisha stopped protecting her story and started to tell her truth, something in her seemed to shift. Owning her part in this allowed her to step out of her defensive position. She dropped the armor, softened, and validated May's experience. In this crucial moment, Keisha had finally taken responsibility for the things that hurt her partner's feelings. Prior to this, their conversations on this topic outside of therapy had stalled. Today, however, was different. They had taken a small step forward.

When our partner's defenses are down, sometimes we will take this as an opportunity to strike. This is where taking responsibility for our need to win the fight becomes extremely important. If May were to use this as an opportunity to crush Keisha, if she hit her when she was open and vulnerable, all of the traction we had gained this day would be lost. Keisha's defenders would come out fighting, or she would go into a protective shell, and untold amounts of trust would be lost. "Apologies call for a continued balance between accountability and acceptance. They call for compassion for the apologizer toward their self, as well as compassion for the apologizer from the other person. It's a dual process; it's also a continual one."[1]

May wanted to respond, but I needed her to do it mindfully and carefully while still delivering her truth. "May, I'm going to guess you've got something to say, but, if you can, I'd like you to try and use the strategies you've learned. Take your time, take a breath but ask yourself what thoughts and feelings are in there? What part of you is present? What stories are you telling, if any?"

This might sound overly "coachy," because it is. As I said, this was a pivotal point for these two. This couple needed to know what it was like to have this conversation in a new way and know they could experience a unique outcome. Now it was May's chance to practice personal responsibility by pushing herself to tell her truth but do it skillfully. Anything less would be a recapitulation of what brought them into my office in the first place.

May took yet another breath to steady herself and to get into her body. "I'm not going to lie, I'm a lot of things right now, and I just want to say them out loud. First, I'm angry that it took this long for you to finally say that. I've felt incredibly unsafe. It has been crazy-making for you to deny what has really been going on. *But*, and it's a big but, I'm also thankful that you finally owned it. Look, I get it. It's nice to be noticed. I find other people attractive, too, and I like it when they pay attention to me. And let's face it, there is room for some of that in our relationship. We blur that line a bit, but I only feel safe when we do it together. And that is especially true when things between us have not been great physically."

"Is there any part of this you can own?" I ask her.

May replies, "I can own that I have not felt great in my body lately and I have not felt very sexual. I intended to tell her about how I was feeling and to make sure she knew it wasn't about her, but I didn't. I need to communicate with her more."

There is no arguing that both of these women had the best of intentions when it came to their partner and their relationship. However, this is where I find so many couples, mired in the argument over their good intentions and never really owning how they made their partners feel.

THE BEST OF INTENTIONS

He watched as she tried desperately to hide her disappointment, not sure how he'd managed to fuck this up. She had complained on several occasions that he never did special things for her, but today he had finally done the thing and bought her flowers. As he bought them, he thought of how much he loved her and how much she meant to him. But when he got home, his girlfriend's initial delight at the sight of the bouquet was quickly replaced with dejection. He'd had the best of intentions when he purchased them, but, in the end, they were yellow flowers.

She had told him several times how much she hated yellow flowers. In a few intimate and important conversations that lasted well into the night, she shared the deep pain she associated with that color flower. They reminded her of the wallpaper in her childhood bathroom, a place where she would run and hide out as a child when her mom and dad would fight, and later when her stepfather would come home drunk. She'd stared at that floral pattern for hours that seemed to stretch into days.

When she became hurt and then angry by his gesture, my client, her boyfriend, said in his session, "But I bought flowers. She asked for flowers, and I bought them. Why can't she just be happy that I made the effort? Why does she have to be so damn picky?"

Was his girlfriend uptight and picky? Could she have simply focused on the fact that he made the effort? Could she have smiled and accepted the gift, knowing he had the best of intentions? Sure, an argument could be made. However, this would be asking her to bury her feelings, and my client would miss an opportunity to truly know and understand his partner. Silencing her real feelings and accepting the gift would be a patronizing pat on the head for my client that said, "Nice try" or "You did the best you could." I, for one, thought he should hold himself to a higher standard than that.

My client had bought his girlfriend flowers. That was factually true. The fact that he did it with the best of intentions was also true. However, these facts are immaterial and, like with Keisha and May, fall into the category of true but not necessarily helpful. There are innumerable examples of when couples have argued over hurt feelings and best intentions. These are situations where one partner has tried to the best of their ability to fulfill an expectation or a promise only to have life swoop in and somehow impede their stated objective. In cases like these, partners become polarized. One of them feels hurt and disappointed because their efforts were not seen. The other feels much the same way because their needs were not met.

The answer to these conundrums is personal responsibility. Like my client and his flowers, we can get caught up in what our intentions were. The fact is, our intentions and our feelings about our intentions are all about us and overlook the disappointment felt on the other side. Arguing for our intentions might seem legitimate, even logical. However, most people fail to understand that when we argue for our intentions, we make the other person feel like they have no right to feel the way they do. Have you ever tried telling someone who is feeling strong emotion to stop feeling what they are feeling? How did that go?

My client had it backward, as so many of us do. If he had simply acknowledged his faux pas, said he was sorry, and/or spoken to his girlfriend's experience, all could have been saved. Holding ourselves accountable for the hurt feelings is of paramount importance. It should be mentioned that this in no way invalidates our good intentions. In fact, when we take personal responsibility, it paves the way and clears the lens, so to speak, so our intentions can be seen and understood.

CIRCLE BACK AND SAY IT FIRST

Circling back and saying it first means we intentionally bring up a topic that is not currently on the table. It is usually an issue both partners are aware of but for various reasons are not speaking about. These topics can span the gamut from mundane, day-to-day issues that can be couched as mildly annoying to much larger problems that threaten the survival of the relationship itself. A common problem in this day and age is cell phone use or screens coming between and stealing time and attention away from romantic partners. Let's say you've begun to recognize that you have spent more face-to-face time with your phone than your mate. Thus far they haven't said anything, though you are quite sure they've noticed. Circling back and saying it first would mean acknowledging the issue with your partner by calling yourself out preemptively before feelings get hurt and emotions run high. In this example, you could say, "Hey, I know I've been on my phone too much. I also know I haven't been as connective lately because of it. This isn't healthy for us, and I want to call myself out before you have to." When you speak to an issue that has gone unspoken but is obviously sitting between you, you afford your partner an opportunity to talk about their feelings. Owning it in this way gives them permission to call you out on it in the future. This type of personal responsibility resets the bar on "adulting" in the relationship and makes the space between us safer for this type of discourse.

It never feels like a perfect time to circle back and say it first. Clients will say, "I didn't bring it up this week because things were going so well, and I didn't want to ruin it." This is often followed by "Well, I didn't bring it up this week either because things were not going very well, and I didn't want to make it worse." There will always be a good reason not to own our bad behavior, especially if there isn't someone calling us on it. This *is* a preemptive strike on ourselves, and although some part of us knows it to be an important and necessary step, it runs contrary to all of our basic instincts to defend and to win.

I'll admit this one is not easy. To call attention to a behavior we need to change, or one that has caused our partner some level of pain or discomfort is like throwing ourselves under the proverbial bus, and most of us don't know how to do it or wouldn't want to if we could.

Having said all that, circling back and saying it first has extraordinary healing potential. When we take personal responsibility on this level, we save our partners from having to do it for us. It says there is an adult in the room, I got your back, and it is safe to be vulnerable here; I'm playing a zero-sum game, that I am thinking of "we" and not "me," and it is an incredible act of choosing.

Circling back and saying it first has proven to be an elixir of healing, especially for the clients I work with who have experienced a profound breach of trust. These kinds of breaches are often acts of infidelity but can also include hidden addictions, secret spending, the loss of large sums of money, or some form of larger-scale lying.

For those that try to work things out, infractions on this level leave partners wondering how or if they can ever trust again. One of the best and most healing exercises in these situations is circling back and saying it first. I tell clients who have transgressed to this degree, do not be afraid to talk about what they've done. I encourage them to bring it up often and especially in those moments when it is obvious you are both thinking about it. Again, this runs counter to our every instinct. However, when we take the initiative to call it out, our partners know it is on our mind, that we are not hoping it goes away and that it is okay to talk about it. When we are unafraid to broach subjects that have been deemed taboo, off-limits, or dangerous, it takes the charge off of the matter and brings that issue out into the light of day, and it puts us in the waiting room of healing.

THIS IS HARD

There is an old story of a potato farmer who hired a new helper to work on his farm. The hired hand was amazing and proficient at all that he did. When he was put to work sawing wood, he cut more logs in one day than anyone ever had. The next day he was sent to mend the fences surrounding the farmer's property. Just as he had with the wood, the helper mended more fences in a single day than anyone could have imagined. The farmer then put him to work sorting his main crop, giving him arguably one of the most important jobs on the farm. His instructions were to put the potatoes in one of three bins, the bin for selling, the bin for planting, or the bin for disposal. After the day was through, the hired hand came to the farmer and said, "I'm sorry, but I have to quit." The farmer began to panic at the prospect of losing his best worker. "What can I do?" the farmer exclaimed. "I'll do anything. I'll double your pay." "No, this job isn't for me," the hand replied. "I'm fine chopping wood and mending fences, but this potato business is decision, after decision, after decision."[2]

Personal responsibility is hard. Accepting the mantle of ownership and accountability often proves to be too much for some. Most people understand its importance in theory but, like the hired hand, shy away from actually doing it. This is especially so in romantic relationships. It's easy to shirk responsibility and hope our partner picks up the slack. In other areas of our lives, accountability seems a less jagged pill. At work, for instance, a number of my clients are hard-chargers when it comes to owning things. There is a budding ethos in the corporate world around accepting personal responsibility. In some circles, it is taught as a professional skill because it is viewed as a strength and powerful way to manage people. There are articles, books, talks, and training on the advantages of taking personal responsibility in the workplace. However, being held accountable for someone's hurt feelings is another matter altogether and is where this practice falls desperately short. Responsibility is synonymous with blame. Short on the heels of blame comes shame and a sense that we've gotten it all wrong. For the ego, this is an experience tantamount to death. Personal responsibility is a direct threat to our self-concept that creates a state called "cognitive dissonance." Cognitive dissonance is the stress we experience when we hold two conflicting thoughts, beliefs, feelings, or opinions. For example, you might consider yourself to be a kind, loving, and thoughtful person, only to be surprised when your mate's feelings are hurt by something you did or said that they deemed thoughtless or inconsiderate. Your partner's feelings challenge your beliefs about who you are. The anxiety created by these two opposing understandings is your cognitive dissonance, and you will employ all manner of defense in order to shirk responsibility, relieve this stress, and salvage your self-concept.[3] This is the place where so many couples struggle. However, when we learn to push past our natural inclination to fight or run and instead own and validate, moments that once served to divide us now bring us together.

Personal responsibility is challenging. What tends to make it even more difficult is the notion that we might have to agree with our partners when maybe we actually don't. There are plenty of occasions when couples find themselves at odds due to lack of agreement. One partner might think, for example, that their mate was being intentionally hurtful during an argument. From this point, the tennis match is on. Back and forth, over and over the same ground: "You said . . .," "No I didn't," "Yes, you did," "Well, that's not how I said it." I cannot tell you how many couples come through my door locked in battles like this. The fix is to understand that empathy for someone's feelings does not require agreement. Most people think they are arguing over the details in any given situation, but that view is shortsighted. What couples are actually arguing over in these moments are feelings. Here is a simple but effective rule; if someone tells you their feelings have been hurt, they probably have been. It does you little to no good to argue that fact. It is important to validate that your partner's feelings have been hurt and understand that on some level you had something to do with it. Like it or not, in relationships we are charged with validating our partner's feelings, even when we don't agree with why they feel the way they do. When you start with validation, the difficult practice of personal responsibility becomes very easy.

MAY AND KEISHA'S PRACTICE

Keisha and May were two people having thoughts, feelings, and experiences that ran counter to who they believed themselves to be. Both were having feelings that their partner didn't want to validate. For Keisha to own that she let her work relationship go too far meant she was admitting that she had danced dangerously close to being unfaithful. Explaining her behavior away as "no big deal" or standing on the faulty ground of plausible deniability was far preferable to taking responsibility for the hurt feelings she had created in her partner.

Alternately, May's feelings about her body had manifested in a lack of communication and connectivity in the bedroom. Nearing forty, May was beginning to see changes in her body that she was having a hard time dealing with. She had always been in top physical shape and had felt sexy and attractive. These new feelings ran counter to how she had seen herself and resulted in her shutting down sexually to her partner.

These women moved out of their defensive positions into a place of compassion and empathy for the other when they learned to point the finger back at themselves and take responsibility. They began implementing strategies like circling back and saying it first as well as recognizing when their good intentions were true but not necessarily helpful. They tried seeing their relationship as a zero-sum game and from a "we" perspective rather than a "me." All of this served to salve the pain that originally brought them through the door.

Historically, this is where Keisha and May would disappear only to resurface when they once again hit a rough patch. However, this time was different. Emboldened by the feelings of closeness they found through personal responsibility and some light urging from me, Keisha and May decided to continue with their work and try to deepen their bond. They began to entertain a closeness that went beyond the warm feelings found when they made up after an argument and even dared to ask for more than the "good enough connectivity" found in so many mundane and unfulfilling relationships.

In addition to using the exercises offered earlier in this chapter, Keisha and May accepted the challenge that is offered at large in this book, to take responsibility for using the first four practices of Mindfulness, Parts of Self, the Narrative, and Choosing. As they did, they moved out of their knee-jerk responses, began showing up in their wise selves, formed more compassionate narratives, and began loving each other the way they each needed to be loved. It wasn't that problems didn't come up because they did. It simply meant that when issues presented themselves, this couple had a game plan, tools and skills they could employ, and a road map that helped them find the true north of their relationship. Ultimately, I saw less and less of Keisha and May. As they became more proficient at using my system, they simply did not need me as much. It's strange, but a part of my job description is to make my job obsolete. My intention is to help clients find a sense of resilience and self-sufficiency that rarely calls for weekly guidance.

These are the gifts that come with personal responsibility. They are not acquired by osmosis or by moving passively through your life or your relationship. They are gained in the effort it takes to push past your comfort level and the status quo. Rather than getting caught in the crossfire of finger-pointing, the "how" of personal responsibility is about the willingness to own everything you did or did not do and everything you said or did not say. We need to understand that no matter our intent, we may still hurt the ones we love and for that, we must hold ourselves accountable rather than wait to be called out. Often, in conjunction with the term "responsibility," we use the word "accept," saying we must "accept our responsibility." I think acceptance is difficult for the Western mind. Acceptance is viewed as a pejorative term synonymous with surrender or giving up or giving in. From this perspective, anything we accept, we do so reluctantly or apprehensively with our tail tucked. In the implementation of this practice, we experience a shift in connotation for these concepts. This represents a metamorphosis in perspective and thinking and takes both the terms "acceptance" and "personal responsibility" out of the realm of the shameful and derogatory and into the province of the heroic and intrepid.

WHAT IF THEY REFUSE TO OWN IT?

What if someone cannot make that perspective shift? What if one partner refuses to take personal responsibility in their relationship? Sometimes I run into people who will not or cannot buy into the idea that accountability is good for their relationship. Instead, they adhere to blaming, judging, finger-pointing, and lecturing, again and again resisting both mine and their partner's entreaties to own their part. They do this for many reasons ranging from simple stubbornness and selfishness to protection of self and fear of vulnerability. Whatever the reason, the effects are the same: it leaves their partner angry, hurt, and frustrated, questioning the viability of the relationship—and question its viability they should. If your partner stays steadfast in their willingness to foist their responsibility onto you, you essentially have two choices. First, you could stay in the relationship, however, it will be necessary to adjust your expectations of your mate and the amount of accountability they will take on. You will have to remember the inherent unfairness of your relationship and that you and your partner have essentially agreed to play by a different set of rules. Second, you can leave and find a partner who is willing to work on themselves and their wounding in order to meet you in the place of equitable ownership of personal responsibility. This might sound too cut-and-dry, possibly too harsh, but in my experience, there is no healing for a relationship where partners refuse to hold themselves personally responsible for what they do and what they say.

20

CONCLUSION

Absorb what is useful, discard what is useless, and add what
is specifically your own.

—Bruce Lee

Throughout this book, I have referenced the notion of creating a
relational culture, the idea that when romantic partners come together, they forge a culture with its own behaviors, norms, and customs.
Most of the time, this is done tacitly. Most of the time, we rely upon
assumptions and expectations. We do this with little to no conversation
or bargain, save a few of the bigger-ticket issues such as money, sex, the
kids, or religious affiliations. Some couples engage in premarital counseling. However, in my experience, most of those lessons don't make it
beyond their allotted number of sessions. We are comfortable enough in
our dopamine haze to leave the boundaries of how we behave and communicate up to the presumption that love conquers all, and if we love
each other enough, everything will work out. Those old sayings prove
brittle and unreliable outside of the limerence of new love.

Imagine for a moment two people standing, facing in opposite
directions, with a large soup pot between them. Each is reading from
a recipe on how to be in a relationship. Each has brought their recipe
from past relationships and their families of origin. Each is mindlessly and
with little discussion throwing ingredients blindly over their shoulders
and into the relational pot hoping against hope that it all works out,
that the ingredients will somehow blend and that the soup will taste
good. If we were actually making soup together, we would discuss the

ingredients. We would talk about the carrots, the onions, and the peas. In the same respect, we should make mindful decisions about what goes into the cultural soup of our romantic relationships. We should come to terms with how we interact, communicate, and relate to each other and how we handle each other's thoughts, feelings, and beliefs. If concrete decisions on these aspects prove too difficult, we should at the very least have a framework to operate from. The Five Practices offer that framework. Life will provide suffering in all its forms, and couples should have a plan of action, a tool kit, and a practice that will sustain them through their struggles. Couples can stand the test of time, and they can do it with their love and their reverence for each other intact. They can learn to manage mistakes and missteps with kindness and compassion, and they can learn to ford the gap created by poor communication and love embargoes. All of this is made possible through this process and this practice. However, it all hinges on one thing: You've gotta want to. You've gotta want to bad, and you have to want to when everything inside tells you to blow it up and let it go. You have to want to more than you want to be right and more than you want to win. If you don't, these practices will bring you only nominal success at best. When I think of this truth, I feel so incredibly fortunate to have been challenged both personally and professionally to bring these practices together and offer them not only to my clients but also to myself and my partner. If I had not, I, too, would be, as John O'Donohue put it, left to "linger in the lowlands of complacency and partial fulfillment."[1]

A long time ago, I was told never to ask a client to walk a path you are unwilling to walk yourself. If you decide to take up this challenge in your relationship and put your feet to this path, know that I am on the path with you, navigating my mistakes and missteps, my mindlessness and wounded parts, forever trying to own my shit and do it a little better tomorrow than I did it today. With this, I honor you, your effort, and your process. I encourage you to practice. I say practice well and practice badly but practice every day and practice all of the time.

21

PERSONAL RESPONSIBILITY EXERCISES

> When you're practicing accountability, you adopt a viewpoint that says, no matter what happens to me, it is my responsibility to manage my own feelings and behavior. I make my own decisions and have choices about almost everything. I am only a victim if I choose to be one.
>
> —Karyl McBride

Practicing personal responsibility is a call to action. It might feel dangerous and, from time to time, things can get messier before they get better. When the goal is to create new habits and ways of interacting, the old ways must first die. Whenever we invite change on this level, we also invite the possibility of discomfort. However, the connection and trust that is produced from this practice is well worth it. Some of these exercises can be performed on your own; however, a few will need time set aside with your partner. Still others will require use in the moment, meaning, you might have to wait to execute them when the opportunity arises. For those exercises, keep them in your back pocket, as it were, and be mindful of your intention to use the tool or skill so as not to miss your chance. From here I ask that you practice and practice well.

APOLOGIZING WELL

Learning to apologize effectively is an important aspect of being personally responsible in a relationship. When we are unafraid to take accountability for our mistakes, it tells our partners that the space between us is a safer one, that they are with an adult and that their feelings matter to us. For this exercise think of a time in your relationship where you might not have apologized when you needed to, or a time when you could have apologized more effectively by taking on more responsibility. Below are several elements that make for compelling apologies. Either through meditation or in your journal, run through your "I'm sorry" scenario. Note where you might take more responsibility with your mate in the future by using these tools.

Expression of Empathy, Validation, and Regret

Apologies are easier when you agree that your words or deeds caused pain. It is another matter when you do not agree you are at fault. The good news is that you do not actually have to agree with the person you hurt to try to understand their pain and validate their suffering. Empathy does not require that we see eye to eye on the subject we are arguing over; it simply means that you acknowledge that your partner is suffering and that what you did or said had a hand in their pain. You might say something like, "I'm so sorry that what I did or said hurt you." The beauty of this statement is that we acknowledge their pain without getting caught up in our intentions. As I covered in Practice 5, our intentions might have been good, but that is not always helpful, at least not at first. Our first step is to express our empathy for their pain, as well as validation of their right to have their experience.

Explanation of Where I Went Wrong and How I Hurt Your Feelings

This is an opportunity to truly accept your responsibility. Beyond acknowledging our partner's pain, this step says I see where my actions caused your suffering and I am willing to own it by saying so. Apologies fall short when they only include the obligatory "I'm sorry" or the dreaded "I'm sorry *you* feel that way." We take it a step further when we explain where we went wrong. In chapter 18's "A Boiling Pot" section, I said, "I *did* hear him screaming. I should have come in to help you, and I didn't. I didn't want to deal with it, and I left you hanging. But more than anything I never, *never* should have spoken to you that way." This was a full-scale acknowledgment of where I went wrong and how I hurt my partner's feelings. Often we will avoid saying it out loud and stating our transgression. However, if we are unwilling to name it, it can play as if we are not sincere. When we explain where we went wrong and how we hurt our partner's feelings, it says you do not have to convince me that I hurt you, which is incredibly validating because it acknowledges responsibility.

Explanation of Why the Violation Occurred

You would be shocked at how far saying, "I was just tired," "frustrated from work," "stressed," or "simply being a big jerk" can go in an apology. When you state that you are aware of where your bad behavior came from, it means you have given it some thought instead of not firing off admission of guilt so your partner will leave you alone. This part of the apology also demonstrates that you are willing to call the penalty on yourself. Note, this is not an opportunity to make an excuse for bad behavior. This is a chance to own the origins of what you did or said.

A Plan for Repair

When you ask if there is anything you can do to make things right, you help the healing process along. It shows that you are willing to go the extra mile and change your behavior in an effort to protect your partner's feelings. The next-best step is to follow through and actually do those things.

Request for Forgiveness

This step may be more than you need for small infractions but it is a must for the larger ones. Having said that, you cannot expect everyone to come around in your time. When you add the statement "When you are ready," or "When it feels right for you" to your request for forgiveness, it shows that you are not making this apology so that your mate will relieve your guilt.

If empathy means being willing and able to put yourself in someone else's shoes to better understand their pain, compassion is the want to do something about that pain. A good apology is a great step in that direction. It should be noted that all of these steps are important, but what might be most important is your intention. Apologies need to be from the heart if they are to be effective.

STEPS TO A COMPELLING APOLOGY

When considering your apology, take into account the following:

- Where could you express more empathy?
- Where can you offer more validation for your partner's experience?
- What do you regret most about your behavior and what would you change if you could?
- Why did you behave the way you did? Remember, this is not a chance for excuses.
- What would you like to do better in the future?
- Request forgiveness.

RESPONSIBLE COMMUNICATION

As we learned in Practice 2, good communication begins with mindfully paying attention to our thoughts and feelings as well as knowing what part of self shows up to that conversation. Practice 5, Personal Responsibility, asks us to own a little bit more when we are attempting to connect with our partners over historically difficult subjects. For this exercise consider your last heated or difficult discussion with your partner. Now, either through meditation or in your journal, consider how you might have taken a bit more responsibility in that communication.

Steps

This is not an exercise in what your partner did wrong but in what you could have owned and what you might take responsibility for in the future. As best as you can, remember a difficult discussion with your partner. Bring to mind what you were thinking and feeling.

Using what you have learned about your parts, name what part or parts of you were present.

- What parts of self could you have invited into the discussion?
- What could you have done to ensure that the wisest, most emotionally intelligent parts came to that discourse?
- Were you engaged in any negative storytelling about your mate or their intentions toward you?
- Can you own any competition or a need to win the argument?
- What would have changed if you moved from a "me" centered way of thinking to a "we" centered way of thinking?
- Were you listening with a mind that could have been changed?
- What would have been different if you had taken responsibility for trying to connect with your partner through this communication?
- Now try to use these same personal responsibility techniques in your next difficult or emotional communication with your partner. You don't have to use all of them; just try a few and notice what happens.

PERSONAL RESPONSIBILITY FOR PROBLEMATIC PATTERNS IN COMMUNICATION: WHAT *NOT* TO DO

Which of the following do *you* need to take responsibility for? Check the box next to the statements that *you* need to work on and change.

- ☐ I finish sentences for my partner.
- ☐ I tend to dismiss my partner's feelings if I don't agree with them.
- ☐ I will stop my partner in mid-sentence if I don't agree with them.
- ☐ I fight to win.
- ☐ When I do apologize, I also use the "but"; for example, "I'm sorry for what I said *but* I said it because you made me angry."
- ☐ I'm unable to show empathy, especially when I'm hurt or angry.
- ☐ I don't often think of things from my partner's position.
- ☐ I rarely stop and ask what part of me is present.
- ☐ I don't listen with a mind that is open to change.
- ☐ I repeat myself often.

- ☐ When I don't understand what my partner is saying, I don't ask for clarification.
- ☐ I postpone bringing up difficult topics and I hope they will just go away.
- ☐ I talk over my partner.
- ☐ I escalate arguments when I'm angry.
- ☐ I blame and attack my partner.
- ☐ I use global language: "You always . . .," "You never . . ."
- ☐ I don't stop and attune to my partner.
- ☐ I rarely lead with my curiosity about my partner's experience.
- ☐ I try to avoid or end conversations that don't interest me.
- ☐ When I feel misunderstood, I escalate.
- ☐ I bring up my complaints when I'm angry.
- ☐ I have a hard time talking about my feelings.
- ☐ I compete for the victim position.

CIRCLING BACK AND SAYING IT FIRST

This exercise requires a ton of personal responsibility and a fair bit of courage. It requires these because it asks us to bring up a subject that is not currently on the table. It means mentioning an issue that some parts of us would say is better left alone. This is a topic that you don't want to broach because it has the potential to ruin what might otherwise be a perfectly good day or could make an already bad day even worse. For this exercise think of a topic or a situation that feels difficult or is left unfinished between you and your partner. This could be anything from a tough discussion about money, sex, the kids, or a breach of trust, or something as small as mentioning that you didn't like the way you spoke to them last night at dinner. Whatever the matter, make sure it is something that is important to your mate and is an area where you feel you could own more responsibility.

Steps

Circle back on a subject that is important, especially to your partner, that is left unfinished or has been historically difficult for you as a

couple. Notice your thoughts, feelings, parts of self, and narratives that come up around this subject. What aspect of these interactions can you own? Examples could include:

- I shut down emotionally.
- I become very defended.
- I don't want to talk about it so I get angry.
- I tell a story in my head that is unfair, untrue, or lacks compassion.
- I often fight to win on this topic.
- I have not listened with an open mind.
- I am only thinking about myself.
- I filibuster the conversation.
- I have behaved in the manner I have because a part of me knows you won't say anything.
- I have not chosen you in this.
- I am moving through fear and not love.

Now that you have the aspect you want to take responsibility for, it's time to bring it up. You can start by saying as an example, "Hey, I know that sex, money, the kids have been difficult topics and I want to start by owning that I have not been an open-minded listener and I have only thought about myself in this."

The tough part is saying it first. You might feel some internal pushback around talking about this issue. However, very often when one partner shows a willingness to broach historically difficult subjects and takes responsibility, there is an immense amount of validation that happens. Often with this validation comes an opening and a softening. Having said that, be warned, there is a good chance your partner will not know how to react the first time you try this exercise. Circling back and saying it first might represent a dramatic shift in the way you have typically interacted. Also, your partner may have some pent-up feelings that come pouring out now that they have the green light to share them. If this happens remember to validate their experience.

Next, when applicable, use the tools offered in the "Apologize Well" section to attempt to make amends where necessary.

THE SMARTEST PERSON IN THE ROOM

Competition between romantic partners can seep in fast. Before we know it, we can go from a relationship of passion and compassion to one of rivalry and one-upmanship. Leaving room for your partner to be the smartest person in the room helps root out problematic competitiveness that can steal the softness between partners. It makes us take a pause to truly take our partners in. We can see for the first time, or for the first time in a long time, what makes them special when we stand back and let them shine. I learned this one firsthand as I wrote this book. Ashley has edited the vast majority of its content. In the process of writing, I found myself pushing back on her suggestions. I saw myself getting protective and competitive over word choices and placement of concepts. At one point I remembered a practice I use with couples where you let your partner be the smartest person in the room. When I did it, I was amazed at what came out both on the page and between us. At once I saw again her talent and her intellect shine through. What was more, I think it made this book that much stronger. This is a practice to take with you and to use in the moment.

Steps

Whenever you and your mate are at odds or of differing opinions, step back, take a breath, and mindfully make room for your partner to be the smartest person in the room. Let them shine and be in the spotlight. Notice what comes up for you.

- Pay attention to your thoughts and feelings as your partner speaks.
- Notice what happens when they say something you do not agree with.
- Pay attention to any parts of you that come up that are spoiling for a fight.
- Ask those parts to step aside.
- Notice what happens when you don't push back or you let go of any attachment you've had to being right or winning the argument.

- Ask clarifying questions that come from curiosity and not a competitive edge, such as, "What was that like for you?" "How did that feel?" "Where did you learn that?"
- This exercise is the essence of nonreactivity.

"ME" TO "WE"

In this exercise, you are to take a look at your relationship and consider where you have been too self-focused or even selfish. It is a chance to notice where you might need to be more generous with your mate. As I said earlier, when we argue we can become quite contracted. When a relationship becomes oppositional and we feel a need to compete to have our feelings considered, we start taking things off of the table and become less open and less magnanimous. Answer the following questions as honestly and as self-critically as you can. Even if you have not been particularly self-focused, we can still fall into these traps. These questions can help you move from a "me"-centered mindset to a "we"-centered mindset.

Steps

Set aside some time with your partner to ask these evocative questions. About forty-five minutes should be enough. Please take a minute to invite your most loving and wisest selves to this exercise. Take turns asking each other these questions. Alternately, you can answer these questions in written form and then share them with your partner.

- Are there subjects or instances in our relationship that I need to circle back on, apologize or take responsibility for?
- Do I shy away from difficult conversations and, if so, what are they? These would be subjects that either you or your mate is uncomfortable with, topics that cause difficult feelings, anger, shame, or embarrassment. These are issues that "we" need to talk about and resolve to make a better relationship but make you or "me" uncomfortable in some manner.

- Are there any issues between us where I am buying into my good intentions rather than listening to how you feel?
- Do I fight fair? Is our relationship a zero-sum game?
- Do I engage in love embargoes when I am hurt, frustrated, or angry?
- Is there any area of our relationship where I could take more personal responsibility?

These are not easy questions. They are not meant to push buttons but to facilitate open and honest communication. If this exercise causes an argument or a fight, one or both of you is not showing up in your wisest and most emotionally mature parts. Refer to Practice 2 if this becomes problematic.

WILDERNESS CAMP EXERCISE

When I was thirty, my life imploded. I was overweight, drinking too much, and smack in the middle of a divorce. I decided I needed to strip it all away and went to a wilderness camp for adults. Two weeks of no showers, pooping outside, cold food, no coffee, no booze, sleeping in the snow in the North Carolina mountains in November, and, oh yeah, lots of personal responsibility. There was one exercise in particular that stayed with me. Every morning we would get up and set our intention for the day. It might be nonjudgment, mindful communication, anger management, learning acceptance, practicing compassion, or simply not kicking the shit out of ourselves internally. Whatever the prime directive was, at the end of the day we would process. In that process group, fellow campers would let you know how they thought you did. It was enlightening and sometimes hard, but we helped hold one another accountable for what we wanted to change in our lives and it made a difference. It especially made a difference to know that at the end of every day we were going to have to talk about how we did. It is in this light that I offer you this exercise.

Steps

- Set a time for this exercise with your partner. You will need twenty to thirty minutes to discuss the initial phase of this exercise.
- *First Meeting*—Set an intention for the week. It could be any of the intentions I offered in the introduction to this exercise, something of your own, or one of the first four practices. For example, you could take responsibility for your mindfulness or attunement, your parts of self, or your narrative. You could also decide to be more accountable for choosing your partner, be less competitive, or move from a "me" mindset to a "we" one. Whatever aspect you choose to own, those are your marching orders for the week. You are to take full and 100 percent responsibility for the execution of this intention. No excuses, it is all on you.
- At the end of your first meeting, set a time for your follow-up meeting, five to seven days after the first.
- During the week, keep a journal of how it is going. Make notes of points at which you notice a difference in your behavior and how it seemed to register in your mate. Also, record when it was hard or you felt you might have stumbled or forgotten your intention altogether.
- *Second Meeting*—Your second meeting is a time to talk about how the exercise went. Discuss in general your experience. What did you find challenging? What did you learn?
- Then ask your partner how they feel you did with respect to your intention.
- When you are offering your assessment of your partner's effort, it is not a time to argue or to be hurtful. This is a time to offer constructive criticism. If it is possible, front-load your critique with what they did well. Then gently offer encouragement in the areas they struggled.
- When it is time for you to receive your partner's assessment, invite your wisest self to the table and hold as open a mind as possible. This is an opportunity to allow your partner to be the smartest person in the room.

CULTURAL SOUP

Like companies and sports teams, couples need to have a mission statement, a shared vision of what their relationship is going to look like.
In my experience, it is a rare couple that actually does. Most assume
their partner has the same outlook, ideals, boundaries of behavior, and
understanding of how we treat each other and communicate. Many
couples are, like my cultural soup analogy, backs to each other, blindly
throwing ingredients over their shoulders into the relational pot, hoping the final product is a good one. In this exercise I have couples turn
toward each other. Here they mindfully and with intention decide
what will go and what will not go into their relational culture. This
is a time to discuss which behaviors are acceptable and which are not.
It is a time to be honest with your partner and with yourself, to take
responsibility as well as to request it.

Steps

- Set aside some time to work on this exercise. You will need
  about an hour.
- Remember you and your partner are not necessarily writing laws
  or rules but agreements. Agreements mean both partners choose
  this and both agree to do the best they can to follow through.
- First, begin with what you would like to do better. What areas
  are you aware of that you need to work on? For example, you
  can agree not to lose your cool and storm out of the room.
  Instead, if you need a break, you will practice a mindful leave
  where you set a time to return. Storming out is not a part of
  our relational culture. Another example might be name-calling
  or speaking disrespectfully toward each other. Here you might
  decide that name-calling is out of bounds and no longer a part of
  your relational culture and will not be accepted.
- After stating what you would like to work on personally, it
  is time to request something you need your partner to take
  responsibility for. These requests can look something like this:
  "In the interest of making our connection better, I would like

to ask that you take more responsibility for the way you communicate when you're angry." Or: "I would like to request that when you say you are going to be home at a certain time, that you are realistic about that time and that if you are going to be late you let me know."

- When you are the person receiving the request, do your best to show up in the wise self, listen with an open mind, and practice letting your partner be the smartest person in the room.
- At the end do a check-in to see how each partner is feeling. If there is anything left to process, give those subjects some time to be expressed and validated.

NOTES

CHAPTER 1. WHAT IS MINDFULNESS?

1. "Ellen Langer: Mindfulness over Matter." Pop Tech, YouTube, November 5, 2013. www.youtube.com/watch?v=4XQUJR4uIGM.
2. Poerio, Giulia L., Peter Totterdell, and Eleanor Miles. "Mind-Wandering and Negative Mood: Does One Thing Really Lead to Another?" *Consciousness and Cognition* 22, no. 4 (2013): 1412–21. doi:10.1016/j.concog.2013.09.012.

CHAPTER 2. WHY IS MINDFULNESS SO IMPORTANT FOR COUPLES?

1. Pang, Jo. "How Mindfulness Transforms." YouTube, June 13, 2018. https://www.youtube.com/watch?v=9gi2ER4pSaU.
2. Taren, A. A., J. D. Creswell, and P. J. Gianaros. "Dispositional Mindfulness Co-Varies with Smaller Amygdala and Caudate Volumes in Community Adults." *PLoS One*, May 22, 2013: 8(5): e64574. doi: 10.1371/journal .pone.0064574. PMID: 23717632; PMCID: PMC3661490.
3. Poe, Edgar Allan, and Edwin Markham. *The Works of Edgar Allan Poe.* Funk & Wagnalls, 1904.
4. Dispenza, Joe. *Breaking the Habit of Being Yourself: How to Lose Your Mind and Create a New One.* Hay House, 2016.
5. Doyle, Glennon. *Love Warrior: A Memoir.* Two Roads, 2017.
6. Siegel, Daniel J. *The Mindful Therapist: A Clinician's Guide to Mindsight and Neural Integration.* Norton, 2010.

CHAPTER 3. HOW TO PRACTICE
MINDFULNESS IN YOUR RELATIONSHIP

1. Spoon, M. "Meditation Affects Brain Networks Differently in Long-Term Meditators and Novices." News.wisc.edu. https://news.wisc.edu/meditation-affects-brain-networks-differently-in-long-term-meditators-and-novices/. Accessed March 20, 2021.

2. Johanson, Gregory J., and Ron Kurtz. *Grace Unfolding: Psychotherapy in the Spirit of the Tao-te ching*. Harmony Books, 1991.

3. Thích Nhất Hạnh. *Fidelity: How to Create a Loving Relationship That Lasts*. Parallax Press, 2011.

CHAPTER 4. MINDFULNESS EXERCISES

1. Thích Nhất Hạnh. *Fear: Essential Wisdom for Getting through the Storm*. HarperOne, 2014.

CHAPTER 5. WHAT ARE OUR PARTS?

1. Brown, Brené. *Daring Greatly: How the Courage to Be Vulnerable Transforms the Way We Live, Love, Parent, and Lead*. Penguin, 2012.

2. Hendrix, Harville, and Helen Hunt. *Getting the Love You Want: A Guide for Couples*. Simon & Schuster UK, 2020.

3. Bradshaw, John. *Healing the Shame That Binds You*. Health Communications, 2015.

4. Borderline Personality Disorder (BPD) is a condition characterized by difficulties regulating emotion. This means that people who experience BPD feel emotions intensely and for extended periods of time, and it is harder for them to return to a stable baseline after an emotionally triggering event. This difficulty can lead to impulsivity, poor self-image, stormy relationships, and intense emotional responses to stressors. Struggling with self-regulation can also result in dangerous behaviors such as self-harm.

CHAPTER 6. WHY ARE OUR PARTS SO IMPORTANT?

1. Johanson, Gregory J., and Ron Kurtz. *Grace Unfolding: Psychotherapy in the Spirit of the Tao-te ching*. Harmony Books, 1991.

2. Rogers, Carl R. *On Becoming a Person: A Therapist's View of Psychotherapy.* Robinson, 2016.

3. Rogers, Carl R. *On Becoming a Person: A Therapist's View of Psychotherapy.* Robinson, 2016.

CHAPTER 7. HOW OUR PARTS WORK

1. Judith, Anodea. *Eastern Body, Western Mind: Psychology and the Chakra System as a Path to the Self.* Alchemy, 2006.

2. Earley, Jay, and Richard C. Schwartz. *Self-Therapy: A Step-by-Step Guide to Creating Wholeness and Healing Your Inner Child Using IFS, a New, Cutting-Edge Psychotherapy.* Pattern System Books, 2009.

3. Thích Nhất Hạnh. *Anger: Buddhist Wisdom for Cooling the Flames.* Riverhead, 2001.

4. Bradshaw, John. *Healing the Shame That Binds You.* Health Communications, 2015.

5. Symptoms for those diagnosed as oppositional defiant include but are not limited to irritable mood, argumentative and defiant behavior, aggression, and vindictiveness that last more than six months and cause significant problems at home or school. Treatment involves individual and family therapy.

CHAPTER 8. PARTS EXERCISES

1. Singer, Michael A. *The Untethered Soul: The Journey Beyond Yourself.* New Harbinger Publications, 2013.

PART 3: PRACTICE 3: THE NARRATIVE

1. The relationship life cycle is a series of stages through which a couple may go through over time. Stages in the development cycle include becoming newly coupled, newly married, a family with young children, a family with adolescents, launching children into the world, and a family in later life. Shifts and changes in the family are thought to cause predictable stress on the marital connection.

2. Narrative therapy helps separate the patient from their narratives. Once the problem has been externalized, the therapist helps the patient to author a new narrative by searching their history for "unique outcomes"—experiences that run counter to the current, problematic story line.

CHAPTER 9. WHAT IS THE NARRATIVE?

1. Limerence, a term coined by American psychologist Dorothy Tennov, is defined as a period in a relationship known as the falling in love and lust stage.

CHAPTER 10. WHY OUR NARRATIVES ARE SO IMPORTANT

1. Dispenza, Joe. *Breaking the Habit of Being Yourself: How to Lose Your Mind and Create a New One.* Hay House, 2016.

2. Even-Chen, Nir, et al. "Mental Rehearsal Prepares Our Brains for Real World Actions." *Neuroscience News*, February 16, 2018. neurosciencenews.com/mental-rehearsal-action-8505/.

3. Iyer, Pico, and Eydís Einarsdóttir. *The Art of Stillness: Adventures in Going Nowhere.* TED Books/Simon & Schuster, 2014.

4. Perel, Esther. *Mating in Captivity: Reconciling the Erotic and the Domestic.* HarperCollins, 2006.

5. Birnbaum, Gurit E., et al. "What Fantasies Can Do to Your Relationship: The Effects of Sexual Fantasies on Couple Interactions." *Personality and Social Psychology Bulletin* 45, no. 3 (2018): 461–76. doi:10.1177/0146167218789611.

CHAPTER 11. HOW TO USE THE NARRATIVE

1. "The Tale of Two Wolves." Nanticoke Indian Association. https://www.nanticokeindians.org/page/tale-of-two-wolves.

2. Singh, Guru. *Buried Treasures: The Journey from Where You Are to Who You Are.* Re-Evolution Publishing, 2014.

3. Gordon, Amie M., et al. "To Have and to Hold: Gratitude Promotes Relationship Maintenance in Intimate Bonds." *Journal of Personality and Social Psychology* 103, no. 2 (2012): 257–74. doi:10.1037/a0028723; Even-Chen, Nir, et al. "Mental Rehearsal Prepares Our Brains for Real World Actions." *Neuroscience News*, February 16, 2018. https://neurosciencenews.com/mental-rehearsal-action-8505/.

4. Metta, taken from Sanskrit, meaning benevolence, friendliness, amity, goodwill, and active interest in others.

5. Chapin, Heather L., et al. "Pilot Study of a Compassion Meditation Intervention in Chronic Pain." *Journal of Compassionate Health Care* 1, no. 1 (2014). doi:10.1186/s40639-014-0004-x.

6. Leppma, Monica. "Loving-Kindness Meditation and Counseling." *Journal of Mental Health Counseling* 34, no. 3 (2012): 197–204. doi:10.17744/mehc.34.3.955g218; Boellinghaus, Inga, et al. "The Role of Mindfulness and Loving-Kindness Meditation in Cultivating Self-Compassion and Other-Focused Concern in Health Care Professionals." *Mindfulness* 5, no. 2 (2012): 129–38. doi:10.1007/s12671-012-0158-6; Klimecki, Olga M., Susanne Leiberg, Claus Lamm, and Tania Singer. "Functional Neural Plasticity and Associated Changes in Positive Affect after Compassion Training." *Cerebral Cortex* 23, no. 7 (2012): 1552–61. doi:10.1093/cercor/bhs142.

7. Gordon, Amie M., et al. "To Have and to Hold: Gratitude Promotes Relationship Maintenance in Intimate Bonds." *Journal of Personality and Social Psychology* 103, no. 2 (2012): 257–74. doi:10.1037/a0028723; Barton, Allen W., Ted G. Futris, and Robert B. Nielsen. "Linking Financial Distress to Marital Quality: The Intermediary Roles of Demand/Withdraw and Spousal Gratitude Expressions." *Personal Relationships* 22, no. 3 (2015): 536–49. doi:10.1111/pere.12094.

8. Suddeath, Eric G., et al. "Narrative Family Therapy: Practical Techniques for More Effective Work with Couples and Families." *Journal of Mental Health Counseling* 39, no. 2 (2017): 116–31. doi:10.17744/mehc.39.2.03.

9. Tolle, Eckhart. *A New Earth: Awakening to Your Life's Purpose.* Penguin Books, 2016.

PART 4: PRACTICE 4: CHOOSING

1. Gurman, Alan S., and David P. Kniskern. *Handbook of Family Therapy.* Brunner/Mazel, 1981.

CHAPTER 13. WHAT IS CHOOSING?

1. EFT is a therapeutic approach for couples developed by Sue Johnson and Les Greenberg and is rooted in research on love as an attachment bond.

2. Attachment theory is a psychological theory that focuses on relationships between humans. It stipulates that young children need to develop a relationship with at least one primary caregiver for normal social and emotional development.

3. Torrent, Lair. "Why Would I Want to Do Dishes? The Importance of 'Choosing' Your Partner in Relationships." *Elephant Journal.* https://www.elephantjournal.com/2015/11/why-would-i-want-to-do-dishes-the-importance-of-choosing-your-partner-in-relationships/.

4. Chapman, Gary D., and Randy Southern. *The 5 Love Languages.* North-field Publishing, 2014.

5. Bunt, Selena, and Zoe J. Hazelwood. "Walking the Walk, Talking the Talk: Love Languages, Self-Regulation, and Relationship Satisfaction." *Personal Relationships* 24, no. 2 (2017): 280–90. doi:10.1111/pere.12182.

6. Cole, Tim. "Speaking Your Partner's Love Language May Not Matter." *Psychology Today,* April 5, 2017. https://www.psychologytoday.com/us/blog/intimate-portrait/201704/speaking-your-partners-love-language-may-not-matter.

CHAPTER 14. WHY CHOOSING IS
SO IMPORTANT TO CONNECTION

1. Sinek, Simon. "How to Make an Impact." Interview by Tom Bilyeu, Motivation2Study, YouTube, November 21, 2017, 3:36. https://www.youtube.com/watch?v=7MR0ZqyhSAA.

2. "Oxytocin." *Psychology Today.* https://www.psychologytoday.com/us/basics/oxytocin.

3. "'Love Hormone' Is Two-Faced: Oxytocin Strengthens Bad Memories and Can Increase Fear and Anxiety." *ScienceDaily,* July 22, 2013. https://www.sciencedaily.com/releases/2013/07/130722123206.htm.

4. "Oxytocin: The Love Hormone?" *Medical News Today.* https://www.medicalnewstoday.com/articles/275795.

5. "Oxytocin Can Improve Compassion in People with Symptoms of PTSD." *ScienceDaily,* March 10, 2016. https://www.sciencedaily.com/releases/2016/03/160310112400.htm.

6. Grebe, Nicholas M., et al. "Oxytocin and Vulnerable Romantic Relationships." *Hormones and Behavior,* March 12, 2017. https://www.sciencedirect.com/science/article/abs/pii/S0018506X1630157X.

7. "The Science of Kindness." Cedars. https://www.cedars-sinai.org/blog/science-of-kindness.html.

8. McLeod, Saul. "Maslow's Hierarchy of Needs." *Simply Psychology,* March 20, 2020. https://www.simplypsychology.org/maslow.html.

9. Seltzer, Leon F. "Feeling Understood—Even More Important Than Feeling Loved?" *Psychology Today,* June 28, 2017. www.psychologytoday.com/us/blog/evolution-the-self/201706/feeling-understood-even-more-important-feeling-loved.

10. Lun, Janetta, Selin Kesebir, and Shigehiro Oishi. "On Feeling Understood and Feeling Well: The Role of Interdependence." *Journal of Research*

in Personality, December 2008. https://www.ncbi.nlm.nih.gov/pmc/articles /PMC2652476/.

11. Morelli, S. A., J. B. Torre, and N. I. Eisenberger. "The Neural Bases of Feeling Understood and Not Understood." *Social Cognitive and Affective Neuroscience.* https://pubmed.ncbi.nlm.nih.gov/24396002/.

12. Gordon, A. M., and S. Chen. "Do You Get Where I'm Coming From? Perceived Understanding Buffers against the Negative Impact of Conflict on Relationship Satisfaction." *Journal of Personality and Social Psychology.* https:// pubmed.ncbi.nlm.nih.gov/26523997/.

13. Hendrix, Harville, and Helen Hunt. *Making Marriage Simple: 10 Relationship-Saving Truths.* Harmony Books, 2013.

14. Johnson, Sue. *Hold Me Tight: Seven Conversations for a Lifetime of Love.* Little, Brown Spark, 2008.

15. Winter, Julie. Personal email to the author, December 5, 2020.

16. Kavar, Louis F. *The Integrated Self: A Holistic Approach to Spirituality and Mental Health Practice.* O-Books, 2012.

17. O'Donohue, John. *Anam Cara: A Book of Celtic Wisdom.* Harper Perennial, 2004.

CHAPTER 15. HOW TO CHOOSE

1. O'Donohue, John. *Anam Cara: A Book of Celtic Wisdom.* Harper Perennial, 2004.

CHAPTER 17. WHAT IS PERSONAL RESPONSIBILITY?

1. Yalom, Irvin D. *Existential Psychotherapy.* Basic Books, 1980.

2. Quotes.net, STANDS4 LLC, 2021. "Sydney Harris Quotes." Accessed July 17, 2021. https://www.quotes.net/quote/7872.

CHAPTER 18. WHY PERSONAL RESPONSIBILITY IS INTEGRAL TO RELATIONSHIPS

1. "The Cornerstone of Any Mature Relationship." *Elephant Journal.* https:// www.elephantjournal.com/2017/11/the-cornerstone-of-any-mature-relation ship/.

2. "What's So Tough about Apologizing?" *Psychology Today*, June 2, 2013. https://www.psychologytoday.com/us/blog/time-out/201306/what-s-so -tough-about-apologizing.

3. Engel, Beverly. "Why We Need to Apologize." *Psychology Today*, June 12, 2020. https://www.psychologytoday.com/us/blog/the-compassion-chron icles/202006/why-we-need-apologize.

4. Peck, M. Scott. *The Road Less Traveled: A New Psychology of Love, Traditional Values and Spiritual Growth*. Simon & Schuster, 2003.

5. Hendricks, Gay. *The Big Leap: Conquer Your Hidden Fear and Take Life to the Next Level*. HarperCollins, 2010.

6. Beecher, Willard, and Marguerite Beecher. *Beyond Success and Failure: Ways to Self-Reliance and Maturity*. Willard & Marguerite Beecher Foundation, 1986.

7. Beecher, Willard, and Marguerite Beecher. *Beyond Success and Failure: Ways to Self-Reliance and Maturity*. Willard & Marguerite Beecher Foundation, 1986.

8. Frost, Robert. *The Poems of Robert Frost*. Modern Library, 1946.

CHAPTER 19. HOW TO TAKE PERSONAL RESPONSIBILITY

1. Frye, Devon. "Why Apologies Are So Hard, and So Necessary." *Psychology Today*, July 28, 2020. https://www.psychologytoday.com/us/blog/brain storm/202007/why-apologies-are-so-hard-and-so-necessary.

2. Watts, Alan. "Letting Go to Gain Control." YouTube Video, 3:48, January 29, 2017. https://www.youtube.com/watch?v=D2FIcF4kv4s.

3. Wong, Kristin. "Why It's So Hard to Admit You're Wrong." *New York Times*, May 22, 2017. https://www.nytimes.com/2017/05/22/smarter-living /why-its-so-hard-to-admit-youre-wrong.html.

CHAPTER 20. CONCLUSION

1. O'Donohue, John. *Anam Cara: A Book of Celtic Wisdom*. Harper Perennial, 2004.

BIBLIOGRAPHY

Barton, Allen W., Ted G. Futris, and Robert B. Nielsen. "Linking Financial Distress to Marital Quality: The Intermediary Roles of Demand/Withdraw and Spousal Gratitude Expressions." *Personal Relationships* 22, no. 3 (2015): 536–49. doi:10.1111/pere.12094.

Basu, Tanya. "Feeling Like Your Partner 'Gets' You Really Is a Big Deal." *The Cut.* March 2, 2016. https://www.thecut.com/2016/03/feeling-like-your -partner-gets-you-really-is-a-big-deal.html.

Beecher, Willard, and Marguerite Beecher. *Beyond Success and Failure: Ways to Self-Reliance and Maturity.* Willard & Marguerite Beecher Foundation, 1986.

Birnbaum, Gurit E., et al. "What Fantasies Can Do to Your Relationship: The Effects of Sexual Fantasies on Couple Interactions." *Personality and Social Psychology Bulletin* 45, no. 3 (2018): 461–76. doi:10.1177/0146167218789611.

Boellinghaus, Inga, et al. "The Role of Mindfulness and Loving-Kindness Meditation in Cultivating Self-Compassion and Other-Focused Concern in Health Care Professionals." *Mindfulness* 5, no. 2 (2012): 129–38. doi:10.1007 /s12671-012-0158-6.

Bradshaw, John. *Healing the Shame That Binds You.* Health Communications, 2015.

Brown, Brené. *Daring Greatly: How the Courage to Be Vulnerable Transforms the Way We Live, Love, Parent, and Lead.* Penguin, 2012.

Bunt, Selena, and Zoe J. Hazelwood. "Walking the Walk, Talking the Talk: Love Languages, Self-Regulation, and Relationship Satisfaction." *Personal Relationships* 24, no. 2 (2017): 280–90. doi:10.1111/pere.12182.

Chapin, Heather L., et al. "Pilot Study of a Compassion Meditation Intervention in Chronic Pain." *Journal of Compassionate Health Care* 1, no. 1 (2014). doi:10.1186/s40639-014-0004-x.

Chapman, Gary D., and Randy Southern. *The 5 Love Languages.* Northfield Publishing, 2014.

Cole, Tim. "Speaking Your Partner's Love Language May Not Matter." *Psychology Today*. April 5, 2017. https://www.psychologytoday.com/us/blog/intimate-portrait/201704/speaking-your-partners-love-language-may-not-matter.

"The Cornerstone of Any Mature Relationship." *Elephant Journal*. https://www.elephantjournal.com/2017/11/the-cornerstone-of-any-mature-relationship/.

Dispenza, Joe. *Breaking the Habit of Being Yourself: How to Lose Your Mind and Create a New One.* Hay House, 2016.

Doyle, Glennon. *Love Warrior: A Memoir.* Two Roads, 2017.

Earley, Jay, and Richard C. Schwartz. *Self-Therapy: A Step-by-Step Guide to Creating Wholeness and Healing Your Inner Child Using IFS, a New, Cutting-Edge Psychotherapy.* Pattern System Books, 2009.

"Ellen Langer: Mindfulness over Matter." Pop Tech. YouTube. November 5, 2013. www.youtube.com/watch?v=4XQUJR4uIGM.

Engel, Beverly. "Why We Need to Apologize." *Psychology Today*. June 12, 2020. https://www.psychologytoday.com/us/blog/the-compassion-chronicles/202006/why-we-need-apologize.

Even-Chen, Nir, et al. "Mental Rehearsal Prepares Our Brains for Real World Actions." *Neuroscience News*. February 16, 2018. https://neurosciencenews.com/mental-rehearsal-action-8505/.

Frost, Robert. *The Poems of Robert Frost.* Modern Library, 1946.

Frye, Devon. "Why Apologies Are So Hard, and So Necessary." *Psychology Today*. July 28, 2020. https://www.psychologytoday.com/us/blog/brainstorm/202007/why-apologies-are-so-hard-and-so-necessary.

Gordon, A. M., and S. Chen. "Do You Get Where I'm Coming From? Perceived Understanding Buffers against the Negative Impact of Conflict on Relationship Satisfaction." *Journal of Personality and Social Psychology*. https://pubmed.ncbi.nlm.nih.gov/26523997/.

Gordon, Amie M., et al. "To Have and to Hold: Gratitude Promotes Relationship Maintenance in Intimate Bonds." *Journal of Personality and Social Psychology* 103, no. 2 (2012): 257–74. doi:10.1037/a0028723.

Grebe, Nicholas M., et al. "Oxytocin and Vulnerable Romantic Relationships." *Hormones and Behavior*. March 12, 2017. https://www.sciencedirect.com/science/article/abs/pii/S0018506X1630157X.

Gurman, Alan S., and David P. Kniskern. *Handbook of Family Therapy.* Brunner/Mazel, 1981.

Hendricks, Gay. *The Big Leap: Conquer Your Hidden Fear and Take Life to the Next Level.* HarperCollins, 2010.

Hendrix, Harville, and Helen Hunt. *Getting the Love You Want: A Guide for Couples.* Simon & Schuster UK, 2020.

Hendrix, Harville, and Helen Hunt. *Making Marriage Simple: 10 Relationship-Saving Truths.* Harmony Books, 2013.

Iyer, Pico, and Eydís Einarsdóttir. *The Art of Stillness: Adventures in Going Nowhere.* TED Books/Simon & Schuster, 2014.

Johanson, Gregory J., and Ron Kurtz. *Grace Unfolding: Psychotherapy in the Spirit of the Tao-te ching.* Harmony Books, 1991.

Johnson, Sue. *Hold Me Tight: Seven Conversations for a Lifetime of Love.* Little, Brown Spark, 2008.

Judith, Anodea. *Eastern Body, Western Mind: Psychology and the Chakra System as a Path to the Self.* Alchemy, 2006.

Kavar, Louis F. *The Integrated Self: A Holistic Approach to Spirituality and Mental Health Practice.* O-Books, 2012.

Klimecki, Olga M., Susanne Leiberg, Claus Lamm, and Tania Singer. "Functional Neural Plasticity and Associated Changes in Positive Affect after Compassion Training." *Cerebral Cortex* 23, no. 7 (2012): 1552–61. doi:10.1093/cercor/bhs142.

Leppma, Monica. "Loving-Kindness Meditation and Counseling." *Journal of Mental Health Counseling* 34, no. 3 (2012): 197–204. doi:10.17744/mehc.34.3.955g218.

"'Love Hormone' Is Two-Faced: Oxytocin Strengthens Bad Memories and Can Increase Fear and Anxiety." *ScienceDaily.* July 22, 2013. https://www.sciencedaily.com/releases/2013/07/130722123206.htm.

Lun, Janetta, Selin Kesebir, and Shigehiro Oishi. "On Feeling Understood and Feeling Well: The Role of Interdependence." *Journal of Research in Personality.* December 2008. https://www.ncbi.nlm.nih.gov/pmc/articles/PMC2652476/.

McLeod, Saul. "Maslow's Hierarchy of Needs." *Simply Psychology.* March 20, 2020. https://www.simplypsychology.org/maslow.html.

Morelli, S. A., J. B. Torre, and N. I. Eisenberger. "The Neural Bases of Feeling Understood and Not Understood." *Social Cognitive and Affective Neuroscience.* https://pubmed.ncbi.nlm.nih.gov/24396002/.

O'Donohue, John. *Anam Ċara: A Book of Celtic Wisdom.* Harper Perennial, 2004.

"Oxytocin." *Psychology Today.* https://www.psychologytoday.com/us/basics/oxytocin.

"Oxytocin Can Improve Compassion in People with Symptoms of PTSD." *ScienceDaily.* March 10, 2016. https://www.sciencedaily.com/releases/2016/03/160310112400.htm.

"Oxytocin: The Love Hormone?" *Medical News Today.* https://www.medicalnewstoday.com/articles/275795.

Pang, Jo. "How Mindfulness Transforms." YouTube. June 13, 2018. https://www.youtube.com/watch?v=9gi2ER4pSaU.

Peck, M. Scott. *The Road Less Traveled: A New Psychology of Love, Traditional Values and Spiritual Growth*. Simon & Schuster, 2003.

Perel, Esther. *Mating in Captivity: Reconciling the Erotic and the Domestic*. HarperCollins, 2006.

Poerio, Giulia L., Peter Totterdell, and Eleanor Miles. "Mind-Wandering and Negative Mood: Does One Thing Really Lead to Another?" *Consciousness and Cognition* 22, no. 4 (2013): 1412–21. doi:10.1016/j.concog.2013.09.012.

Rogers, Carl R. *On Becoming a Person: A Therapist's View of Psychotherapy*. Robinson, 2016.

"The Science of Kindness." Cedars. https://www.cedars-sinai.org/blog/science-of-kindness.html.

Seltzer, Leon F. "Feeling Understood—Even More Important Than Feeling Loved?" *Psychology Today*. June 28, 2017. https://www.psychologytoday.com/us/blog/evolution-the-self/201706/feeling-understood-even-more-important-feeling-loved.

Siegel, Daniel J. *The Mindful Therapist: A Clinician's Guide to Mindsight and Neural Integration*. Norton, 2010.

Sinek, Simon. "How to Make an Impact." Interview by Tom Bilyeu, Motivation2Study, YouTube. November 21, 2017, 3:36. https://www.youtube.com/watch?v=7MR0ZqyhSAA.

Singer, Michael A. *The Untethered Soul: The Journey Beyond Yourself*. New Harbinger Publications, 2013.

Singh, Guru. *Buried Treasures: The Journey from Where You Are to Who You Are*. Re-Evolution Publishing, 2014.

Spoon, M. "Meditation Affects Brain Networks Differently in Long-term Meditators and Novices." News.wisc.edu. https://news.wisc.edu/meditation-affects-brain-networks-differently-in-long-term-meditators-and-novices. Accessed March 20, 2021.

Taren A. A., J. D. Creswell, and P. J. Gianaros. "Dispositional Mindfulness Covaries with Smaller Amygdala and Caudate Volumes in Community Adults." *PLoS One*. May 22, 2013: 8(5): e64574. doi: 10.1371/journal.pone.0064574. PMID: 23717632; PMCID: PMC3661490.

Thích Nhất Hạnh. *Fear: Essential Wisdom for Getting through the Storm*. HarperOne, 2014.

Thích Nhất Hạnh. *Fidelity: How to Create a Loving Relationship That Lasts*. Parallax Press, 2011.

Thích Nhất Hạnh. *Anger: Buddhist Wisdom for Cooling the Flames*. Riverhead, 2001.

Tolle, Eckhart. *A New Earth: Awakening to Your Life's Purpose*. Penguin Books, 2016.

Torrent, Lair. "Why Would I Want to Do Dishes? The Importance of 'Choosing' Your Partner in Relationships." *Elephant Journal*. https://www.elephant journal.com/2015/11/why-would-i-want-to-do-dishes-the-importance-of -choosing-your-partner-in-relationships/.

Watts, Alan. "Letting Go to Gain Control." YouTube Video, 3:48. January 29, 2017. https://www.youtube.com/watch?v=D2FIcF4kv4s.

"What's So Tough about Apologizing?" *Psychology Today*. June 2, 2013. https:// www.psychologytoday.com/us/blog/time-out/201306/what-s-so-tough -about-apologizing.

Winter, Julie. Personal email to the author, December 5, 2020.

Wong, Kristin. "Why It's So Hard to Admit You're Wrong." *New York Times*. May 22, 2017. https://www.nytimes.com/2017/05/22/smarter-living/why -its-so-hard-to-admit-youre-wrong.html.

Yalom, Irvin D. *Existential Psychotherapy*. Basic Books, 1980.

INDEX

ABOUT THE AUTHOR

Born to a fifteen-year-old mother in abject poverty, **Lair Torrent** saw few examples of connective, loving, functional relationships. As a young man he began recapitulating those same behaviors of disfunction in his own life. Committed to change, Lair began a lifelong journey of self-exploration and healing, which has culminated in his work as a therapist. Less than an "expert," he considers himself a fellow practitioner of the principles he offers, trying to do it a little better tomorrow than he did it today.

Lair is a clinically trained and licensed marriage and family therapist and a mindfulness-based relationship therapist. He attended the Helix Training Program, a rigorous, four-year, multidiscipline training in psycho-spiritual counseling and work in personal transformation based in New York City. His graduate work was conducted at Mercy College under Dr. Evan Imber-Black, world-renowned marriage and family therapist, where his research focused on couples and the work of Susan Johnson's Emotionally Focused Therapy.

Lair is a DailyOM best-selling author and has been a contributing columnist at Inc.com. He writes, speaks publicly, and holds workshops and seminars on relationships and mindfulness, as well as mindfulness and its effects on racism and children. Lair has published articles on his work and has been resourced and interviewed by such notable news outlets and publications as NPR, *Rolling Stone,* and the *New York Times* for his expertise in working with struggling relationships.

CPSIA information can be obtained
at www.ICGtesting.com
Printed in the USA
BVHW061922080122
624556BV00002B/2